Female Piety

or

The Young Woman's Friend and Guide through Life to Immortality

by
John Angell James

Edited by Dr. Don Kistler

Soli Deo Gloria Publications
. . . for instruction in righteousness . . .

Soli Deo Gloria Publications
A division of Soli Deo Gloria Ministries, Inc.
P.O. Box 451, Morgan, PA 15064
(412) 221-1901/FAX 221-1902
www.SDGbooks.com

*

*

ISBN 1-57358-103-8

Contents

Foreword to the 20th-Century Edition

Whenever I read the Puritans, I am reminded of that statement of Francis Bacon: "Some books are to be tasted, others to be swallowed, and some few to be chewed and digested."

This book deserves to be chewed and digested. The author is practical. He is sensitive. He is informational.

Take for example his practical ability. In his chapter "To Young Mothers," he stresses that emphasis should be placed on rearing the first child right. "If a mother begins well, she is likely to continue well . . . her conduct towards the first child is likely, of course, to determine her conduct with respect to all the following ones." The first child, if undisciplined, makes the others fall over like dominoes.

And how practical is his admonition on discipline: "Do not make them learn Scripture as a punishment for offenses, and thus convert religion, which is the foretaste of heaven, into penances." And then he adds, "Especially do not make the Sabbath a day of gloom instead of gladness." He would, no doubt, approve of a friend of mine who would let her children eat candy *only* on the Sabbath!

The author is sensitive. In his description of Jesus dealing with Mary and Martha on the death of their brother, he focuses on how differently Christ deals with the personalities of the two sisters: "Martha's distress was of such a nature that it admitted of discussion and discourse. Jesus accordingly spoke to her, and led her to speak to Him, as suited her circumstances, some of the sublimest communications touching the resurrection of the body and the life of the soul. To Mary, who is wrapped in such deep grief, He shows His sympathy in a different way . . . Jesus wept." We see the "Son of God in tears."

He is informational. His first chapter abounds in data on how much feminists owe to the gospel: "It is enough to demand her thankfulness that in common with man she is the object of divine love, redeeming mercy, and the subject of immortal hope; but in addition to this she is rescued from oppression and exalted to honor in this present world." He points out that the Bible is a friend of women in both worlds: "How, then, shall woman discharge her obligations? In two ways. First, in yielding up her heart and life to the influence and service of her Benefactor, in faith, in holiness, and in love. Female piety is the best, the only sincere expression of female gratitude to God. An irreligious woman is also an ungrateful one."

And also she ought to be very energetic in missionary enterprises, anxious to give to others what she has received. As a child growing up in India of missionary parents, I can still see the awe on the women's faces as my mother would share with them the surprising good news: the gospel is not for men only!

The author is very up-to-date in his reason for writing the book. He writes: "Can any good and valid reason be assigned for shutting out from the house of God instructions to so important a class of the community? Many persons almost instinctively shrink from such addresses, from a fear lest matters should be introduced at which modesty would blush, and by which the finer sensibilities would be wounded. There is a prudishness in such feelings which can be justified neither by reason nor revelation."

Our author writes of women: "She not only renders smooth or rough our path to the grave, but helps or hinders our progress to immortality." To crib, with a minor alteration, a line from the quotable G. K. Chesterton, I would say, "Forward to the nineteenth century!"

Edna Gerstner
Ligonier, PA
May 1994

Chapter 1

The Influence of Christianity on the
Condition of Woman

"There is neither Jew nor Greek; there is neither bond nor
free; there is neither male nor female; for ye are all one
in Christ Jesus." Galatians 3:28

Woman was the finishing grace of the creation. Woman
was the completeness of man's bliss in paradise. Woman was
the cause of sin and death to our world. The world was redeemed by the seed of the woman. Woman is the mother of
the human race; she is either our companion, counselor, and
comforter in the pilgrimage of life or she is our tempter,
scourge, and destroyer. Our sweetest cup of earthly happiness
or our bitterest draught of sorrow is mixed and administered by
her hand. She not only renders smooth or rough our path to
the grave, but helps or hinders our progress to immortality. In
heaven we shall bless God for her aid in assisting us to reach
that blissful state; or, amidst the torments of unutterable woe
in another region, we shall deplore the fatality of her influence.

This work was delivered originally in a course of monthly
sermons, to which I was led by a conviction that woman, as
regards her specific duties, is too much neglected in the ministrations of the sanctuary—an omission which must be traced
to a morbid delicacy unworthy of the pulpit. Happily this reproach does not appertain to the press, to which, perhaps, in
the opinion of some, this subject ought to be exclusively consigned. But why? Can any good and valid reason be assigned

for shutting out from the house of God instructions to so important a class of the community? Many persons almost instinctively shrink from such addresses from a fear that matters would be introduced at which modesty would blush, and by which the finer sensibilities would be wounded. There is a prudishness in such feelings which can be justified neither by reason nor revelation.

It may be as well to announce in this opening chapter that the whole course will be of a decidedly religious nature. For all the general directions and excellences of female character, I shall refer to the various works which have issued from the press on these topics. My subject is religion; my object is the soul; my aim is salvation. I view you, my female friends, as destined for another world; and it is my business to aid and stimulate you by patient continuance in well-doing to seek for glory, honor, and immortality, and to obtain eternal life. I look beyond the painted and gaudy scene of earth's fading vanities to the everlasting ages through which you must exist in torment or bliss; and, God helping me, it shall not be my fault if you do not live in comfort, die in peace, and inherit salvation.

I can think of no subject with which more appropriately to commence this work than the influence of Christianity on the condition of woman.

Our first attention must be directed of course to the condition of the sex beyond the boundaries of Christendom.

It would seem from the words of the original denunciation upon Eve for her transgression in eating the forbidden fruit that while yet the first pair was innocent, there was a more entire equality of condition and rights between the sexes than there has been after the fall. "Thy desire shall be to thy husband, and he shall rule over thee." This sounds like something penal, though perhaps some would regard it as merely predictive, and intended to describe the cruel and brutalizing tendency of sin in turning man, who ought to be the loving companion of his wife, into a tyrant. How fearfully, if predictive, this sentence has been fulfilled the degradation of woman—her wrongs, her sorrows, and her vices, in many cases—most painfully attests.

History, which will ever be found to corroborate revelation, proves that in most pagan and Mohammedan nations, whether ancient or modern, woman has been cruelly and wickedly sunk below her proper level in social and domestic life, hated and despised from her birth, and her birth itself esteemed a calamity; in some countries not even allowed the rank of a moral and responsible agent; so tenderly alive to her own degradation that she acquiesces in the murder of her female offspring; immured from infancy; without education; married without her consent; in a multitude of instances sold by her parents; refused the confidence of her husband, and banished from his table; on his death, doomed to the funeral pyre, or to contempt that renders life a burden. In such a condition she has been the household drudge, or the mere object of passion. She has ministered to the gratification of man's indolence or appetite, but has not been his companion, his counselor, or his comforter. In barbarous countries she has been a slave, in civilized ones very generally little better than a kept mistress. Her mind has been left untaught, as if incapable or unworthy of instruction. She has been not only imprisoned in seclusion by jealousy, but degraded and rendered vicious and miserable by polygamy. Sometimes worshipped as a goddess, next fondled as a toy, then punished as a victim, she could never attain to dignity, and even with all her brightest charms could rarely appear but as a doll or a puppet.

Exceptions, to some extent, may be made in favor of the polished Greeks and proud Romans, but only to some extent; for (if time permitted and necessity required) it could be shown that neither Athenian refinement nor Roman virtue gave to woman her just rank by the side of her husband, or her proper place in his affection, esteem, and confidence. The laws of Rome, it is true, secured greater liberty and consideration for her than she had previously received; but still she was so treated even there as to sink into a degradation disgraceful to her purity and destructive to her happiness. In his book *Female Scripture Biography,* my late friend Dr. Cox wrote: "No happy influence did she exert on the public or private welfare of the state. Politicians were intrigued by her instrumentality, ambition combined with passion to corrupt her, and her liberty degenerated in licentiousness. Through her influence the streets of the capitol were sometimes deluged with its best blood; and to such an extent was her profligacy carried that among the decrees against the licentiousness of female manners, enacted by the Senate during the reign of Tiberius, was one 'that no woman whose grandfather, father, or husband was a Roman knight should be allowed to make her person venal.' The laws of a nation are an instructive and faithful history of its manners. If such was the condition of a Roman lady, what must have been that of the subordinate classes? Neither paganism nor Mohammedanism ever yet understood the female character, or conceded woman's just claims. In many nations the degradation has been excessive. You remember probably the reply of a pagan mother who, having been expostulated with for the murder of her female child, contended that she had performed an act of mercy in sparing the babe the miseries of a woman's life. All travelers and all missionaries attest to the fact of woman's humiliation, beyond the boundaries of revelation."

If we go to the Bible, we shall learn that it is to Christianity, as contrasted even with Judaism, that woman owes her true elevation. Polygamy is, and ever must be, fatal to female dignity and happiness; this, or at any rate concubinage, was practiced, no doubt under mistaken views, by the patriarchs. Not that it was ever positively sanctioned by God, for from the beginning He made one woman for one man, and by the providential and remarkable fact of the general equality of the sexes as to numbers He still proclaims in unmistakable language the law of monogamy; but to use an expression of the apostle, He "winked at" these things. He did not regard it as innocent or convenient, yet He did not say much about it or punish it, but left it to punish itself, which it most certainly did. If we examine the Levitical code we shall find that even it, though a divine dispensation, contained some regulations which evidenced that the time of woman's full emancipation from a state of inferiority had not yet arrived, and that it was reserved for the glorious and gracious economy under which we are placed to raise the female sex to its just position and influence in society. Christianity as in other things, so in this, is an enlargement of human privileges; and among other blessings which it confers is its elevation of woman to her proper place and influence in the family and in society.

Let us now consider what there is in Christianity that tends to elevate and improve the condition of woman.

To the oppressive and cruel customs of Mohammedanism and paganism in their treatment of the female sex, Christianity presents a beautiful and lovely contrast, while to the partial provisions for female rights in Judaism it adds a complete recognition of their claims. It is the glory of our holy religion, and a proof of its emanation from the divine beneficence, that it is the enemy of oppression in every form and every condition, and gives to everyone his due. It tramples on no right; it resents and resists all wrong; but no one of all the sons of men is so indebted to its merciful and equitable reign as woman. From Christianity woman has derived her moral and social influence, yea, almost her very existence as a social being. The mind of woman, which many of the philosophers, legislators, and sages of antiquity doomed to inferiority and imbecility, Christianity has developed. The gospel of Christ in the person of its divine Founder has descended into this neglected mine, which even wise men had regarded as not worth working, and brought up many a priceless gem, flashing with the light of intelligence, and glowing with the lovely hues of Christian graces. Christianity has been the restorer of woman's plundered rights, and has furnished the brightest jewels in her present crown of honor. Her previous degradation accounts, in part at least, for the instability of early civilization. It is impossible for society to be permanently elevated where woman is debased and servile. Wherever females are regarded as inferior beings, society contains within itself the elements of dissolution and the obstruction of all solid improvement. It is impossible that institutions and usages which oppose and stifle the instincts of our nature, and violate the revealed law of God, can be crowned with ultimate success. Society may change in its external aspect; it may exhibit the glitter of wealth, the refinements of taste, the embellishments of art, or the more valuable attainments of science and literature; but if the mind of woman remains undeveloped, her tastes uncultivated, and her person enslaved, the social foundations are insecure and the cement of society is weak. Wherever Christianity is understood and felt, woman is free. The gospel, like a kind angel, opens her prison doors and bids her walk abroad and enjoy the sunlight of reason, and breathe the invigorating air of intellectual freedom. And in proportion as pure Christianity prevails, this will be ever found to be the case.

But all this is vague and general assertion, and I will bring forward proofs of it.

Christianity elevates the condition of woman by its genius

as a system of universal equity and benevolence. When it descended from heaven to earth, it was heralded into our world by the angel's song, "Glory to God in the highest; and on earth, peace and good will to man." The offspring of infinite love, it partakes of the spirit and reflects the character of its divine Parent. It is essentially and unalterably the enemy of all injustice, cruelty, and oppression, and the friend of all that is just, kind, and courteous. The rough, the brutal, and the ferocious are alien to its spirit, while the tender, the gentle, and the courteous are entirely in unison with its nature. It frowns with indignant countenance upon tyranny, whether in the palace or the parlor, while it is the friend of liberty and the patron of right. The man who understands its genius, and lives under its inspiration, whether he is a monarch, a master, a husband, or a father, must be a man of equity and love. Christianity inspires the purest chivalry, a chivalry shorn of vanity, purified from passion, elevated above frivolity; a chivalry of which the animating principle is love to God, and the scene of its operation the domestic circle and not the public pageant. He who is unjust or unkind to anyone, especially to the weaker sex, betrays a total ignorance of, or a manifest repugnance to, the practical influence of the gospel of Christ. It is a mistake to suppose that the faith of Jesus is intended only to throw a dim religious light over the gloom of the cloister, or to form the character of the devotee. On the contrary, it is preeminently a social thing, and is designed as well as adapted to form a character which shall go out into the world in a spirit of universal benevolence. To such a character the oppressor or degrader of woman can make no pretensions.

The incarnation of Christ tended to exalt the dignity of the female sex. His assuming humanity has given a dignity to our nature which it had never received before, and could not have received in any other way. Christ is "the Pattern Man" of our race, in whom all the lines of humanity converge and unite so far as the existence of our race goes. When He took man's nature, He promised to ally Himself to all the members of the race by the actual adoption of a body, which gave Him a relationship to them. He not only became like men and dwelt among them, but He became man himself, an actual descendant from their first progenitor. He was made man. Human nature became more precious. By the manner of His birth, He associated Himself with our nature. This appears to be the meaning of the apostle in his quotation of Psalm 8 in the epistle to the Hebrews: to show the dignity conferred upon humanity by its being assumed by so glorious a person as was our Lord Jesus Christ in His divine nature.

If, then, manhood is honored by Christ assuming it, how much more is woman exalted who, in addition to this, was made the instrument of giving birth to the humanity of Christ? It is emphatically said by the apostle, "When the fullness of the time was come, God sent forth His Son, made of a woman, made under the law." In the person of the Virgin Mary, and by her giving birth to the holy Being born of her, the sex was elevated. True, it was a personal distinction that she should be the mother of our Lord's humanity; and (while she has been, by the apostate Church of Rome, wickedly exalted into an object of idolatrous homage) all generations justly call her "blessed." Yet the honor is not limited to herself, but passes over to her sex, which she represented; and it is to this the apostle alludes. He does not mention her, but dwells upon the abstract general term "made of a woman." Every female on earth, from that day to this, has had a relative elevation by and in that wonderful transaction. Woman was not the mother of God, as the Papists absurdly, and, as I think, blasphemously say; but she was the mother of that humanity which was mysteriously united with divinity. And does not this great fact proclaim, "Let the sex which alone was concerned in giving birth to the Son of God and Savior of the world be ever held in high estimation"?

The personal conduct of our Lord during His sojourn upon earth tended to exalt the female sex to a consideration before unknown. Follow Him through the whole of His earthly career, and mark the attention which He most condescendingly paid to, and as condescendingly received from, the female sex. He admitted them to His presence, conversed familiarly with them, and accepted the tokens of their gratitude, affection, and devotedness. See Him accompanying His mother to the marriage feast of Cana in Galilee. See Him conversing with the woman of Samaria, instructing her ignorance, enduring her petulance, correcting her mistakes, awakening her conscience, converting her soul, and afterwards employing her as a messenger of mercy and salvation to her neighbors. See Him rebuking His disciples for discouraging the approach of mothers and their infants. See Him showing compassion to the widow of Nain, and restoring her son to life. See Him in the little family of Bethany, blending His sympathies with the bereaved sisters, and on another occasion entering into familiar conversation with this same Martha and Mary, and faithfully rebuking one and kindly commending the other. See Him receiving the offerings of those women who ministered to Him of their substance. Witness the attendance of pious women upon Him in the last scenes of His life. It was to Mary Magdalene that the honor of the first manifestation of the risen Savior was made; and thus a woman was preferred to apostles, and made the messenger of the blissful news to them.

"The frequent mention," says [Philip] Doddridge, "which is made in the evangelists of the generous courage and zeal of pious women in the service of Christ, and especially of the faithful and resolute constancy with which they attended Him in those last scenes of His suffering, might very possibly be intended to obviate that haughty and senseless contempt which the pride of men, often irritated by those vexations to which their own irregular passions have exposed them, has in all ages affected to throw on that sex, which probably in the sight of God has constituted by far the better half of mankind; and to whose care and tenderness the wisest and best of men generally owe and ascribe much of the daily comfort and enjoyments of their lives."

Compare this behavior towards the sex—this chaste, holy, dignified conduct of our Lord—with the polygamy, licentiousness, and impurities of Mohammed, not merely as evidence of their respective claims, but as regards their influence upon the condition of woman. While the one did everything by example and by precept to corrupt, to debase, and to degrade them, the other did everything to purify, to elevate, and to bless them. The conduct of the Arabian enthusiast and impostor, and the boasts of his followers and admirers in respect of him, are too revolting for description, almost for allusion. But on the contrary, what one syllable of the Savior's utterances, or what one scene of His life, was there which tainted the immaculate purity of His language, or left the slightest stain upon the more than snow-like sanctity of His character? What part of His conduct might not be unveiled and described before a company of the most modest, most delicate, and even most prudish-minded females in existence? But His treatment of woman raised her from her degradation without exalting her above her level. He rescued her from oppression without exciting her vanity, and invested her with dignity without giving her occasion for pride. While He allowed her not only to come into His presence, but to minister to His comfort, and while He conciliated her grateful and reverent affection, He inspired her with awe; and thus He taught man how to behave toward woman, and what return woman was to make to man.

The conduct of Jesus Christ towards the female sex was one of the most attractive excellences of His beautiful character, though perhaps it is one of the least noticed. To Him they must ever point not only as the Savior of their souls, but as the Advocate of their rights and the Guardian of their peace.

The actual abolition of polygamy by Christianity is a vast improvement in the condition of woman. Wherever polygamy prevails, the female sex must ever be in a state of degradation and misery. Experience has abundantly and painfully proved that polygamy debases and brutalizes both the body and the soul, and renders society incapable of those generous and refined affections which, if duly cultivated, would be found to be the inheritance even of our fallen nature. Where is there an instance in which polygamy has not been the source of many and bitter calamities in the domestic circle and in the State? Where has it reared a virtuous and heaven-taught progeny? Where has it been distinguished for any of the moral virtues, or rather where has it not been distinguished for the most fearful degeneracy of manners? By this practice, which has prevailed so extensively through nearly all countries and all ages in which Christianity has not been known or has not been paramount, marriage loses all its tenderness, its sanctity, and its reciprocal confidence. The cup of connubial felicity is exchanged for that of mere animal pleasure; woman panders to the appetite of man instead of ministering to his comfort, and the home assumes much of the character of a brothel. There may be several mistresses, but there can be only one wife; and though there may be many mothers, they are without a mother's affection, presenting a scene of endless envy and jealousy, before which domestic comfort must ever retire, leaving mere sensual gratification. No stimulus to improvement, no motive to fidelity, and no ambition to please can be felt by a wife who may be supplanted the next month by a new favorite. And in such circumstances there is no room and little occasion for the display of those virtues which constitute female honor.

Here, then, is the glorious excellence of Christianity: it revived and re-established the original institution of marriage, and restored to woman her fortune, her person, her rank, and her happiness, of all of which she had been cheated by polygamy. It thus raised the female sex to the elevation to which they were destined by their wise and beneficent Creator. It is true that Christianity has not effected this great change—so beneficial not only to the sex, but to society—by direct, explicit, and positive precept; yet it has done so by an implication so clear that there can be no mistake as to the reality of the command or the universality of its obligation; for all its provisions, precepts, and promises proceed on the supposition of each husband being the husband but of one wife. And the springs of national prosperity rise from beneath the family hearth, and the domestic constitution is the mold where national character is cast, and that mold must of necessity take its form from the unity, sanctity, and inviolability of marriage.

The jealousy with which Christianity guards the sanctity of the marriage tie must ever be regarded as having a most favorable influence upon the condition of woman. Let this be relaxed or impaired, and that moment woman sinks in dignity, in purity, and in happiness. There have been nations in which the facility of divorce took the place of polygamy, and of course was accompanied with some of its vices, and many of its miseries too. This was eminently the case with ancient Rome after the early times of the Republic; and most instructive are the examples in the annals of its history, and the allusions to them in the pages of its poets. Let the nuptial tie be weakened, and the wife lives in perpetual fear because her union to her husband is placed in jeopardy by a law under which he may at any time, at the instigation of passion or caprice, dissolve the bond between them, and without either penalty, remorse, or shame dismiss her from his home; and there is an end to her peace, and perhaps to her purity. For it is to be recollected that it is she who has most to dread from the license of divorce. She is likely to be the victim of such a liberty. With what devout and reverential gratitude should she then turn to that divine Teacher who has interposed His authority to strengthen the marriage bond, and to guard it from being severed at the demand of illicit passion or the dictates of temperament or caprice. How should she rejoice to hear Him say, "Whoever shall put away his wife except it be for fornication, and shall marry another, committeth adultery; and whoso marrieth her that is put away doth commit adultery." The indulgence of greater latitude and liberty in this matter granted to the Jews was thus superseded by Christianity; a greater security was provided for woman's honor and felicity, and a broader basis laid for domestic harmony and happiness. If it were only for this, Christianity deserves the gratitude of mankind. But it is only half its glory that it has abolished the custom of having many wives. Its crowning achievement is that it has protected the rights, the dignity, and the comfort of the one wife. It has shut out intruders from her home, and guaranteed the safe and permanent possession of it to herself.

I may surely mention the equal participation in religious blessing to which women are admitted by the Christian religion. How explicitly and how firmly has the apostle claimed for women all the blessings obtained by Christ for the human race when he says, "There is neither Jew nor Greek; there is neither bond nor free; there is neither male nor female; for ye are all one in Christ Jesus." There is the charter granting to woman all the blessings of salvation; there is the proof of woman's equality in the sight of God; there is woman's claim to her just rank in the institutes of man. There is not a blessing necessary to eternal life which she does not receive in the same measure and in the same manner as the other sex.

There is a popular tradition among the Mohammedans, prevalent among them to this day, that women are not permitted to enter paradise, the *houris* of that region being specially created in their stead. What degradation is there in such an idea! But it is consistent with the spirit, and harmonizes with the attitude of Mohammedanism, which regards woman more as the slave of man's passions than as the companion of his life. Christianity places the wife by the side of the husband, the daughter by the side of the father, the sister by the side of the brother, and the maid by the side of the mistress at the altar of the family, in the meeting of the church, at the table of the Lord, and in the congregation of the sanctuary.

Male and female meet together at the cross, and will meet in the realms of glory. Can anything more effectually tend to raise and sustain the condition of woman than this? God in all His ordinances, Christ in His glorious undertaking, and the Holy Spirit in His gracious work gave woman her proper place in the world by giving her a proper place in the church. It is for her with peculiar emphasis to say, "God, who is rich in mercy, for His great love wherewith He loved us, hath raised us up together, and made us sit together in heavenly places." And well have women understood their privileges, for look into our congregations and churches and see how largely they are composed of females. How many more of their sex than of the other avail themselves of the offer of gospel mercy, and come under the influence of religion! It is in the female bosom, however we may account for the fact, that piety finds a home on earth. The door of woman's heart is often thrown wide open to receive the divine Guest, when man refuses Him an entrance. And it is by this yielding to the power of godliness, and reflecting upon others the beauties of holiness, that she maintains her standing and her influence in society. Under the sanctifying power of religion she ascends to the glory not only of an intelligent, but of a spiritual existence; she not only gladdens by her presence the solitary hours of man's existence, and beguiles by her conduct and sympathy the rough and tedious paths of his life, but in some measure modifies, purifies, and sanctifies him by making him feel how wonderful goodness is.

But the finishing stroke which Christianity gives in elevating the condition of women is by inviting and employing their energies and influence in promoting the spread of religion in the world, and by thus carrying out, through them as well as men, the great purposes of God in the redemption of the world by the mission of His Son. To them, in common with men, the apostle says, "That ye also may have fellowship with us; and truly our fellowship is with the Father and with His Son Jesus Christ." The honor so liberally bestowed upon the pious women of antiquity of ministering to the personal wants of the Savior, and of being so constantly about His person, was the least of the distinctions designed for them by our holy religion. They bear an exalted place in the labors and offices enjoined and instituted in apostolic times for setting up Christ's Kingdom in the world. How instructive and impressive it is to hear Paul say, "Help those women which labored with Me in the gospel." What a register of names and offices of illustrious females we find in Romans 16. Priscilla, Paul's helper; "Mary, who bestowed much labor on us"; "Tryphena and Tryphosa, who labored in the Lord"; "Phoebe, the servant of the church at Cenchreae," who was sent to the church at Rome, and entrusted with so momentous a commission as to bear to that community of Christians that epistle of the apostle, which, if we may lawfully compare one portion of Scripture with another, is the most precious portion of divine revelation.

In addition to all this, there can be but little doubt that in the primitive church not only were women occasionally endowed by the Spirit with the miraculous gifts of prophesying, but they were also employed in the office of deaconesses. The Christian church in modern times has gone backward in the honor put upon the female character. The primitive age of Christianity was in advance of ours in the respect paid to the female sex by officially employing them in the services of the church, and in the wisdom which made use of their available and valuable resources. It has been said that the usages of society have somewhat changed since that time, so as to render the services of women to their own sex less necessary now than they were then, when the friendly and social intercourse of the sexes was more restricted and females were kept in greater seclusion. Some truth, no doubt, there is in this assertion; but perhaps not so much as is imagined by some. Both general and sacred history represent women in the times referred to as mingling in the society and sharing the occupations of the other sex.

I now remark that not only does Christianity thus tend, by its own nature and provisions, to exalt the female character, but it has accomplished this wherever it has prevailed. If we consult the pages of history, whether ancient or modern, whether eastern or western, we shall find that wherever the religion of our Lord Jesus Christ has been successful, there it has achieved the emancipation of woman from her thraldom and rescued her from degradation. I refer to modern Europe and America in proof of this. What a contrast in this respect do those countries present to all pagan and Mohammedan nations! Is it not a triumph and a trophy of Christianity to be able to point to the most polished nations of the globe as being, at any rate, professedly Christian, and at the same time to say, "Look at the improved condition of the female sex"? And may I not affirm that woman's emancipation and elevation are in proportion to the purity of that Christianity which has thus been diffused?

If we refer to the records of modern missions, we shall find abundant proof of what the gospel does for the elevation of the female character. It has abolished the suttee in India, and the widow is no longer immolated on the pile which consumes her departed husband. It has stopped the drudgery of the wives of all savage tribes, the incarcerating seclusion of Mohammedan and Papal nations, the polygamy, the infanticide, and the concubinage of all countries whither it has gone. Yes, Christianity has in modern times proved itself, in all parts of the world, woman's emancipator and friend. It has brought her from under the disastrous influence of the pale crescent of the impostor of Mecca, and placed her in all the irradiating and enlivening splendor of the Sun of Righteousness. It has rescued her from the baleful power of the crucifix, and brought her within the elevating attraction of the cross.

But there is another way in which we may see that Christianity, even in this Christian and Protestant nation, has benefited and raised the condition of millions of once wretched and degraded women, made such not by their own misconduct, but by the vices and cruelty of their husbands. How many wives have been reduced to a kind of domestic slavery by the drunkenness, infidelity, and tyranny of those who had pledged themselves to love and cherish them? Christianity in its power has in myriads of instances laid hold of the hearts of such men, and changed them from vice to holiness—and the husband at home appeared as much changed as the man in his other duties. Among other evidences of the reality of the change, and the manifestations of its excellence, was his altered conduct at home, where his wife became his companion instead of being his drudge, his slave, and his victim. Christianity has thus carried out its genius and its precepts in the actual elevation of the female character wherever it has gone.

The chivalry of the Middle Ages which combined religion, valor, and gallantry, whimsical as the institution seems, no doubt did something to accomplish this end. I do not dispute the truth of the remark made by a French writer, quoted in a popular work entitled *Woman's Mission,* where he says that women shut up in their castle towers civilized the warriors who despised their weakness, and rendered less barbarous the passions and the prejudices which these men shared. It was they who directed the savage passions and brute force of the men to an unselfish aim—the defense of the weak—and added humanity to courage, which had been the only virtue previously recognized.

But even chivalry derived its existence in some measure from religion. And, after all, how inferior in its nature and how different in its influence was that system of romance compared to the dignified principles and holy influence of Christianity? It did very well to figure at the joust and the tournament, in the hall of the baron, and in the circle of the fair; but its influence in the domestic scene was very slight compared with that of the institutions of the New Testament. It was rather the exaggeration to extravagance of female rights and privileges than an intelligent concession of them under a sense of justice, and in obedience to the divine authority; and it may be questioned whether many an illustrious knight did not (when the hour of imagination had passed away, and the ardor of passion had cooled, in the absence of Christian principles) crush and break the heart which he had been so anxious to win. It is the glory of Christianity that, instead of appealing to the imagination, the senses, and the passions, it supplies principles which are rooted in the soul and sway the conscience; and that instead of leading its possessor to expend his

admiration of woman in the exciting scenes of public amusement, it teaches and influences him first of all to contemplate
her where her charms are less meretriciously adorned, in the
retirement of social intercourse, and then to enjoy them within
the hallowed circle of domestic life. It allows for no senseless
adoration like that which chivalry promoted, and which from
its very excess is likely to be followed by recoil or collapse. What
Christianity does for woman is to fit her to be neither the
goddess nor the slave, but the friend and companion, of man,
and to teach man to consider her in this honorable and
amiable aspect.

Do we not see in all this a beautiful exhibition of the tran-
scendent excellence of our holy religion? In every view that we
can take of Christianity, whether we contemplate it in its aspects towards another world or towards this one, in its
relations to God or society, in its sublime doctrines or its pure
morality, we see a form of inimitable beauty sufficient to captivate every heart but that which is petrified by false philosophy, avowed infidelity, or gross immorality. But never does it
appear more lovely than in its relation to woman. With what
equity does it hold the balance between the sexes! With what
kindness does it throw its shield over the weaker vessel! With
what wisdom does it sustain the rank and claims of those
whose influence is so important to society, and yet so limit
their claims that they shall not be carried to such a length as to
defeat their end! With what nice discrimination does it fix
woman's place where her power can be most advantageously
employed for the cultivation of her own virtues and the benefit
of society! In the work previously mentioned, Dr. Cox wrote:
"Behold Christianity, then, walking forth in her purity and
greatness to bless the earth, diffusing her light in every
direction, distributing her charities on either hand, quenching
the flames of lust and the fires of ambition, silencing discord,

spreading peace, and creating all things new. Angels watch her
progress, celebrate her influence, and anticipate her final triumphs! The moral creation brightens beneath her smiles and
owns her renovating power. At her approach man loses his
fierceness, and woman her chains; each becomes blessed in the
other, and God is glorified in both."

May we not affirm that the treatment of woman by
Judaism and Christianity is one of the proofs of their divine
origin? We have seen already how much superior the later dispensation was to the earlier one—as in other particulars, so in
respect of the matter I am treating here. But they must always
be associated together. The spiritual religion of Christ was the
development of the great truths prefigured in the symbols of
the ceremonial religion of Moses. I have shown how both
Mohammedanism and paganism degrade the female character
and sex. It would seem therefore that man, left to himself,
would never have set up a religion which dealt equitably and
kindly with them. And what has infidelity, without a religion,
done for them? What would it do for them? Degrade them by
demoralizing them. The patrons of impurity and licentiousness, infidels at heart, have put on the cloak of the philosopher,
and the most licentious maxims have found their way into
works making high pretensions to morality, and assuming the
office of teachers of the age. Atheism, the most undisguised,
has made its appearance, and, alas, that it should boast of a
priestess entitled to distinction on other grounds to conduct its
worship at the shrine and upon the altar of chance!

Before skepticism had reached this depth of error, and arrived at the gloomy region of a godless void, while yet it lingered on the shores of Deism, it manifested its demoralizing
tendency. Hume taught that adultery, when known, was a
slight offense, and, when unknown, no offense at all.
Bolingbroke openly and violently attacked every important

truth and every serious duty; particularly he did what he could to license lewdness, and cut up chastity and decency by the roots. Lord Herbert, of Cherbury, the most serious of the early English deists, declared that the indulgence of lust is no more to be blamed than the thirst of a fever or the drowsiness of lethargy.

Nor have modern infidels been behind their predecessors. Godwin and Owen attacked the marriage tie. And let the annals of the first French revolution, that terrible eruption from the volcano of atheism, tell by the history of Mirabeau the type of its morals, what infidelity would do to corrupt and degrade the female sex. Woman's virtue, dignity, honor, and happiness are nowhere safe but under the protection of the Word of God. The Bible is the aegis of the female sex. Beneath this protection they are secure in their rights, their dignity, and their peace. It is their vine and fig tree, under which, in calm repose, they may enjoy the shade and relish the fruit. It protects their purity from taint and their peace from disturbance. Let woman know her friend and her enemy too. An infidel of either sex is the foe of our species, either individually or collectively viewed; but a female infidel is the most dangerous and destructive of the furies from whom, in her suicidal career, the virtuous of her own sex recoil with horror, and whom the vicious regard as the abettor, though it may be unintentionally, of their crimes. Woman! regard your Savior for the next world as your Emancipator for this present one. Love the Bible as the charter of your liberty and the guardian of your bliss. And consider the church of Christ as your asylum from the wrongs of oppression and the arts of seduction.

Let woman seek to discharge her obligations to Christianity. Grateful she ought to be, for immense are the favors which have been conferred upon her by it. It is enough to demand her thankfulness that, in common with man, she is the object of divine love, redeeming mercy, and the subject of immortal hope; but, in addition to this, she is rescued from oppression and exalted to honor in the present world. In regard to this, your obligations to Christianity are immense. You owe infinitely more to it than you ever reflect upon, or than you will ever be able to cancel. Often, as you look around upon your condition in society, and especially as often as you contrast your situation with that of women in pagan countries, let a glow of gratitude warm your heart and add intensity to the fervor with which you exclaim, "Precious Bible." Yes, doubly precious to you as your friend for both worlds.

How, then, shall woman discharge her obligations? In two ways: first, in yielding up her heart and life to the influence and service of her benefactor in faith, holiness, and love. Female piety is the best, the only sincere expression of female gratitude to God. An irreligious woman is also an ungrateful one. She who loves not Christ, whomsoever else she may love, and however chaste and pure that love may be, is living immeasurably below her obligations, and has a stain of guilt upon her heart and her conscience, which no other virtue can efface or conceal.

Woman's obligations should also be discharged by seeking to extend to others that benign system which has exerted so beneficial an influence upon herself. Of all the supporters of our missionary schemes, whether they are formed to evangelize the heathen abroad or reform the sinful at home, women should be, as indeed they generally are, the most zealous, liberal, and prayerful supporters. Wherever she turns her eye over the distant regions of our earth, at least wherever paganism and Mohammedanism throw their baleful shadows (and alas, how large a portion of the earth that is!), there she beholds her sex degraded and oppressed. From China's vast domain, from India's sunny plains, from Persia's flowery gardens, from the snows of Arctic regions, from the sterile deserts of Arabia, and beneath the burning line in Africa, woman lifts her voice amidst her wrongs, her woes, and her miseries, piteously imploring, "Come over and help us." The whole creation groans and travails in pain together until now, but her groans are deeper, her cries louder, than any others. Borne upon the wings of every breeze, and floated on every wave that touches our shores from those regions of sin and sorrow, comes her petition to Christian females in this country for the blessings of Christianity. Cold, thankless, and unfeeling must be that heart which is unaffected by such an appeal and makes no effort to respond to it; which prompts no interest in our missionary schemes, and leads to no liberality in their support. The Millennium will be especially woman's jubilee, and as no groan is deeper than hers during the reign of sin and sorrow, so no joy will be louder than hers under the reign of Christ. It belongs, therefore, to her to be most fervent in the cry of the church, "Come, Lord Jesus, come quickly."

Chapter 2

*The Conspicuous Place Which Woman
Occupies in Holy Scripture*

"In the old time the holy women also . . ." 1 Peter 3:5

It will probably be objected against some of the subjects selected for this work that they are not exclusively appropriate for the class of persons to whom they are addressed, that is, young women. This, however, so far from being a fault, is an excellence. Most conditions of human life are prospective, and have not only some proximate objects and duties connected with them, but also some ultimate ones to which the others are preparatory; and he who would lead persons to the right discharge of the whole range of their obligations must set before them the future as well as the present, especially when due preparation for later years must not only be made in the present, but must be considered, to a considerable extent, the object and design of the present. Neither childhood nor youth is an ultimate condition of human existence, but each leads on, looks to, and prepares for manhood or womanhood. Surely it must be appropriate, then, to those who are already arrived at adult age, or are fast approaching it, to have the whole view of their future condition laid before them, at least in general outline. How else can they prepare for it?

Those to whom this volume is addressed are supposed to have arrived at that period of youth when the judgment is sufficiently matured and reflective to be capable of studying and appreciating their future relations and duties, and therefore ought to have the subject laid before them. Who can be rightly educated for any future situation if it is concealed till all its obligations and responsibilities burst suddenly upon them? True, there is in some minds an almost instinctive kind of perception of what is proper to be done in any new conjuncture of circumstances, so that, almost without training, they are prepared for whatever situation is before them. But this is not the case with all. The greater number of mankind must, as far as possible, be trained for their various situations in life. Just as, in the education of a boy, especially when learning a trade or profession, the future tradesman, master, father, and citizen must be set before him as that for which he must prepare himself, so in the training of young women the whole of womanhood in its full expansion, ripened excellences, and complete relations, obligations, and responsibilities must be laid before them.

We know that there is much which can be learned only from experience, yet there is much also that may be learned by observation, reading, and reflection. Mothers, governesses, authors, and preachers who take up the subject should ever bear in mind that the girl is to develop into the woman; and in teaching the girl, they should ever have their eye fixed ultimately upon the woman, and should with all possible earnestness fix the eye of the girl also upon her future womanhood. Not that she is to be so taken up with the remote as to neglect the proximate, with the future as to neglect the present, or to acquire a precocious matronly air and gravity which will repress the ardor and vivacity of youth, and, by anticipated cares and solicitudes, go out to meet halfway the coming troubles of life. But remember, my young female friends, and the lesson cannot be too deeply impressed upon your minds, that the seeds of woman's lifelong excellences must be sown in the springtime of existence; and it must be done in part by her own hand, when aided and taught by others to prepare the soil. The flowers of womanly excellence, which she would wish to grow in her future character, must be previously and carefully selected, and be contemplated and anticipated by her in all their full-blown beauty and their richest fragrance, even while she is yet in youth.

With these remarks as my justification in presenting to the younger of the sex what in fact appertains to the more advanced in years, I now proceed to the subject of the present chapter.

When we consider the importance of woman in the great human family, it would be strange if, in a volume given by inspiration of God for regulating the conduct and promoting the happiness of mankind, she had no place assigned to her commensurate with the influence she is formed to exert. The Bible gives us an account of the origin and construction of society, and is designed, among other and still higher purposes, to direct its movements and promote its welfare. This it could not do if it left out woman, failed to bring her prominently forward, or did not prescribe with much form and detail her rank, her mission, and her duties. In the coins which were struck in the reigns of our William and Mary, when the wife was reigning as queen, the busts of both husband and wife were represented—the king in front and the queen behind. And if a frontispiece were designed for the history of our race as recorded in the Bible, man and woman should be exhibited in something of a similar manner, with this inscription around the twofold portrait: "Male and female created He them."

The subject of this chapter was entered upon in the last one; it will be here continued and expanded into wider dimensions. Man, of course, is the chief subject of revealed truth. He occupies there, as he does in society, the first place. More is said of him, to him, and by him than applies to woman. He is the prime actor—but not the sole one—in the great drama of Providence, as it is developed in the pages of inspiration. His companion in pilgrimage is brought forward into notice, and is neither lost in his shadow, nor only occasionally peeps out from behind his more portly form and loftier stature. Her name and history, her virtues and vices, her services and sorrows occupy a considerable space in the holy book. She has no right to complain that she is overlooked or forgotten, or that she is thrust into a corner and hidden from observation. There is more than enough said about her to make her contented. She ought to be thankful and, without divine grace, may even be tempted to be vain. She cannot be deprived of self-respect, or of the respect of others, on account of the manner in which she is treated in the Scriptures. In this respect the Bible stands in bright and beautiful contrast to the Koran.

We shall first of all advert to the account which the Bible gives of woman's creation and fall in the book of Genesis. We would, in passing, remark that it is to revelation, and to that alone, that we are indebted for our knowledge of the origin of the human species. Without the Mosaic account of the creation, we should know neither the date nor the source of the family of man. There is no other oracle which can give a response to the question, "Whence came we?" This furnishes an answer and satisfies the inquirer, not as some would pretend, with a mere allegorical history, but with a veritable fact.

I need not recite the details of the scenes of Paradise, but only refer to them. It is at once a beautiful and melancholy record. We there see woman as she came from the hand of the Creator, with a body combining every charm which could captivate the being for whose companionship she was designed, and a soul possessing every virtue that could adorn her character and make her an object of reverent affection. Her creation was peculiar, but not unworthy of the Great Being who made her,

of herself, or of him from whose own body she was derived.
Her origin seemed to dignify both her husband and herself.
She was formed of organized and vitalized matter, and not of
mere dust; here was her distinction. Who can describe or conceive the thoughts or emotions of this holy pair at their first
interview! Our great bard has attempted it in his immortal
verse, where he says,

> I beheld her, not far off,
> Such as I saw her in my dream, adorned
> With what all earth or heaven could bestow
> To make her amiable; on she came,
> Led by her heavenly Maker, though unseen,
> And guided by His voice—
> Grace was in all her steps, heaven in her eye,
> In every gesture dignity and love.
> I, overjoy'd, could not forbear aloud:—
> Thou hast fulfill'd
> Thy words, Creator bounteous and benign,
> Giver of all things fair! but fairest this
> Of all Thy gifts! nor enviest. I now see
> Bone of my bone, flesh of my flesh, myself
> Before me: Woman is her name; of man
> Extracted: for this cause he shall forego
> Father and mother, and to his wife adhere;
> And they shall be one flesh, one heart, one soul.

Painters and sculptors have joined with poets to represent
to the senses and the imagination the first woman in all her
untainted loveliness. It is the Scriptures, be it recollected, that
supply to them the enrapturing subject of their art.

Thus far we see woman, man's companion in holiness and
bliss, inhabiting with him the garden of Eden, enjoying its

beauties, and helping to preserve them. Together they joined in the morning hymn and vesper song, confessed no sin (for they had committed none), and unburdened themselves of no care, for none pressed upon them. All was praise, while their own notes of thanksgiving, blended with the melodies of the grove and the music of the fields, led even the ear of God to listen with delight, and to say, "It is good."

Alas, how soon and how suddenly changed was this scene of Paradisaic bliss! Man was placed in Eden not (as we shall be in heaven, if we are so happy as to reach it) in a state of confirmed happiness, but as we are now upon earth, in a condition of trial. His submission to God must be tested; and this was done in a manner that exactly suited his condition. A garden as a residence became his state of innocence, and the fruit of a particular tree equally well suited his circumstances for the proof of his entire and implicit subjection. The test was as easy as it was rational and suitable. Traditions of the state of primeval felicity are current among many nations. They are discoverable in Grecian and Roman poetry, in the fables of the gardens of the Hesperides, and in the pleasing fiction of the poet's golden age. To induce Adam to eat of the forbidden fruit was the scheme of Satan for his fall. It is difficult to conceive in what other way he could tempt them. And how did he succeed? You know the melancholy sequel. The assault of the tempter was made upon woman. She was the selected victim of his wiles. It is evident, therefore, that he regarded her, while in a state of innocence, as more easily vanquished than man, and considered her even then as the weaker vessel. At the same time, does it not seem as if he had marked her out from the beginning as the chief instrument for accomplishing his future purposes of mischief towards the family of man? Events have justified the sagacity of his malice; for to her influence how much may be traced of the crimes and calamities which desolate our earth! He saw in the conduct of the first pair the love which woman inspires and cherishes, and was confident that, if he could subdue her, he might leave her to subdue the man.

The Apostle Paul, in referring to this event, says, "Adam was not deceived, but the woman being deceived was first in the transgression." From the very creation, woman has shown a feebler power of resistance, a greater pliancy of disposition, than man. How Satan knew this we are not informed; but that he did know it is evident from his commencing the assault on Eve instead of Adam. The passage just quoted seems to imply all this. It does not mean that Adam did not sin, and was not deceived by the tempter, but that the woman posed a feebler resistance to the temptation than he would have done, and that the temptation, as applied to her mind, would have been ineffectual on him. To tempt and seduce him to sin there were needed all the soft persuasions, the entreaties, and the example of his wife. Satan understood this, and approached man not with the specious argument of the serpent, but through her irresistible allurements.

Some have supposed that Adam was not at all deceived by the tempter (that he saw at once all his suggestions were lies), but that foreseeing what Eve had done, how she had plunged herself into ruin, he, out of mere love to her, and with his eyes open, determined to share her fate. But the apostle's words do not necessarily convey this; they indicate that he was not deceived first, nor directly, by the tempter, but afterwards, and by his wife. Her fall was occasioned by the deception of Satan alone; his by the deception of Satan, aided by the persuasion of the woman (see Albert Barnes's *Notes* on the passage).

Having considered the Scriptural account of woman's condition at the creation, and the means by which, through her, the human race was brought into its present state of sin and misery, we may next notice the very explicit and frequent mention which is made in the Scriptures of her numerous relations in social life, with the descriptions they give of the various characters of women. It certainly tends deeply to impress us with the importance of woman, and to raise her in her own and in our estimation, to see how constantly she is brought before us on the sacred page, in every part which she fills in life, as if the duties connected with each were of vast consequence to society. Not one is omitted; all are recognized and dwelt upon. Woman is ever before us in one or another of her many relations to the community.

Not only is there much said about the son, but also about the daughter. This relationship is not only included in the generic term of "children," but it is also set out by itself. How commonly is it mentioned in connection with the children of the other sex, as "the sons and the daughters" are spoken of. A beautiful instance of this we have in the words of the psalmist: "that our sons may be as plants grown up in their youth, and our daughters may be as cornerstones, polished after the similitude of a palace," or "as corner-pillars, wrought like those of a palace," that is, in their fittest and best proportions, combining strength, beauty, and symmetry both of body and of soul. No comparison can be more elegant and delicate than this. In the exquisite poetry of the Hebrews, how commonly is this relationship employed as the metaphor of countries, states, and cities! Jerusalem comes before us as "the daughter of Zion," sometimes jubilant in her prosperity, at other times, as in the Lamentations of Jeremiah, covered with sackcloth and bathed in tears.

The word "sister" occurs in almost every portion of the Word of God, like a floweret, lowly and lovely amidst others of larger growth and more imposing form and color. How sweet and gentle a spirit is sometimes seen in a sister's form amidst her brothers' more robust ones; and what a softening influence does the spell of her fascinating tenderness throw over their ruder natures. We are thus reminded by Scripture that the younger female branches of the family are to be thought of as having their separate claims upon parental regard and brotherly affections. Many families are laid open in the Bible to our view of which the sisters, as well as the brothers, are brought prominently into notice.

How much may it be supposed would be said about the wife—and how much is indeed said about that close and endearing relation! To form the character and direct the conduct of the wife is worth all the pains that have been bestowed by innumerable writers; and we might have been very sure, even before we had read a page of revelation, that much would be there found concerning this relationship. The book of Proverbs, that admirable directory for domestic and social life, is quite a manual for wives, as well as for every other member of the family. Unusual pains seem taken for the right formation of her character. How frequently and impressively does Solomon refer to woman as sustaining this close and tender relation. In what exalted and glowing terms does he speak of her when she comprehends the graces and the excellences which she should always possess. "Whoso findeth a wife findeth a good thing." "A prudent wife is from the Lord." Who has ever read, or can read, without admiration, the beautiful description of a virtuous woman in the closing chapter of Proverbs? Can we wonder that he who had this elevated idea of the value of such a companion should again and again exhort a husband to live joyfully with the wife of his youth and, forsaking all others, cleave to her alone? In this he merely copied the beautiful and poetic picture of connubial happiness which had been furnished to him by his father David, if indeed he was the author of the Psalm: "Thy wife shall be as a fruitful vine by the sides of thine house; thy children like olive plants round about thy table."

"The vine," says Bishop Horne, "a lowly plant raised with tender care, becoming by its luxuriance, its beauty, its fragrance, and its clusters the ornament and glory of the house to which it is joined, and by which it is supported, forms the finest imaginable emblem of a fair, virtuous, and faithful wife. The olive trees planted by the inhabitants of eastern countries round their banqueting places in their gardens, to cheer the eye by their verdure and to refresh the body by their cooling shade, do no less aptly and significantly set forth the pleasure which parents feel at the sight of a numerous and flourishing offspring."

On the other hand, Solomon directs all the powers of his bitter eloquence and irony against the degraded woman, whose deadly work none has ever depicted with more holy indignation. How does he brand the crime of the harlot in the second and fifth chapters of the book of Proverbs, and with what awful correctness does he describe the conduct of the adulteress in the seventh! Nor does he stop here, but descends to the characters of women who, though less guilty than those to whom we have just alluded, are still deserving of severe reprobation: the foolish woman who plucks her house down with her hands; the brawling woman, whose society is more intolerable than dwelling in a corner of the housetop, or in the wilderness; the woman who makes ashamed, who is a rottenness in the bones of her husband; the odious woman, whose marriage is one of the four things for which the earth is disquieted, and which it cannot bear; the fair woman without discretion, whose beauty is like a jewel of gold in a swine's snout; the contentious wife, who is like a continual dropping on a very rainy day.

This same Solomon, at the period when he had reached a penitent and reformed old age, and when all the events of his life had passed in review before him, is compelled to confess that he had sought in vain for a woman after his own heart: "I find more bitter than death the woman whose heart is snares and nets, and her hands as bands; whoso pleaseth God shall escape from her, but the sinner shall be taken by her. Behold, this have I found (said the Preacher), counting one by one, to find out the account, which yet my soul seeketh, but I find not; one man among a thousand have I found, but a woman among all those have I not found."

Let not this passage, however, be mistaken, as if it meant that it was Solomon's opinion that the number of good women is inferior to the number of good men. Observation and general testimony assure us that this is not the truth. We are to consider where he made his inquiry for female virtue, and under what circumstances it was made. He who had crowded his court with wives and concubines could little expect to find female excellence in such a situation. Instead of concentrating his affections on one woman as his wife, the partner of his joys and sorrows, and seeking his happiness in drinking with her the sweet cup of connubial bliss, he had gathered round him in his harem, for pride and sensuality, a multitude of women amidst whose jealousies and contentions he could no more find happiness than he could virtue amidst their illicit pleasures. From such a scene virtue would retire abashed and weeping. If, therefore, in this passage he satirized the sex, he did it on unjust, unwise, and unmanly grounds. "But," says Dr. [Ralph] Wardlaw, "I am far from thinking that he here speaks the language of a disappointed and waspish satirist. He rather utters the feeling of an abased and self-dissatisfied penitent, of one who had felt it to be 'an evil and a bitter thing' to depart as he had done from God; who remembered 'the wormwood and the gall'; who perceived and lamented the folly and the wickedness of all those 'inventions' by which he and others had sought to find out happiness apart from the favor and the ways of God."

If we speak of woman as a mother, how often does that endearing relationship come before us in holy Scripture, both literally and metaphorically, in the Old Testament and in the New, in the way of example and of precept. The maternal relationship is the theme of constant reference, both for the sake of illustrating other subjects and for enforcing its own claims as those of the female head of the household. Had this character been omitted, or only introduced occasionally, and then invested with no more than a second-rate importance, the Bible would have been wanting in one of its sweetest harmonies with the feelings of nature, and one of its strongest appeals to the sympathies of humanity; and we would have doubted if it had come from Him who created woman and gave her as a help-meet for man. The paternal character and relation are maintained in their primary rank, authority, and dignity. No invasion is made upon the prerogative, nor is there any usurpation of the rights of the father; he is not called to yield his place of rule, his supremacy of condition, to the mother—and yet all her proper rank and station and influence are maintained. There she is exhibited as being in the family circle, if not the circumference which includes all, yet in one sense as the center in which husband, children, and servants all meet. How resonant are the Scriptures with that sweet and tender name, how redolent with the fragrance of that odoriferous word, how rich with the ornament of that beautiful term "mother." There is sustained the poet's declaration:

> A mother is a mother still,
> The holiest thing alive.

If the mother's importance is not known, her claims not conceded, her influence not felt, and her duties not rightly discharged, it is not the fault of the Bible, which is the friend of society by exalting that relationship. Nor is the mistress of the family overlooked or forgotten, nor her duties left out of consideration.

The widow, that name of desolation, that sorrowful epithet, that type of woe, meets us at every turn. She passes before us in her weeds and in her tears, leading in her hand her fatherless children, and saying to us, "Pity me; pity me, O my friends, for the hand of God hath touched me." More is said about, for, and to, this bereaved one than any other class of women—a circumstance which exhibits with uncommon force and beauty the compassion of God. But there is a discrimination on this subject which shows the wisdom as well as the tenderness of God. Young widows are admonished, while aged and helpless ones are comforted.

Nor is the female servant left out. A place for her is found among the various other and higher ranks and conditions of her sex. Her humble lot is recognized amidst the provisions and commands of the Law, and was announced and defended by the thunders of Mount Sinai. We find it protected by precept and illustrated by example, as if woman in the lowest grade of society should not be overlooked in the Bible, that blessed and glorious charter of rights and privileges. There the little maid lifts up her head among the queens and princesses of Scripture history.

But the most impressive and important point of view in which the subject can be placed, and the most convincing proof of the effect produced by the Scriptures with regard to woman, is the very great number and variety of female examples which they contain. It is one of the surpassing excellences of the Bible that it is replete with narrative, history, and biography, and thus, apart from its sacred character and its momentous importance, is one of the most interesting books in the world. It is full not only of precept, but of living, acting patterns of the virtues which it inculcates and the vices which it prohibits. It is a complete picture gallery in which we see portraits of every size, from the miniature to the full-length painting, and in every degree of representation, from the mere outline to the most finished production of the artist's pencil. Among these it would have been strange if female characters had been wanting; and they are not wanting. There, amidst kings, priests, warriors, and prophets, are to be seen the portraits of "the holy women of the old time, who trusted in God," as well as of those who disgraced themselves and dishonored their sex. In the great drama of life, as it passes before us in the Bible, no mean or inconsiderable part is assigned to female characters. Woman's place among the *dramatis personae* is not that of some airy vision which lights upon our path, and after surprising and dazzling us for a moment straightway vanishes and is seen no more, but of one of the veritable actors in almost every place and every scene.

The sacred volume opens, as we have already seen, with Eve in Paradise, all beauty, innocence and smiles, as its lovely frontispiece; and then it shows us that same Eve, impelled by the vanity which she has bequeathed as a mournful legacy to her daughters, reaching forth her hand, at the instigation of the tempter, to pluck that fruit which was the test of her obedience and the seed of all our woe, and thus exhibiting to us the sad association of beauty with sin.

In tracing woman's history, as it is set forth on the pages of Scripture, from Paradise as the starting point, we will look first at the darker side of the narrative. How soon do we see Adah and Zillah consenting to be the joint wives of Lamech, and thus giving, for all we can tell, the original pattern of that bane of domestic happiness, polygamy! Then come the "daughters of men," the women in the line of Cain who made no profession of religion, but lived in atheism, seducing and corrupting the "sons of God," the male line of Seth and the professors of godliness, and thus, by their unsuitable and incongruous marriages and the universal corruption that followed, creating the necessity for the waters of the deluge to wash away the moral filth of the old world. Hagar comes next, troubling the faith, charity, and peace of Abraham, persecuting the child of promise and, at the same time, punishing by her waywardness the weakness of the patriarch, whose concubine she was. Then comes the family of Lot: the poor, earthly-minded mother, who was so wedded to Sodom as to cast the lingering, longing look behind, which transformed her into a pillar of salt, and the disgusting conduct of her incestuous daughters, who showed too well how they had been corrupted by the place of their abode, and how careful all parents should be to remove their children from the polluting influence of evil examples.

What a revolting pattern of an adulterous woman, and of a cruel slanderer to hide her shame, is Potiphar's wife! Then there was the ensnaring and successful temptation offered by the daughters of Moab to the children of Israel in the wilderness. How mighty and fatal were the powers of harlotry in Delilah to subdue the strength and extort the secrets of Samson! And what a forcible picture of man's weakness before woman's vicious wiles have these furnished to all coming ages! Who does not think of Bathsheba consenting to David's wicked proposals, and thus causing him for a while to cease to be David? Then come the strange women who threw even the mighty intellect of Solomon into the awful eclipse of idolatry; Jezebel, that Zidonian idolatress, who instigated her husband to the murder of Naboth, and exasperated the mind of Ahab to a more intense degree of wickedness than he would otherwise have attained to; and Athaliah, that turbulent and idolatrous queen-mother, who counseled her son to do wickedly, and was put to death by command of Jehoiada the priest.

I have not been anxious, of course, to dwell on the examples and descriptions of female delinquency recorded in the Scriptures. It has been a matter of surprise, perhaps almost of regret, to some that such instances of depravity should have been left on record. But shall we dispute either the wisdom, goodness, or purity of God in these histories? Are not important ends to be answered by them in the moral government of God, and in the religious history of man? A profligate woman is at once the most odious, mischievous, and hateful member of the community. Is it not in every way proper, and even desirable, that such a character should be held up to detestation and scorn as a warning to her sex, and that God should thus set a brand upon her with His own hand, and bear His indignant testimony against her vices?

The examples of this kind are all for our warning, to show in instances from actual life the excessive odiousness of female depravity. This is done in a manner least likely to do harm and most likely to do good. The descriptions of female turpitude in the Word of God contain nothing to inflame the imagination or stimulate the passions; nothing to make vice seductive by a half-concealment of its odiousness; nothing to beat down the guards of virtue by associating sin with an amiable or interesting character, or to screen it by sophisticated and insidious excuses or defenses. Vice is left in all its naked and revolting deformity, all its nauseating loathsomeness, to inspire disgust and cause even ordinary virtue to recoil from the ugly and filthy object. How different is the case with many works of fiction, both prosaic and poetic, in which, though there may be less particularity of sinful detail, there is immeasurably more to corrupt the moral principles, to pollute the heart, and to lead astray the youthful mind from the paths of virtue! What female reader of the Word of God can rise from contemplating even the worst characters, and perusing the most vivid descriptions of the sins of her sex, without a stronger love of purity and a more deeply rooted hatred of iniquity? This is the answer we would give to infidels who sometimes affect to be prudish, and complain of the descriptions and examples of female criminality which are contained in the sacred volume. The use which every virtuous woman will make of them is to be inspired with a greater abhorrence of transgression, and a more holy and intense desire to be kept from the most distant approach to it.

Coming to the New Testament, we meet with Herodias, exhibiting the malignant and vengeful passions of a shameless woman against the servant of God, who had dared to reprove her paramour, and impelling Herod, against the protest of his judgment, heart, and conscience, to put John the Baptist to death, and so involve them both in murder. And here also we read of the Jewish women who encouraged and stimulated to violence the mob that persecuted Paul and Barnabas, and "that woman Jezebel, who called herself a prophetess, and taught and seduced God's servants to commit fornication, and to eat things sacrificed to idols."

In such instances as these, female pride, wherever it exists, may find some check upon its exercise, and some motive to humility. To those females who are prone to think of their sex more highly than they ought, we present these examples of woman's frailty, which the pen of inspiration has drawn upon the pages of Scripture. To those of the other sex, if there are any, who are apt to glory over fallen women, we would, after reminding them that some of these instances are the result of their own seductions, present the brighter side of the picture. We would also call upon women to contemplate for their own encouragement the beautiful specimens of female excellence, with which, like so many stars of various magnitudes, the firmament of Scripture is studded.

There is Sarah, who, notwithstanding her many failings, was unquestionably a good and even a great woman. In her case, as in many others, her beauty became a snare to others, if not dangerous to her own virtue, and placed the life of her husband in peril. Still she is presented by the Apostle Peter as one of the holy women of old who were patterns of domestic virtue and piety. Her defect, which consisted of a weakness of faith, leading to some strange domestic arrangements that brought their own punishment, was surrounded with the brightness of many excellences in which, if they were not entirely lost, they were at any rate diminished. She was a pattern of conjugal fidelity, sweet simplicity, and a just, matronly jealousy towards the stranger who had been brought for a while so unwisely into her place. Her faith in God's promise was strong, though shaken for a moment by the improbabilities of the promised blessing.

Rebekah's earlier and latter life present to us a somewhat painful contrast. None can read the beautiful account of the mission of Abraham's servant to her father without admiration of the good qualities of the damsel who is the heroine of the story, her industrious habits, her unaffected and artless simplicity, her genuine yet not silly modesty, her graceful courtesy, and her humane consideration of the comfort of the brute creation. What a bright pattern is here for the imitation of young people. But, oh! her unbelieving, injudicious, and sinful contrivances to bring about the bestowal of the divine blessing upon the heir of promise by the wicked imposition which she practiced upon her aged and blind husband! Mothers, read it, and learn to guard against sinful contrivances to get good for your children. Rebekah, however, was a good, though mistaken, woman.

In Miriam, the watchful sentinel beside the waters of the

Nile of the ark which contained the infant Moses, we see first the dutiful daughter and anxious sister, and, in later life, the co-adjutor of her illustrious brother, leading the chorus of women by her timbrel and her voice in his triumphal song on the borders of the Red Sea. Afterwards, in conjunction with Aaron, she became his opponent through envy; but we may hope she was restored to her better and earlier mind through the chastisement she received from the Lord. How much mischief may envy do to spoil the best of characters, and to poison the happiness of families!

In Deborah, we contemplate the religious heroine and the inspired poetess, raised up by the special providence of God for the deliverance of His people—an instance of exalted piety in an age of depressed religion, and still deeper national distress.

Should anyone ask what we are to say of Jael, celebrated by the poetess Deborah in her lofty strain of praise, I scarcely know what answer to give. Nothing less than a divine mandate, which she may have received in some unknown and unrecorded manner, could have justified the deed. Apart from this, even the stratagems of war would not clear the heroine from the charge of treachery of the blackest kind. True, Sisera was an enemy, but he had trusted himself to her protection, and she slew him while he slept under her guardianship. I leave the matter therefore as I find it, without either justifying or condemning it, for I know not all the facts of the case.

What a pattern of filial obedience, piety, and patriotism we have in Jephthah's daughter, over whose affecting story hangs so deep a mystery. Whether, according to the opinions of some, she was actually offered up in sacrifice, or, according to others, was only consecrated by perpetual virginity to God, her beautiful character shines out with equal brightness, in all that is amiable, dutiful, and submissive.

But now turn to that touching and melancholy group of

widows in the land of Moab: Naomi, Ruth, and Orpah. What
pen but that which has done it, and done it with such inimitable simplicity, could do justice to this sweet and pathetic
story? Rarely in the history of families does such a scene of affliction as this occur: a widowed mother, and the widows of
her two sons! A sad proof how precarious are all the scenes of
dear domestic bliss we fondly call our own. How tender, how
dignified, and how thoughtful is the conduct of Naomi! What
nobleness of resolution, what daughter-like attachment, and
what piety do we see in Ruth! If in her later conduct there was
that which would not suit the meridian of our age and country, there was nothing contrary to the strictest purity of intention or modesty of conduct, if we take into account the circumstances of her time, and the provisions of the Jewish law
under which she lived. The whole narrative presents a beautiful
episode in Jewish history, and an attractive specimen of the
simplicity of early manners.

Can we fail to sympathize with Hannah in her sorrows,
her insults, and her joys, or to admire her zeal for the Lord in
devoting her child of promise to His service? What a pattern
for parents willingly to give up their sons as ministers and missionaries! Abigail furnishes us with a striking example of the
singular prudence of a woman who was unhappily associated
with a drunkard and a churl, and of her diligence and tact in
averting from her family the evils impending over it from her
husband's vices.

What an instance of respect, gratitude, and affection for
the ministers of religion, of female influence rightly exerted
over the mind of her husband in the cause of religion, and of
submission to the will of God is the Shunammite! Who can
read that touching account of the death of her only son, and
her own collected, composed, and energetic conduct on the
occasion, without deep feeling and high admiration? We find

in her no overwhelming or distracting grief preventing her from adopting the best and only means for obtaining relief, but a faith which sustained her courage and directed all her actions. Multitudes in every age and country, where the story has gone, have been instructed by her language and stimulated by her example, and, amidst their deepest sorrows, have echoed her few noble monosyllables in reply to the question, " 'Is it well with thee? With thy husband? With thy child?' And she answered and said, 'It is well.' "

And then what a pattern of fidelity, piety, and kindness do we find for female servants in the very next chapter, in the simple and beautiful story of the little Hebrew captive girl who was nursemaid in Naaman's family! All, and especially those who occupy a similar situation, may learn by what weak and humble instruments God may accomplish His purposes and work out the schemes of His providence. To many a charity sermon in these remote days has that incident furnished a text; and thus the little Jewish slave not only brought healing to her master, and a knowledge of the true God into Syria, but became a pattern to myriads of children in our own country!

No less to be admired are the generosity and faith of the widow of Sarepta, whose barrel of meal and cruse of oil stand out in such relief among the brightest pictures of Old Testament history. In what a glimmer of glory does the name of Esther blaze forth upon us for conjugal fidelity, piety uncorrupted by prosperity, and queenly influence consecrated to the cause of true religion!

Now open the pages of the New Testament. Is Christianity destitute of female worthies, women of holy renown? It would be very strange if it were. Strange, indeed, if His religion, who, though He was the Son of God, was born of woman, did not raise up many who would shine forth in all the mild and heavenly radiance of female piety.

Though, as I said in the last chapter, we ascribe no divine honors and offer no idolatrous homage to the Virgin Mary, nor set her forth in the beauties of painting and sculpture, nor call her, with a singular mixture of absurdity and blasphemy, "the Mother of God," we revere her as blessed and exalted among women, to give birth to the humanity of Christ, the Savior of the world; and we ascribe to her every holy and general excellence as a woman, wife, mother, and saint.

In an age when Popery is lifting up its head in triumph and hope, no fair opportunity should be lost to expose its pretensions and refute its errors. There is no part of this dreadful system more contrary to Scripture or more insulting to God than its Mariolatry, or worship of the Virgin Mary. She is called "Mother of God," "Queen of Seraphim, Saints, and Prophets," "Advocate of Sinners," "Refuge of Sinners," "Gate of Heaven," and "Queen of Heaven." And as the same titles are ascribed to her, or nearly so, as are ascribed to Christ, so is the same worship paid to her as to the Savior. Churches are built to her honor; her shrines are crowded with devotees, enriched with their gifts, and adorned with their votive offerings. Prayers are offered to her; her praises are chanted in hymns; thanksgivings are addressed to her, and blessings are asked from her, as one who has power to bestow them. Seven annual festivals celebrate her greatness, and keep alive the devotion of her worshippers. In this way Papists almost shut out the worship due to the Father and the Savior by their idolatry of her.

Now where, I ask, is one single example, command, or even hint for all this in the Word of God? Is it any wonder that the Scriptures are kept from the people, when the most common understanding could see that nothing of all this is to be found in that volume? The Acts of the Apostles make mention of her name but once, and that without any mark of eulogy; and in the epistles she is not mentioned at all. Yes, how

contrary is all this to the declaration that there is only one
Mediator between God and man, the Man Jesus Christ. "This
doctrine of the worship due to the Virgin," says Wylie, in his
admirable work on the Papacy, "has been exhibited in symbol,
and that in so grotesque a way that for a moment we forget its
blasphemy. In the dream of St. Bernard, which forms the
subject of an altar-piece at Milan, two ladders were seen
reaching from earth to heaven. At the top of one of the ladders
stood Christ, and at the top of the other stood Mary. Of those
who attempted to enter heaven by the ladder of Christ, not
one succeeded; all fell back. Of those who ascended by the ladder of Mary, not one failed. The Virgin, being prompt to suc-
cor, stretched out her hand, and, thus aided, the aspirants ascended with ease."

We cherish also a high veneration for Elizabeth, Mary's
cousin, the wife of Zechariah and the mother of John the
Baptist. In the piety of old Anna, we see a bright pattern for
aged widows in her posture, believing and waiting for the
consolation of Israel, and an example for an aged saint, ready
for the coming of the Lord Jesus Christ; we see the zeal, so
worthy to be imitated by every reclaimed sinner, of the woman
of Samaria, after she had believed in Christ, for His honor and
the conversion of her countrymen; we see the melting penitence of the woman who had been a sinner, whose history
teaches us that the most abandoned persons may be reclaimed
and find mercy, and that penitence, gratitude, and love should
be in proportion to the guilt contracted and forgiven; we see
the invincible faith of the Syrophoenician woman, which received such admiration from Christ, and will teach the latest
generations of mankind the power of importunate, persevering, and believing prayer; we see the generosity of the poor
widow who cast two mites, the whole of her substance, into
the treasury of the temple; we see the beautiful account of the

two sisters, Martha and Mary, and the delineation in it of the characters of the careful and troubled housewife, and the anxious inquirer after salvation; we see the pouring out of the box of spikenard by one who loved Christ so much as to give her costliest offerings to His person; we see the grateful, devoted attention and ministrations of Mary Magdalene and the other Mary to Christ. What an array of female excellence is here!

Passing on to the Acts of the Apostles, what delightful mention is made of Dorcas, full of good works and almsdeeds which she did, as evidenced by her coats and garments for the poor and the tears which were produced by her death, and which embalmed her memory; Lydia, who resorted to the place of prayer at Philippi, whose heart the Lord had opened to attend to the things spoken by Paul, and who afforded the rites of hospitality to the apostle and his companion; and the chief women, not a few at Thessalonica, who believed in the apostle's doctrine concerning Christ.

Nor are the epistles barren of female names deserving ever to be held in remembrance for their piety, zeal, and good works. There we find Phoebe, the deaconess and bearer to Rome of the epistle to the church in that city, Euodia and Syntyche; Lois and Eunice, the mother and grandmother of Timothy, renowned for the unfeigned faith which dwelt in them; and those women also who labored with Paul in the gospel. And what shall we say more of Priscilla, Paul's helper in Christ, and the instructress of the eloquent Apollos; and Mary, "who bestowed much labor upon him"; and Tryphena, and Tryphosa, and Julia, "who labored in the Lord"?

No, my female friends, you see, I repeat, the Scriptures of truth have not passed over your sex in silence, nor thrust it into a corner, nor thrown it into the shade. On the contrary, the sacred page is rich and luminous with bright and beautiful examples of female excellence. You stand there side by side with man in the practice of piety, and are exhibited as not a whit behind him in all that appertains to the glory of humanity.

In the Bible, we have now proven that woman is seen in every gradation of rank, from the queen upon the throne to the menial grinding at the mill; in every variety of condition, the maid, the wife, the mother, and the mistress; in every circumstance of grief and joy, the happy bride and the mourning widow; in every phase of moral character, the faithful spouse and the shameless adulteress; in every scene of active duty, whether in the family, the church, or the world; in every change-filled aspect of fortune, rolling in affluence or pining in want. There she is seen enlivening the sacred page with her narrative and adorning it with her beauty, sometimes darkening it with her crimes, at others brightening it with her virtues; now calling us to weep with her in her sorrows, then to rejoice with her in her joys. In short, woman is everywhere to be found wrought into the details of God's Scriptures, a beacon to warn us or a lamp to guide us. And all the notices written by the inspiration of the Holy Spirit are to be considered as His testimony to the excellence and importance of your sex, and the influence it is intended and destined to exert upon the welfare of mankind.

Had the Bible (I will not say had it been against you) passed you over in silence, or only referred to you incidentally, or looked at you with sidelong glances, you would have sunk in general estimation, and man's neglect of you would have been defended or excused by that of God Himself. But now no one can plead the example of the Bible for any attempt to neglect, despise, or oppress you. While it protects woman from the insults, injuries, and oppression of the other sex, it saves her with no less care and benefit from the sad effects which would arise from the assumption of prerogatives which do not belong to her, and from those excesses of ambition to which her own vanity might otherwise prompt her. It guards her dignity from being trampled down by others, and equally prevents her from lowering it herself by pretensions which would only make her ridiculous. It describes with accuracy the circle within which it is the will of Providence that she should move; presents to her the mission which she is sent into the world to fulfill; furnishes her with the rules by which she is to act; proposes to her the rewards which she may legitimately seek and surely expect if she is faithful to herself; and offers her the assistance necessary for the fulfillment of her high and holy vocation. What this is will be the subject of our next chapter.

In the meantime, let me exhort you not only to study the Scriptures to learn the way of salvation through faith in Christ Jesus, but to study them in order to form your own character as women by their precepts and examples. Many and precious are the volumes that have been written for your benefit by your own sex. Female pens have been most happily and usefully employed in delineating female excellence, in writings which you would do well to read. But, after all, there is no guide for the formation of female character, morally or religiously considered, like the inspired one. A woman unacquainted with the Bible, and ignorant of its contents as affecting her own conduct, character, and history, has yet to know the finest patterns of female loveliness. The Bible is the best mirror by which most accurately to know what you are, and to become what you should be; before which you may adjust all the moral habiliments of the soul, and from which you may go forth adorned with all the beauties of holiness, clothed with the garment of purity, and decorated with the ornament of a meek and quiet spirit.

Chapter 3

Woman's Mission

"And the Lord God said, 'It is not good that the man should be alone. I will make him an help meet for him.' "
Genesis 2:18

"What in the great, diversified, and busy world is my place and my business?" is a question which everyone should ask. For everyone has a place to fill and a part to act. And to act his part well, according to the will of God, in the lofty drama of human life, should be the ambition, solicitude, and prayer of each of us. It is the first lesson of wisdom to know our place, the second to keep it—and, of course, corresponding to this, to ascertain the duties of our place and to discharge them. There are class duties as well as individual ones, and the latter are generally to be more accurately learned by an intelligent apprehension of the former. Woman, as such, has her mission. What is it? What is precisely the rank she is to occupy? What is the purpose she is to fulfill, above which she would be unduly exalted, and below which she would be unjustly degraded? This is a subject which should be thoroughly understood in order that she may know what to claim, and man what to concede; that she may know what she has to do, and that he may know what he has a right to expect.

I shall endeavor to answer this question, and point out the nature of woman's mission. In doing this, I shall consult the infallible oracle of Scripture, and not the speculations of moralists, economists, and philosophers. I hold this to be our rule in the matter before us. God is the Creator of both sexes, the constructor of society, the author of social relations, and the arbiter of social duties, claims, and immunities. And this is admitted by all who believe in the authority of the Bible. You are content, my female friends, to abide by the decisions of this oracle. You have every reason to be so. He who created you is best qualified to declare the intention of His own acts, and you may safely, as you should humbly, allow Him to fix your position and make known your duties. In common with man, woman has a heavenly calling to glorify God as the end of her existence, and to perform all the duties and enjoy all the blessings of a religious life. Like man, she is a sinful, rational, and immortal creature, placed under an economy of mercy, and called, by repentance towards God and faith in our Lord Jesus Christ, to eternal life. Religion is as much her vocation as that of the other sex. In Christ Jesus there is neither male nor female, but all are on a level as to obligations, duties, and privileges.

In common with man, she is called, where she is unmarried and dependent, to labor for her own support—a condition to which large portions of the community are necessarily subject by the circumstances of their birth. Industry is as incumbent upon her as upon the other sex, and indolence is as inexcusable in her as in man. But in the married state, her sphere of labor, as we shall presently show, is her family; and it belongs to the husband to earn by the sweat of his brow not only his own bread, but that of the household. In many of the uncivilized tribes, where the ameliorating condition of Christianity is not felt, the wife is the drudge of the family while the husband lives in lordly sloth; and even in this country, at least in its manufacturing portions, manual labor falls too often and too heavily upon married women, greatly to the detriment of their families. An unmarried woman, however, without fortune, must provide for herself in some way or other, according to the circumstances of her birth and situation; and let her not consider herself degraded by it. Honest industry is far more honorable than pride and sloth.

But neither of these is the peculiar mission of woman, as pertaining to her sex. To know what this is, we must, as I have said, consult the pages of revelation, and ascertain the declared motive of God for her creation. "And the Lord God said, 'It is not good that the man should be alone; I will make him an help meet for him.'" This is further expressed, or rather repeated, where it is said, "And Adam," or "Although Adam had given names to all cattle, and to the fowl of the air, and to every beast of the field, yet for Adam there was not found an help meet for him." Nothing can be more clear from this than that woman was made for man. Adam was created as a being with undeveloped social propensities, which indeed seem essential to all creatures. It is the sublime peculiarity of deity to be entirely independent, for happiness, of all other beings. He, and He only, is the theater of His own glory, the fountain of His own felicity, and a sufficient object of His own contemplation, needing nothing for His bliss but self-communion. An archangel alone in heaven would pine, even there, for some companionship, either divine or angelic.

Adam, surrounded by all the glories of Paradise, and by all the various tribes it contained, found himself alone and needing companionship. Without it his life was but a solitude, Eden itself a desert. Endowed with a nature too communicative to be satisfied from himself alone, he sighed for society, for support, for some complement to his existence, and only half-lived so long as he lived alone. Formed to think, to speak, to love, his thoughts yearned for other thoughts with which to compare and exercise his soaring aspirations. His words were wearisomely wasted upon the wanton air, or at best awoke but an echo which mocked instead of answering him. His love, as regards an earthly object, knew not where to bestow itself, and, returning to his own bosom, threatened to degenerate into a desolating egotism. His entire being longed, in short, for another self, but that other self did not exist; there was no help meet for him. The visible creatures which surrounded him were too much beneath him, and the invisible Being who gave him life was too much above him, to unite their condition with his own. Whereupon God made woman, and the great problem was immediately solved.

It was, then, the characteristic of unfallen man to want someone to sympathize with him in his joys, as it is of fallen man to want someone to sympathize with him in his sorrows. Whether Adam was so far conscious of his wants as to ask for a companion we are not informed. It would appear from the inspired record as if the design of this precious boon originated with God, and as if Eve, like so many of His other mercies, was the spontaneous bestowment of His own free will. Thus Adam would have to say, as did one of his most illustrious descendants many ages afterwards, "Thou preventest me with Thy goodness."

Here, then, is the design of God in creating woman: to be a suitable helpmate to man. Man needed a companion, and God gave him woman. And as there was no other man than Adam at that time in existence, Eve was designed exclusively for Adam's comfort. This teaches us from the beginning that whatever mission woman may have to accomplish in reference to man, in a generic sense, her mission, at least in wedded life, is to be a suitable helpmate for that one man to whom she is united. It was declared from the beginning that every other tie, though not severed by marriage, shall be rendered subordinate, and a man shall "leave his father and mother and cleave unto his wife, and they two shall be one flesh."

If woman's mission in Paradise was to be man's companion and joy, such must be the case still. Her vocation has not been changed by the Fall. By that catastrophe, man needs still more urgently a companion, and God has rendered this mission of hers still more explicit by the declaration, "Thy desire shall be to thy husband and he shall rule over thee." It has been often shown that by being taken from himself, she was equal to man in nature; while the very part of the body from which she was abstracted indicated the position she was intended to occupy. She was not taken from the head, to show she was not to rule over him; nor from his foot, to teach that she was not to be his slave; nor from his hand, to show that she was not to be his tool; but from his side, to show that she was to be his companion. There may perhaps be more of ingenuity and fancy in this than of God's original design; but if a mere conceit, it is at once both pardonable and instructive.

That woman was intended to occupy a position of subordination and dependence is clear from every part of the Word of God. This is declared in language already quoted: "Thy desire shall be to thy husband, and he shall rule over thee." This referred not only to Eve personally, but to Eve representatively. It was the divine law of the relation of the sexes, then promulgated for all time. The preceding language placed woman, as a punishment for her sin, in a state of sorrow; this places her in a state of subjection. Her husband was to be the center of her earthly desires, and, to a certain extent, the regulator of them also; and she was to be in subjection to him. What was enacted in Paradise has been confirmed by every subsequent dispensation of grace. Judaism is full of it in all its provisions; and Christianity equally establishes it.

I shall here introduce and explain the words of the apostle: "I would have you to know that the head of every man is Christ, and the head of the woman is the man." He then goes on to direct that women should not, unveiled and with their hair cut off, exercise the miraculous gifts which were sometimes bestowed upon them, and adds, "A man indeed ought not to cover his head, forasmuch as he is the image and glory of God; but the woman is the glory of the man. Neither was the man created for the woman, but the woman for the man." For the explanation of this passage, I remark that in the times of the apostles there were two recognized characteristic emblems of the female sex when they appeared in public: veils and the preservation of their tresses. It would seem from the apostle's remarks as if some of the female members of the Corinthian church, during the time when the inspiration of the Holy Spirit was upon them, cast off their veils after the manner of the heathen priestesses when they delivered the responses of the oracles. This conduct the apostle reproves, and informs them that if the veil were thrown aside they might as well also cut off their flowing hair, which is one of woman's distinctions from man, and is by all nations considered the ornament as well as the peculiarity of the sex.

We may pause for a moment to observe how constantly and completely Christianity is the parent of order, and the enemy of indecorum of every kind. Why were not the women to lay aside their veils? Because it would be forgetting their subordination and dependence, and assuming an equal rank with man. This is the gist of the apostle's reason. It was not merely indecorous and contrary to modesty, but it was ambitious and violated the order of heaven. The other expressions of the apostle in this passage are very strong. As Christ is the head or ruler of man, so man is the head and ruler of woman in the domestic economy. Man was made to show forth God's glory and praise, to be in subordination to Him and only to Him; woman was created to be, in addition to this, the glory of man by being in subordination to him, as his help and his ornament. She was not only made *out of* him, but *for* him. All her loveliness, comeliness, and purity are not only the expressions of her excellence, but of his honor and dignity, since all were not only derived from him, but made for him.

This, then, is woman's true position, and if anything more need be said to prove it from the records of Christianity we may refer to apostolic language in other places, where wives are enjoined to "be subject to their husbands in all things, even as the church is subject to Christ." Nor is the Apostle Paul alone in this, for Peter writes in the same strain. Let woman then bow to this authority, and not feel herself degraded by such submission. It has been said that in domestic life man shines as the sun, but woman as the moon, with a splendor borrowed from the man. It may be said with greater truth and propriety, and less invidiously, that man shines as the primary planet, reflecting the glory of God, who is the center of the moral universe, and woman, while she equally derives her splendor from the central Luminary and is governed by His attraction, is yet the satellite of man, revolves around him, follows him in his course, and ministers to him.

Behold, then, I say again, woman's position and mission is summed up in love and subjection to her husband. Everything connected with the relationship of man and woman has, however, since the Fall, a more serious character; her love has become more anxious; her humility more profound. Bashful of her own defects, and anxious to reinstate herself in her husband's heart, woman lives to repair the wrong she has inflicted on man, and lavishes upon him consolations which may sweeten the present bitterness of sin, and warnings which may preserve from the future bitterness of hell.

Woman, then, whatever relation she may bear to society at large, whatever duties in consequence of this relation she may have to discharge, and whatever benefits by the right discharge of these duties she may have it in her power to confer upon the community, must consider herself chiefly called to advance the comfort of man in his private relations; to promote her own peace by promoting his; and to receive from him all that respect, protection, and ever assiduous affection to which her equal nature, her companionship, and her devotedness give her so just a claim. She is, in wedded life, to be his constant companion, in whose society he is to find one who meets him hand to hand, eye to eye, lip to lip, and heart to heart; to whom he can unburden the secrets of a heart pressed down with care or wrung with anguish; whose presence shall be to him better than all society; whose voice shall be his sweetest music, whose smiles his brightest sunshine; from whom he shall go forth with regret, and to whose converse he shall return with willing feet when the toils of the day are over; who shall walk near his loving heart, and feel the throbbing of affection as her arm leans on his and presses on his side. In his hours of retired conversation, he shall tell her all the secrets of his heart, find in her all the capabilities and all the promptings of the most tender and endeared fellowship, and in her gentle smiles and unrestrained speech enjoy all to be expected in one who was given by God to be his associate and friend.

In that companionship which woman was designed to afford to man must of course be included the sympathetic offices of the comforter. It is her role, in their hours of retirement, to console and cheer him; when he is injured or insulted, to heal the wounds of his troubled spirit; when he burdened by care, to lighten his load by sharing it; when he groaning with anguish, to calm by her peace-speaking words the tumult of his heart, and to act, in all his sorrows, the part of a ministering angel.

Nor should she be backward to offer, nor he backward to receive, the counsels of wisdom which her prudence will suggest, even though she may not be intimately acquainted with all the entanglements of this world's business. Woman's advice, had it been asked for and acted upon, would have saved thousands of men from bankruptcy and ruin. Few men have ever had to regret their taking counsel from a prudent wife, while multitudes have had to reproach themselves for their folly in not asking, and multitudes more for not following, the counsels of such a companion.

If, then, this is woman's mission according to the representation of her Almighty Creator, to be the suitable helpmate of that man to whom she has given herself as the companion of his pilgrimage upon earth, it of course supposes that marriage, contracted with a due regard to prudence and under all proper regulations, is the natural state of both man and woman. And so, I affirm, in truth it is. Providence has willed it and nature prompts it. But as the exceptions are so numerous, is there no mission for those to whom the exception appertains? Is it married women only who have a mission, and an important one? Certainly not. In these cases, I fall back upon woman's mission to society at large. And is not this momentous? Has it not been admitted in all ages, and by all countries, that the influence of female character upon social virtue and happiness, and upon national strength and prosperity, is prodigious, whether for good or for evil? Is not the declaration with which Adolphe Monod opens his beautiful treatise perfectly true? "The greatest influence on earth, whether for good or for evil, is possessed by woman. Let us study the history of bygone ages, the state of barbarism and civilization; of the east and the west; of Paganism and Christianity; of antiquity and the middle ages; of the medieval and modern times; and we shall find that there is nothing which more decidedly separates them than the condition of woman." Every woman, whether rich or poor, married or single, has a circle of influence within which, according to her character, she is exerting a certain amount of power for good or harm. Every woman, by her virtue or her vice, by her folly or her wisdom, by her levity or her dignity, is adding something to our national elevation or degradation. As long as female virtue is prevalent, upheld by one sex and respected by the other, a nation cannot sink very low in the scale of ignominy by plunging into the depths of vice.

To a certain extent, woman is the conservator of her nation's welfare. Her virtue, if firm and uncorrupted, will stand sentinel over that of the empire. Law, justice, liberty, and the arts all contribute, of course, to the well-being of a nation; beneficial influence flows in from various springs, and innumerable contributors may be at work, each laboring in his vocation for his country's weal. But let the general tone of female morals be low, and all will be rendered nugatory, while, on the other hand, the universal prevalence of womanly intelligence and virtue will swell the stream of civilization to its highest level, impregnate it with its richest qualities, and spread its fertility over the widest surface. A community is not likely to be overthrown where woman fulfills her mission, for by the power of her noble heart over the hearts of others she will raise it from its ruins and restore it again to prosperity and joy. Here, then, beyond the circle of wedded life as well as within it, is no doubt part of woman's mission, and an important one it is. Her field is social life, her object is social happiness, her reward is social gratitude and respect.

"If any female," says Mr. Upham in his life of Madame Guyon, "should think these pages worthy of her perusal, let her gather the lesson from these statements, that woman's influence does not terminate, as is sometimes supposed, with the molding and the guidance of the minds of children; her task is not finished when she sends abroad those whom she has borne and nurtured in her bosom, on their pilgrimage of action and duty in this wide world. Far from it. Man is neither safe in himself, nor profitable to others, when he lives dissociated from that benign influence which is to be found in woman's presence and character—an influence which is needed in the projects and toils of mature life, in the temptations and trials to which that period is especially exposed, and in the weakness and sufferings of age, hardly less than in childhood and youth.

"But it is not the woman who is gay, frivolous, and unbelieving, or woman separated from those divine teachings which make all hearts wise, that can lay claim to the exercise of such an influence. But when she adds to the traits of sympathy, forbearance, and warm affection which characterize her the strength and wisdom of a well-cultivated intellect, and the still higher attributes of religious faith and holy love, it is not easy to limit the good she may do in all situations, and in all periods of life."

If I am right as to the nature of woman's mission, I cannot err as to the proper sphere of it. If she was created for man, and not only for the race of man, but for one man, then the easy and necessary inference is that home is the proper scene of woman's action and influence. There are few terms in the language around which cluster so many blissful associations as that delight of every English heart, the word "home." The elysium of love, the nursery of virtue, the garden of enjoyment, the temple of concord, the circle of all tender relationships, the playground of childhood, the dwelling of manhood, the retreat of age; where health loves to enjoy its pleasures, wealth revels in its luxuries, and poverty bears its rigors; where sickness can best endure its pains, and dissolving nature expire; which throws its spell over those who are within its charmed circle, and even sends its attractions across oceans and continents, drawing to itself the thoughts and wishes of the man who wanders from it to the antipodes—this home, sweet home is the sphere of wedded woman's mission.

Is it any hardship upon woman, any depreciation of her importance, to place her sphere of action and influence there? Is it to assign her a circle of influence unworthy of herself if we call her to preside over that little community of which home is the seat? Can we estimate the importance of such a scene of action? Shall we tell of the varied and momentous interests which are included in that circle? Shall we speak of the happiness of a husband whose bliss, to so considerable an extent, is created by her, and involves her own, or the character and future well-being (for both worlds) of children, if she has them? Or the comfort of servants, and the order and pleasant working of the whole domestic constitution, all which depend so much upon her? Why, to make one such home a seat of holiness and happiness, to fill one such sphere with an influence so sweet and sacred, to throw the fascination of connubial feeling and of maternal influence over one such community, to irradiate so many countenances with delight, to fill so many hearts with contentment, and to prepare so many characters for their future part in life—such an object would be deemed by an angel worth an incarnation upon earth.

Or from this sense of her duties shall we look abroad upon the public good, the strength and stability of the nation? Who knows not that the springs of an empire's prosperity lie in its domestic constitution, and in well-trained families? Even one such family is a contribution to the majestic flow of a nation's greatness. Can such families exist without a woman's care, oversight, and wisdom? Has it not grown into a proverb that home has ever been the nursery of great men, and their mothers their instructresses? It may be said as a general principle that woman is not only the mother of the body, but of the character of her children. To her is first entrusted the instruction of the mind, the cultivation of the heart, and the formation of the life. Thought, feeling, will, imagination, virtue, religion, or the contrary moral tendencies all germinate under her fostering influence. The greatest power in the moral world is that which a mother exercises over her young child. The decisive moment in education is the starting point. The dominant direction which is to determine the whole course of life lies concealed in the first years of infancy; and these belong to the mother.

One of the most hallowed, lovely, and beautiful sights in our world is a woman at home discharging, in all the meekness of wisdom, the various duties of wife, mother, and mistress, with an order that nothing is allowed to disturb, a patience which nothing can exhaust, an affection which is never ruffled, and a perseverance that no difficulties can interrupt, nor any disappointments arrest—in short, such a scene as that described by the writer of the most exquisite chapter of the Proverbs. Eve in Paradise, in all her untainted loveliness, by the side of Adam, propping the lily, training the vine, or directing the growth of the rose—shedding upon him, and receiving, reflected back from his noble countenance upon her happy spirit, such smiles as told in silent language their perfect and conjoint bliss—was, no doubt, a brighter image of perfect virtue and undisturbed felicity. But to me, a woman in our fallen world, guiding in piety, intelligence, and all matronly and motherly excellences the circle of a home made happy chiefly by her influence, presents a scene little inferior in beauty, and far superior as a display of virtue and intelligence, to that of which our first mother was the center even in her original perfections. And it is fancy, and not reason and moral taste, that can revel in the mind's pictures of Eve in Paradise, and not feel warmer admiration in the actual presence of such a woman as I have described.

But it will, perhaps, be asked whether I would shut up every married woman within the domestic circle, and, with the

jealousy and authority of an oriental despot, confine her to her
own home, or whether I would condemn and degrade her to
mere household drudgery. I have, I think, protected myself already from this imputation by representing her as the companion, counselor, and comforter of man. She shall never, with
my consent, sink from the side of man to be trampled under
his feet. She shall not have one ray of her glory extinguished,
nor be deprived of a single honor that belongs to her sex. To be
the instructress of her children, the companion of her husband, and the queen consort of the domestic state is no degradation; and she only is degraded who thinks so.

Still in connection with—though not in neglect of—this,
let her give her influence upon society to the circle of her
friends on all suitable occasions and in all suitable places.
Though the drawing room is not the chief sphere of her influence, it is one of the circles in which she may move; and although incessant parties of pleasure, and a constant round of
entertainments, are not her mission, but oppose and hinder it,
yet she is occasionally to bestow that influence which every
wise and good woman exerts over the tone of morals and
manners among the friends who may court her society.
Woman is the grace, ornament, and charm of the social circle;
and when she carries into it habits that frown upon vice, that
check folly and discountenance levity, she is a benefactress to
the country. And as to the various institutions of our age for
the relief of suffering humanity, the instruction of ignorance,
and the spread of religion, we give her all the room and liberty
for these things which are compatible with her duties to her
own household. What prudent female would ask more, or
what advocate of her rights would claim more? Woman is always in her place where charity presides, except when her time
and attention are demanded at home for those who are more
immediately her charge. But I shall have much more to urge

on this subject in a future chapter.

But what shall I say of those women who claim on their own behalf, or of their advocates who claim for them, a participation in the labors, occupations, rights, and duties which have usually been considered as exclusively appertaining to men? There are those who would expunge the line of demarcation which nearly all nations have drawn between the duties and occupations of men and those of women. Christianity has provided a place for woman for which she is fitted and in which she shines; but take her out of that place, and her luster pales and sheds a feeble and sickly ray. Or, to change the metaphor, woman is a plant, which in the seclusion of its own greenhouse will put forth all its brilliant colors and all its sweet perfume; but if you remove it from the protection of its own floral home into the common garden and open field, where hardier flowers will grow and thrive, its beauty fades and its odor is diminished. Neither reason nor Christianity invites woman to the professor's chair, conducts her to the bar, makes her welcome to the pulpit, or admits her to the place of ordinary magistracy. Both exclude her, not indeed by positive and specific commands, but by general principles and spirit, alike from the violence and license of the camp, the debates of the senate, and the pleadings of the forum. And they bid her beware how she lays aside the delicacy of her sex and listens to any doctrines which claim new rights for her, and becomes the dupe of those who have put themselves forward as her advocates only to gain notoriety or perhaps bread. They forbid us to hear her gentle voice in the popular assembly, and do not even suffer her to speak in the Church of God. They claim not for her the right of suffrage, nor any immunity by which she may "usurp authority over the man." The Bible gives her her place of majesty and dignity in the domestic circle—the heart of her husband and the heart of her family. It is the female supremacy of that domain where love, tenderness, refinement, thought, and feeling preside. It is the privilege of making her husband happy and honored, and her sons and daughters the ornaments of human society. It is the sphere of piety, prudence, diligence in the domestic station, and a holy and devout life. It is the sphere that was occupied by Hannah, the mother of Samuel; by Elizabeth, the mother of John; by Eunice, the mother of Timothy; and by Mary, the mother of Jesus. It is the respect and esteem of mankind. It is that silent, unobserved, unobtrusive influence by which she accomplishes more for her race than many whose names occupy a broad space on the page of history.

A woman who fills well the sphere assigned to her as a good wife, a mother, and a mistress—who trains up good citizens for the state, and good fathers and mothers of other families which are to spring from her own, and so from generation to generation in all but endless succession—need not complain that her sphere of action and her power of influence are too limited for female ambition to aspire to. The mothers of the wise and the good are the benefactresses of their species. What would be gained as for woman's comfort, respectability, or usefulness, or for the welfare of society, and how much would be lost to each by withdrawing her from her own appropriate sphere and introducing her to that for which she has no adaptation? Who but a few wild visionaries, rash speculators, and mistaken advocates of woman's rights would take her from the home of her husband, of her children, and of her own heart, to wear out her strength, consume her time, and destroy her feminine excellence in committee rooms, on platforms, and in mechanics' or philosophical institutions?

But may not woman, in every way in her power, benefit society by her talents and her influence? Certainly, in every legitimate way. Her sphere is clearly assigned to her by

Providence, and only by very special and obvious calls should she be induced to leave it. Whatever breaks down the modest reserve, the domestic virtues, or the persuasive gentleness of woman is an injury done to the community. Woman can be spared from the lecturer's chair, the platform of general convocation, and the scene of public business; but she cannot be spared from the hearth of her husband and the circle of her children. Substitutes can be found for her in the one, but not in the other. In the bosom of domestic privacy she fulfills with truest dignity and faithfulness the first and highest obligations of her sex.

Monod's remarks on this subject are so beautiful, appropriate, and just that I shall be more than forgiven for the following quotation:

> Is not the humble sphere which we assign to woman precisely that for which her whole being is predisposed and pre-constituted? Her finer but more fragile conformation, the quicker pulsation of her heart, the more exquisite sensibility of her nerves, the delicacy of her organs, and even the softness of her features, all combine to make her what St. Peter so aptly designates "the weaker vessel," and render her constitutionally unfit for incessant and weighty cares, for the duties of the state, for the vigils of the cabinet, for all that which yields renown in the world.
>
> Again, are not the powers of her mind equally distinct? The question is sometimes raised whether they are equal to those of man. They are neither equal nor unequal; they are different, being wisely adapted to another end. For the accomplishment of the work assigned to man, woman's faculties are inferior to his; or rather she is not adapted to it. We speak of the general rule, and not of exceptions. It must be conceded that, by way of exception, there are among women some few whose intellects are adapted to the cares reserved, on

principle, to the other sex, and that peculiar situations may arise in which women of ordinary capacities may be called upon to discharge the duties assigned to man, man in that case being a defaulter; it must be seen, however, that these exceptions are clearly indicated by God, or called for by the interests of humanity. For, after all, in the mission of woman, humility is but the means, charity the end, to which all must be subservient. And why should not God, who has made exceptions of this nature in sacred history, do the same in ordinary life?

Be this as it may, we leave exceptions to God, and to the conscience of the individual, and, abstaining from all irritating, personal, or contestable questions, will confine ourselves simply to the general rule.

Generally speaking, enlarged views of politics and science, the bold flight of metaphysics, the sublimer conceptions of poetry, which, bursting every shackle, soar in the boundless regions of thought and imagination, are not in the province of woman.

In that limited sphere, however, of which we are speaking, limited in extent, but boundless in influence, within which, supported by Scripture, we exhort woman to confine her actions, she is endowed with faculties superior to those of man, or rather, she alone is adapted to it. Here she has her requital; here she proves herself mistress of the field, and employs those secret resources (which might be termed admirable, if they did not inspire a more tender sentiment both towards her and towards God, who has so richly endowed her): her practical survey, equally sure and rapid; her quick and accurate perception; her wonderful power of penetrating the heart, in a way unknown and impracticable to man; her never-failing presence of mind and personal attention on all occasions; her constant though imperceptible vigilance; her numerous and fertile resources in the management of her domestic affairs; her ever-ready access and willing audience to all who need her; her freedom of thought and action in the

midst of the most agonizing sufferings and accumulated
embarrassments; her elasticity (may I say her perseverance?) despite her feebleness; her exquisitely tender feelings; her tact that would seem so practiced, were it not
instinctive; her extreme perfection in little things; her
dexterous industry in the work of her hands; her in-
comparable skill in nursing the sick, in cheering a broken spirit, in reawakening a sleeping conscience, in re-
opening a heart that has long been closed—in sum, innumerable are the things which she accomplishes, and
which man can neither discern nor effect, without the
aid of her eye and hand.

Milton has finely expressed the difference between the
original pair:

> For contemplation he, and valour formed;
> For softness she, and sweet attractive grace.

And this difference, by limiting their respective capacities, pre-
scribes their separate duties and spheres of action.

Now look at woman's natural adaptation for her sphere. If
the view here given of woman's mission is correct, we can in a
moment perceive what is required to enable her to fulfill it.
There must be, as indeed there generally is pervading the sex, a
consciousness of subordination, without any sense of degradation or any wish that it was otherwise. Woman scarcely needs
to be taught that in the domestic economy she is second and
not first, that "the man is the head of the woman." This is a
law of nature written on the heart, and coincides exactly with
the law of God written on the pages of revelation. It is, first of
all, an instinct, and then confirmed by reason. Without this
law deeply engraved and constantly felt as well as known, her
situation would be endured as a slavery, and she would be constantly endeavoring to throw off the yoke. Her condition

would be wretched, and she would make all wretched around her. With such a sense of oppression, or even of hardship, pressing upon the mind, no duty could be well performed, and the family would be a scene of domestic warfare. But she generally knows her place, and feels it is her happiness as well as her duty to keep it. It is not necessity, but even choice that produces a willing subjection. She is contented that it should be so, for God has implanted the disposition in her nature.

Then her gentleness is another part of her qualification for her duty. She should have, must have, really has, influence and power of impulsion, if not compulsion. Were she utterly powerless, she could do nothing. Her influence, however, is a kind of passive power; it is the power that draws rather than drives, and commands by obeying. Her gentleness makes her strong. How winning are her smiles, how melting her tears, how insinuating her words! Woman loses her power when she parts from her gentleness. It is this very yielding, like the bulrush lifting its head after the rush of water to which it has bowed, that gives her a power to rise superior to the force of circumstances which, if resistance were offered, would break all before them. She vanquishes by submission. How necessary gentleness is to the fulfillment of her mission in handling the young and tender spirits of her children, in training the first delicate shoots of their infant dispositions, and for directing the feelings of that one heart on which she depends for her happiness. There are many varieties of disposition in women, which may make them sensitive, petulant, irritable, jealous, quick to feel and to resent; but notwithstanding all this, and under all this, there is a gentleness of disposition which indicates this vocation as destined to influence and constrain by love.

Tenderness is another of her characteristics. Gentleness relates more to manner, tenderness more to disposition; the former to habitual conduct towards all persons and all cases, this one to the occasional exercise of sympathy with distress. Tenderness is so characteristic of the female heart that an unfeeling woman is considered a libel upon her sex. If compassion were driven out from every other habitation, it would find there its last retreat. Her heart is so made of tenderness that she is ever in danger of being imposed upon by craft and falsehood. How suitable such a disposition for one who is to be the chief comforter of the domestic commonwealth; who is to mollify the wounds of her husband's heart, and to heal the sorrows of her children; whose ear is to listen to every tale of domestic woe, and whose bosom is to be the lodging place of all the family's grief!

Self-denial is no less necessary for this domestic mission than anything I have yet mentioned. How much ease, comfort, and enjoyment must she surrender who has to consult her husband's comfort and will before her own; whose happiness is to consist, in a great measure, in making others happy; who has first to endure all that is connected with giving birth to her children, and then all that is involved in nursing, watching, comforting, and training them! One of the most striking instances in our world of endurance and self-denial, both as to the extent and the cheerfulness with which it is borne, is the busy, tender, and contented mother of a growing family. God has given the power, yet I sometimes wonder how she can exercise it.

And then see her fortitude in this situation. In that courage which leads man to the cannon's mouth, to mount the breach, or to encounter some terrific danger of any other kind, she is inferior to man; but in the fortitude manifested by enduring bodily suffering, the ills of poverty, the wasting influence of long-continued privations, the gloom of solitude, the bitterness of injustice, the cruelty of neglect, and the misery of oppression, is she not in all these as superior to man as man is to her in all that pertains to brute force?

On the subject of woman's fortitude and power of endurance, I will introduce, though it may be at some length, the most surprising instance of it perhaps on record, whether in inspired or uninspired history, and it will serve as an appropriate illustration of this part of the subject of the chapter. The Apostle John, in his narrative of the events of the crucifixion of our Lord, says with beautiful simplicity, and without a single comment, as if he could not hope and would not attempt to add to the grandeur of the incident: "Now there stood by the cross of Jesus His mother, and His mother's sister, Mary the wife of Cleophas, and Mary Magdalene." That the other women should have been there is less wonderful, though even their presence at such a scene (from which it would seem as if all the apostles had retired except John) was indeed an instance of the fortitude of heroic love. But that His mother should have been there, not far off but beside the cross, not prostrate in a swoon or beating her breast, wringing her hands, tearing her hair, and shrieking in frantic grief, but standing in silent, though pensive, anguish to witness the horrors of crucifixion, so far surpassing those of any modern method of execution; the crucifixion of her Son, and such a Son—oh, wondrous woman! an act surpassing wonder! To whatever length endurance may be carried by attendance at the sickbed of a dying friend, how few of even female heroes could witness the execution of a husband, son, or brother.

I have read of one who, when her lover was executed for high treason, went in a mourning coach to witness the dreadful process, and when the whole was closed by the severing of that head which had leaned on her bosom, simply said, "I follow thee," and, sighing forth his name, fell back in the coach and instantly expired. Here was a power of endurance carried to a point which nature could sustain no longer, and it sunk at length, crushed beneath the intolerable burden of its grief. But behold the scene before us: that mother, in the dignity and majesty of profound, yet composed grief, enduring to the end. Peter had denied his Master; the other disciples, at the sight of the officers of justice and the soldiers, amidst the deep shadows of Gethsemane, had deserted Him, and still kept at a distance from the scene of suffering and danger. But there, standing by the cross, were those dauntless, holy women, sustaining with wondrous fortitude the sight of His dying agonies, and confessing their Lord in the hour of His deepest humiliation, in the absence of His friends and in the presence of His foes—and there among them was His mother. I shall never wonder at anything that female fortitude, when upheld by divine grace, can do after it could stand in the person of Mary at the foot of the cross, when Christ, her Son and her Lord, was suspended upon it. Nor shall I ever despair of the support of any woman, in the hour and scene of her deepest woe, who is willing to be sustained after I have beheld the mother of our Lord upheld in that unutterably awful situation.

Painters and poets have not done justice to the dignity of this most honored of all women. There is a picture of Annibale Carracci's entitled "The Three Marys," the subject of which is those holy women surveying the body of Christ after it was taken down from the cross. As a work of art it is inimitable, and does full justice to the painter's skill. But it does far less justice to the character of the mother of our Lord than the apostle's description of her. In the painting she is represented swooning over the dead body of Jesus, whose head reclines on her lap, while the other figures are represented in the attitude of passionate grief. How different this is from the dignified, majestic, and composed grief which stood beneath the cross. So far must art ever fall beneath nature, still lower below the wonders of grace, and most of all below such grace as was vouchsafed to the mother of our Lord.

Let females study this pathetic and amazing scene, and learn that the deepest love and the noblest grief are not that sickly sensibility, that emotional excitability, which are too tender to bear the sight of suffering, but that which, instead of sinking with hysterical outcries, retiring with averted eyes from agonies, or swooning at the sight of tears and blood, can control the feelings and brace the nerves to perform in the hour and scene of woe a part which none can perform except herself, or at any rate none can perform so well. Let young women set out in life practicing that discipline of their emotions which, without diminishing all of that softness and tenderness of manner which are the most lovely characteristics of their sex, or robbing their hearts of those delicate sympathies and sensibilities which constitute the glory of woman's nature, will preserve their judgment from being enveloped in such a mist of feeling, and their will from being so enervated, as to make them incapable of resolution and render them incompetent in times of their own sorrow and trial for anything besides weeping over the calamities which they might otherwise remove, and to make them altogether unfit for those hardy services of mercy which the miseries of others will sometimes require at their hands.

Arising out of this self-discipline, and as one beautiful display of it, see woman when called to put forth her gentleness, her sympathy, and her self-denial in the hour of affliction and the chamber of sickness. It has been somewhere beautifully said that "In sickness there is no hand like woman's hand, no heart like woman's heart." A man's breast may swell with unquestionable sorrow, and apprehension may rend his mind; yet place him by the sick couch, and in the light (or I should rather say in the shadow) of the sad lamp by which it is watched; let him have to count over the long dull hours of night, and await, alone and sleepless, the grey dawn struggling into the chamber of suffering; let him be appointed to this ministry, even for the sake of the brother of his heart or the father of his being—and his grosser nature, even when most perfect, will tire, his eye will close, and his spirit will grow impatient of the dreary task. And though his love and anxiety remain undiminished, his mind will experience a creeping in of irresistible selfishness, which indeed he may be ashamed of and struggle to reject, but which, despite all his efforts, will remain to characterize his nature, and prove in one respect, at least, the weakness of man. But see a mother, a sister, or a wife in his place! The woman feels no weariness, and has no thought of herself. In silence and in the depth of night, she bears up not only passively, but (so far as the term, with the necessary qualification, may express our meaning) with delight. Her ear acquires a blind man's instinct, as from time to time it catches the slightest stir, whisper, or breath of the now more-than-ever loved one who lies under the hand of human affliction. Her step, as she moves in obedience to an impulse or signal, would not awaken a mouse; if she speaks, her accents are a soft echo of natural harmony, most delicious to the sick man's ear, conveying all that sound can convey of pity, comfort, and devotion. And thus, night after night, she tends him like a creature sent from a higher world, when all earthly watchfulness has failed; her eye never winking, her mind never palled, her nature, which at all other times is weakness, now gaining a superhuman strength and magnanimity, herself forgotten, and her sex alone predominant.

But as woman's mission is, in a special sense, one of charity, love is, above all things, essential to its right performance. Here again, I will give a long quotation from Monod's beautiful work:

But in speaking of love, it is less the degree than the character which is of importance. Love, as we have before said, is the very essence of woman's existence. But what love? Let her reflect, and she will find that it is precisely that love which predisposes her for the vocation of beneficence prescribed for her by the Scriptures. There are two kinds of love: love which receives and love which gives. The former rejoices in the sentiment which it inspires and the sacrifice it obtains; the second delights in the sentiment which it experiences and the sacrifice which it makes. These two kinds of love seldom subsist apart, and woman knows them both. But is it too much to say that in her the second predominates? And that her motto, borrowed from the spontaneous love of her Savior, is "It is more blessed to give than to receive"?

To be loved! This, we well know, is the joy of a woman's heart; but alas, how often is the joy denied her! Yet let her continue to love, to consecrate herself by love; it is the exigency of her soul, the very law of her existence, a law which nothing can ever hinder her from obeying.

Man also is no stranger to this feeling. He, too, must love; but his is the love in which St. Paul sums up the obligations imposed upon the husband in conjugal life, "Husbands, love your wives," even as he sums up the duties of submission on the part of the wife: "Wives, obey your husbands." But what we are treating here is not the obligation, nor the faculty; it is the inclination to love.

Love, it must be remembered, is less spontaneous, less disinterested among men than among women. Less spontaneous in that man is often obliged to conquer himself in order to love; woman need only listen to the dictates of her innate feelings. Hence Scripture, which frequently commands the husband to love, abstains from giving this command to the wife, taking it for granted that nature herself would supply the injunction.

Moreover, the love of woman is more disinterested.

Man loves woman more for his own sake than for hers;
woman, on the contrary, loves man less for her own
sake than for his. Man, because he is not sufficient in
himself, loves that which has been given him of God;
woman, because she feels that she is needed, loves him
to whom God has given her. If solitude weighs heavily
upon man, it is because life has no charms for him
when separated from his help meet; if woman dreads
living alone, it is because life has lost its aim, while she
has none to whom she can be a help meet. Of her it
may be said, if we may be permitted to make the comparison in the emphatic language of Scripture, "We
love her because she first loved us."

If such, then, is woman's mission (and who will deny or
question it?), how immensely important it is that it should be
well understood, and that she should be properly trained to
perform it well. But is it really understood, and is education so
conducted as to qualify woman for her mission? It requires little knowledge of modern society to answer these questions in
the negative.

Parents, and especially mothers, who have daughters, to
you appertains the serious, deliberate, and prayerful consideration of this momentous and deeply interesting subject. Look
upon those girls whom Providence has committed to your care,
and say to yourselves, "I very distinctly perceive, and as impressively feel, the importance of the female character on account
of its influence upon the well-being of society. And it is clear
to me that woman's is a domestic mission, which is to affect
society through the medium of family influence. As she fills up
her place with wisdom and propriety, so will she promote the
well-being of the community. Nor is it society only, but the
Church of Christ, that is concerned in and promoted by the
female character. Now, I have daughters who must contribute
their share of influence to the public weal or woe. How shall

they be educated so as best to fulfill their mission, should they be called to preside over the domestic economy? It depends much upon me whether they fail or succeed in this mission."

These are appropriate, weighty, and necessary reflections, peculiarly belonging to mothers. To them, I say, in all your conduct never let these thoughts and views be long out of your minds. Look beyond the drawing rooms of your friends, where your daughters are to be sometimes seen, perhaps shown. Look higher than to get them married, even well married. Take into account their being well-qualified to fulfill their mission. Set them before you as the future heads of a domestic establishment, and prepare them to preside over it with dignity and efficiency.

How much in modern education is calculated, if not intended, rather to prepare our females to dazzle in the circle of fashion and the lively party than to shine in the retirement of home! To polish the exterior by what are called accomplishments seems to be more the object than to give a solid substratum of piety, intelligence, good sense, and social virtue. Never was a subject less understood than education. To store the memory with facts, or to cultivate the taste for music, singing, drawing, languages, and needlework, is the ultimatum with many. The use of the intellect in the way of deep reflection, sound judgment, and accurate discrimination is not taught as it should be, while the direction of the will, the cultivation of the heart, and the formation of the character are lamentably neglected. I ask not the sacrifice of anything that can add grace, elegance, and ornament to the feminine character; but I do want incorporated with this more of what is masculine in knowledge and wisdom. I want to see woman educated not to be man's plaything, but his companion. I want to see her invested with something higher and better than fashionable littleness, elegant trifles, and fascinating airs. I want her to be

fitted to hold fast her husband's heart by the esteem in which
he holds her judgment; to inspire confidence and reverence in
her children, and, in that home where her influence is so po-
tent, to train up men and women who shall add to the
strength and glory of the nation. In this, let mothers be assisted by those to whom they entrust the education of their
daughters when they pass from their hands. It is melancholy to
think of the incompetence of a large portion of those to whom
the education of females is entrusted. How little has it ever occurred to many of them to inquire into woman's mission, what
is necessary to qualify her for it, and how they shall aid her in
obtaining this fitness! How rarely does it come within their
comprehension that it is their duty, and should be their study,
to impart not only knowledge, but wisdom; not only to train
the performer, the artist, or the linguist, but to lay the foundation for the character of the sincere Christian, the intelligent
woman, the prudent wife, the judicious mother, the sagacious
mistress, and the useful member of society!

And if there is no impropriety in turning aside for a few
moments to address myself as well to fathers, I would urge
them to study deeply, and ponder much, the momentous importance of the domestic constitution. In the present age, how
much has been said and written respecting improvements in
society; but never let it be forgotten that all radical improvement must commence in the homes and hearts of our families.
The inquiries how best to cure existing evils, or to supply existing defects, which do not begin here will be superficial in their
nature and unsatisfactory in their results. It is in the correct
understanding of the nature of parental obligations, and the
right discharge of the duties of man and wife towards each
other and their children, that the chief restorative remedy for
the diseases of a nation must be sought, as well as the best
means of preserving its health. Institutions may be set up to aid

or to supplement a father's efforts, or to alter the nature or widen the sphere of woman's mission; and an artificial state of social life may be produced, varnished and glittering with the showy devices of human wisdom; but it will be found in the end that the purposes of the God of nature, the great Author of human society, cannot be frustrated, and that the parent must still be the educator of the child, and home the school for the formation of character.

And here I would remind you of your privileges as Protestants, in having no intruder thrusting himself into your families, or exerting, without coming there, through the medium of the confessional and from behind the parent's chair, an influence greater than that of the parents, whether father or mother. A French writer, Michelet, in *Priests, Women, and Families,* thus depicts the homes of his country:

> The question is about our family, that sacred asylum in which we all desire to seek the repose of the heart. We return, exhausted, to the domestic hearth; but do we find there the repose we sigh for? Let us not dissemble, but acknowledge to ourselves how things are. There is in our family a sad difference of sentiment, and the most serious of all. We may speak to our mothers, wives, and daughters on any of the subjects which form the topics of conversation with indifferent persons, such as business or the news of the day, but never on subjects that affect the heart or moral life, such as eternity, religion, the soul, and God! Choose, for instance, the moment when we naturally feel disposed to meditate with our family in common thought, some quiet evening, at the family table; venture even there, in your own house, at your own fireside, to say one word about these things. Your mother sadly shakes her head; your wife contradicts you; your daughter by her very silence shows her disapprobation. They are on one side of the table and you on the other, alone. One

would think that in the midst of them, and opposite to you, was seated an invisible personage to contradict whatever you may say.

Enter a house in the evening, and sit down at the family table; one thing will almost always strike you: the mother and daughters are together of one and the same opinion on one side, while the father is on the other side alone. What does this mean? It means that there is some one man at his table whom you do not see, to contradict and give the lie to whatever the father may utter.

Nor should young females themselves be kept in ignorance of woman's mission. Their future destiny, as stated in the last chapter, should sometimes by a wise mother or an able governess be set before them, and they themselves reminded how much is necessary on their part to prepare themselves for their future lot. They must be reminded that above and beyond accomplishments, their character is to be formed, which never can be done without their own aid. They must be early impressed—not indeed in a way to inflate their vanity, but to excite their ambition, to stimulate their energies, and to direct their aim—that they have a mission on earth, for which it becomes them most anxiously and most diligently to prepare themselves.

My young friends, let it be your constant aim, and at the same time your earnest prayer, that you may first of all thoroughly understand your mission, and then diligently prepare for it, and hereafter as successfully fulfill it. Look around and see what women commend themselves most to your judgment as worthy of imitation. You will see some, perhaps, in whom, as Monod says, reserve has degenerated into supineness, activity into restlessness, vigilance into curiosity, tact into cunning, penetration into censoriousness, promptness into levity, fluency into loquacity, grace into coquetry, taste into fastidiousness, aptitude into presumption, influence into intrigue, authority into domination, and tenderness into morbid susceptibility. In some their power of loving is converted into jealousy, and their desire for usefulness into obtrusiveness. From such turn away, as from examples in which the best qualities are metamorphosed into the worst. And equally avoid those whose whole aim seems to be to amuse and to be amused; whose vanity is predominant, even in matronly age, and who appear, in their taste for gaiety, company, and entertainments, to forget that they have any mission upon earth except to flutter in a drawing room and to dazzle its guests. On the contrary, select for your models those who seem to be aware of woman's destiny and mission, as a help meet for man.

If, in closing a chapter already too long, I may suggest a few things which, in preparing to fulfill well your future mission, it is important that you should attend to, I would mention the following:

Consider deeply that character for life is usually formed in youth. It is the golden season of life, and to none more truly and eminently so than to the young woman. Her leisure, her freedom from care, and her protected situation give her the opportunity for this, which it is her wisdom and her duty to consider, embrace, and improve.

It is of immense consequence to consider that whosoever may help you, and whatever appliances from without may be brought to bear upon your mind and heart, you must, to a considerable extent, be the constructor of your own character. Set out in life with a deep conviction of the momentous consequence of self-discipline. Let your mind, your heart, and your conscience be the chief objects of your solicitude.

Lay the basis of all your excellences in true religion, the religion of the heart, the religion of penitence, faith in Christ, love to God, a holy and heavenly mind. No character can be well-constructed, safe, complete, beautiful, or useful without this.

Cultivate those dispositions of mind which have special reference to your future mission as the help meet for man. Improve your mind, and grow in intelligence by a thirst for knowledge; for how can an ignorant woman be a companion for a sensible man? Cherish a thoughtful, reflective turn of mind. Look beneath the surface of things, beyond their present aspect to their future consequences. Be somewhat meditative, and learn to restrain your words and feelings by a rigid self-control. Pay most anxious attention to your temper, and acquire as much as possible its perfect command. More women are rendered miserable, and render others miserable, by neglect of this than perhaps from any other cause whatsoever. Let meekness of disposition and gentleness of manner be a constant study. These are woman's amiabilities, which fit her for her future situation far better than the bold, imposing, and obtrusive airs of those who mistake the secret of woman's influence.

Contentment and patience, self-denial and submission, humility and subordination, prudence and discretion are all virtues, the seeds of which you should sow in early youth so that their rich, ripe fruits might be gathered in later life. Benevolence of heart and kindness of disposition must be among your foremost studies, the most prominent objects of your pursuit and most laborious endeavors; for they are the virtues which in their maturity are to form matronly excellence, and constitute you as the fit companion for a husband.

Make accomplishments subordinate to more substantial excellences. Let the former be to the latter only as the burnish of the gold or the cutting of the diamond. And as matters of mental taste are to be less thought of than the state of the heart and the formation of moral character, so especially let bodily decorations be in low estimation compared with those of the mind.

To prepare you to carry out the duties of your future mission with ease to yourself, with satisfaction to a husband, and with comfort to a household, pay attention to the minor virtues: punctuality, love of order, and dispatch. These are all of immense importance; the want of them in the female head of a family must necessarily fill the home with confusion, and the hearts of its inmates with sadness. Set out in life with a deep conviction of the importance of habits, and a constant recollection that habits for life are formed in youth—and that these habits, if not acquired then, are likely never to be.

Aim at universal excellence. Do little things well. Avoid with extreme dread a loose, slovenly, and careless way of doing anything proper to be done.

Young woman, your whole future life will illustrate and confirm the truth and propriety of this advice, either by the comfort and usefulness which will result from your attending to it, or by the miseries which you will endure yourself and inflict on others if you allow it to sink into oblivion. It is in this way only that you can fulfill with effect that which it has been the object of this chapter to set before you: woman's mission in social life.

Chapter 4

Early Piety

"I love them that love me; and those that seek me
early shall find me." Proverbs 8:17

How fascinating is nature in the second quarter of the year. Spring, lovely, animating spring, then sheds its reviving and gladdening smiles upon us. It is always a season of beauty. "For lo, the winter is past, the rain is over and gone; the flowers appear on the earth; the time of the singing of birds is come, and the voice of the turtle is heard in the land." Nature stands forth dressed in her garb of living green, decorated with the chaste colors and perfumed with the mild fragrance of the violet, the primrose, and the cowslip. It is a season of joy as well as beauty; recently recovered from the gloom of wintry months, the earth smiles and is vocal with delight. The feathered songsters of the grove blend their notes with the lowing of the herds and the bleating of the flocks; and the harmony is completed by the joyful sounds of the husbandman and the gentle music of the breeze. But it is also a season of activity as well as of loveliness and delight; the torpor produced by short days and cold nights is succeeded by universal motion. The farmer is busy in his fields, the florist in his greenhouse, and the horticulturist in his garden, for full well is it known and felt that a seedless spring must be followed by a fruitless autumn. Hope too adds radiance and delight to vernal scenes. The blade springing from the well-cultivated soil, and the blossom on the well-pruned tree, give the promise and prospect of the future crop.

And what is youth but the vernal period of existence? It is the season of beauty and of joy; it should be the season of activity and of hope. It is then that the beauty of the human form is in all its untainted freshness, and the spirits of our animal nature are in all their unchecked vigor. And it is then that all the energies of the soul should be put forth in the way of self-improvement, to awaken the hopes not only of their possessor, but of every observer. Do, my young friends, thus look abroad upon the field of nature, not only to poetize, but to moralize; not only to admire, but to imitate; not only to feel the throb of pleasure and the thrill of delight, but to learn lessons of wisdom and collect motives for self-improvement. You are passing through the spring of your life; and as in nature, so in your existence, there can be but one spring; and in each case, it is the spring that will give the character to the seasons that follow it. It is then that the seeds of intelligence, of prudence, of virtue, and of piety must be sown, or there will be no produce in the later periods of your history. A seedless spring must here also be followed by a fruitless autumn and a destitute, dreary, and cheerless winter, and for this reason this chapter is devoted to the enforcement of early piety.

Your first concern (and deep indeed should that concern be) is, of course, to understand the nature of real religion. This is of momentous importance. No language can exaggerate it. There can be no hyperbole here. Upon a right understanding of this subject is suspended your happiness for eternity. Ponder that word "eternity," and think of the millions of millions of ages beyond comprehension which it includes, all to be filled with torment or bliss according as you understand and practice or mistake the nature and neglect the claims of true religion. Should not this awaken solicitude of the deepest kind? What should increase the concern of your mind to intense solicitude, and almost to distress, is that both our Lord and His apostles, by what they have said, lead us to believe that mistakes on this subject are very common and very destructive, as you may learn by consulting the following passages of Holy Scripture: Matthew 7:13–28; 1 Corinthians 13; 2 Corinthians 13:5–7; Galatians 4:11–18; 6:3–5.

To guard against mistakes, go to the right source of information; consult the only infallible oracle, the Word of God. You have the Bible in your hand; search it for yourselves. Do not be satisfied with merely consulting men's works, but consult God's own Word. All churches, whatever they may boast, may err, have erred, and have no authority or ability to settle this matter for you. Creeds and catechisms, prayerbooks and missals, formularies and confessions, are none of them pure truth; this is true only of the Bible. The Bible, the Bible alone, is the religion of Christians. Not that I would have you reject the help of other things, but only their authority. A humble, docile mind will be thankful for human aid in the great business of religion. There is a middle ground between despising assistance and so depending upon it as to cast off all self-inquiry. The pert and flippant self-sufficiency which would lead a young woman to neglect, or even to despise, the judgment of those whose calling it is to teach the Word of God, and who have studied it more closely than it is possible she can have done, is no proof of that humility which is one of the brightest ornaments of her sex. I do not, therefore, teach young females to think lightly of the assistance rendered by ministers and books in the momentous concerns of religion, but simply remind them of their duty to search for themselves the Scriptures, by whose authority all books and all ministers are to be tried.

Before I dwell on this source of information, as to the nature of religion, I may just remark that there are one or two things which must of necessity characterize religion. Since it has, first of all and chiefly, to do with God, and since God can and does regard, search, and judge the heart, its true seat must be the heart. It is not a mere outward thing, a round of ceremonies, or a course of unintelligent action. The soul must be religious; the whole inner self—the intellect, the will, the affections, the conscience—must be under the influence of piety. Mark this: there must be thought, choice, affection, and conscientiousness. Again, whatever is true religion must primarily relate to God, and must of necessity be a right state of mind and heart towards Him. It must also be to its possessor a very serious, solemn, important matter; it supposes great concern for it as an affair of salvation, eternity, and heaven. It must produce a character very different from that of the person who is not living under its influence. It is too great a matter to leave no mark, to produce no impression, to form no peculiarity. So that we may be sure where it lives properly in the heart, it will develop itself visibly in the outward character.

With these ideas, which are at once obvious, instructive, and impressive, let us open the New Testament and see what descriptions of religion we find there. I beg your very closest attention to them, as in the presence of God and the prospect of eternity. The Apostle Paul, in setting forth the subject and substance of his ministry, describes it thus: "Testifying, both to the Jews and also to the Greeks, repentance towards God, and faith in our Lord Jesus Christ." This, then, is true religion: repentance and faith. If we turn to the gospel of John, we read thus: "But as many as received Him, to them gave He power to become the sons of God, even to them that believe on His name; which were born not of blood, nor of the will of the flesh, nor of the will of man, but of God." This is also repeated: "Jesus answered, 'Verily, verily, I say unto thee, except a man be born of water and of the Spirit, he cannot enter into the kingdom of God.' " This is religion, a new spiritual birth, or, in other words, an entire spiritual renovation of our fallen and corrupt nature. Then again we may quote the apostle's words in that beautiful chapter on charity: "And now abideth faith, hope, charity, these three; but the greatest of these is charity." These also constitute religion: faith, hope, and love. Similar to this is his language in his epistle to the Galatians: "For in Jesus Christ neither circumcision availeth anything, nor uncircumcision, but faith which worketh by love." This is an immensely important passage, showing that no outward ceremonial observance or church relationship constitutes religion, but a true, simple faith in Christ for salvation which produces love to God, to man, and to holiness.

This accords with what our Lord said: "Thou shalt love the Lord thy God with all thy heart, and with all thy soul, and with all thy mind. This is the first and great commandment. And the second is like unto it: Thou shalt love thy neighbor as thyself. On these two commandments hang all the law and the prophets." Then, again, the apostle said, "For the grace of God that bringeth salvation hath appeared to all men, teaching us that, denying ungodliness and worldly lusts, we should live soberly, righteously and godly in this present world, looking for that blessed hope, and the glorious appearing of the great God and our Savior Jesus Christ, who gave Himself for us that He might redeem us from all iniquity, and purify unto Himself a peculiar people, zealous of good works."

Observe then from these passages what is religion and its usual order: true conviction of sin; deep solicitude about pardon and salvation; confession of sin, without defense, excuse, or palliation; genuine repentance; self-renunciation; faith in Christ, or a simple reliance on Him for salvation; the new birth, or an entire change of our corrupt nature; love to God, leading to obedience of His commands and a holy life; and a serious observance of all the ordinances of religion, including baptism and the Lord's Supper. Are these things so? Is this the description of religion given us in the New Testament? Who will pretend to deny it? Search for yourselves! You will see at once how this answers to the general description of it previously given as a thing of the heart, a right state of mind towards God, a matter of deep concern to the mind that possesses it, and making an obvious distinction between her who has it and her who has it not.

You are in danger, my young friends, from the female temperament, from your sensibility, susceptibility, and imaginativeness, of having your minds led astray on the subject of religion, and of considering it rather as a matter of feeling than of principle, as belonging rather to the emotions than to the judgment and the will. You are liable to be seduced from the truth by appeals to the senses and the imagination, as the spurious religion of the present day abounds with them. But I again say, search the New Testament and judge for yourselves, and see what you find there about tasteful architecture, gorgeous ceremonies, splendid dresses, sacerdotal power, sacred days (either of fasting or festivity), church authority, or even the prevalence of devotional observances over moral duties. What you find everywhere is faith, love, peace, hope, and holiness; a religion of which devotion is indeed an element, but only one out of many, being ever associated with self-government, conscientiousness, social excellence, and charity. Nor is the religion of the New Testament merely that state of mind which is moved by a pathetic sermon, which melts at the Lord's Supper, or which is excited by the appeals of a missionary meeting. Religion has to do, I know, with our whole nature, and therefore with its emotional part; but then the degree of sensibility so much depends upon physical constitution that a sense of excitement during religious ordinances is far less to be depended upon as a test of personal godliness than rigid self-government, resolute will in the way of righteousness, and tender conscientiousness exercised in obedience to the divine authority, and under a constraining sense of the love of Christ. None are more in danger, therefore, of self-delusion on this subject than yourselves.

I may now lay before you the obligations you are under to possess, and ever to cultivate and exhibit under the influence of such a religion as this. I say "obligations." This word is stern and hard, but not too much so. The subject is pressed upon your judgment, heart, will, and conscience by all the weight and power of a divine authority. Religion is not one of those matters which is submitted to your option, for which if you have a taste, well, and if not, still well. Nor are you left to form your own religion, and to select for yourself the form in which you will please God and find your way to heaven. This is the dangerous delusion of many in the present day. It is all well enough, they think, to be religious after some fashion; but each must adopt his own way of serving God. Upon this principle of resolving it all into taste, the person of no religion, if his taste is that way, is on nearly the same footing as he whose religion is simply according to his own liking. The truth must be told, and told plainly too, that there is but one religion, and that is the religion of the Bible.

To be pious at all, we must be pious in God's way. It would be a strange thing if, when a master had given strict and explicit written orders to a servant how he should be served, the servant should choose his own way of obedience, and set aside the directions he had received. In all honesty, therefore, I must tell you at once, harsh as the declaration may seem, that without religion, and without the religion of the Bible too, you will perish everlastingly. There is no way to heaven but by the religion of the Bible. "He that believeth on the Son hath everlasting life; he that believeth not on the Son shall not see life, but the wrath of God abideth on him." These are awful words; they roll like thunder and flash like lightning, not from Sinai, but from Calvary, and they should be pondered by all who hear or read them.

The obligations to a life of religion arise out of the relations in which you stand to God. He is your Creator, Preserver, and Benefactor; and you are His creatures, dependents, and beneficiaries. You feel, my young friends, your obligations to your parents, arising out of your relation to them. As a child, you feel bound to love, serve, and please them. What, and do you not feel your relation to God, which is a thousand times closer than your connection with them? Yes, you sustain an individual relationship to God. Do you consider this? Have you considered it? Have you ever yet, in devout seriousness, said, "What and where is God my Maker? What do I owe Him, and how should I conduct myself towards Him?" Is God the only relation you should leave out of consideration and forget? Did you ever yet in all your life devoutly ponder this relationship to God, and the claims which it brings? Why, if He had never commanded you to love and serve Him, you ought to do so on account of this relationship. But He *has* commanded it. Your Bible is His demand upon you. It is God's voice, enjoining you to be truly, constantly, and consistently religious. It is His formal, explicit, frequently and solemnly repeated claim. Its injunctions command, its invitations allure, its promises encourage, its threatenings warn, its judgments alarm you to be truly pious. It is given to teach you what religion is, how it is to be practiced, and how it will be rewarded.

And then this is all addressed to you. Religion is not merely the concern of the middle-aged and the old, but of the young; not of the other sex only, but of yours. Indeed, it has ever flourished more among persons of your sex and age than among any other class. To imagine it is only the business of old age and a deathbed is an insult both to it and to God. Ought He not to have the first and the best of our days? Should He be put off with the dregs of life? Will you dare entertain such an idea as offering those dying remains of existence that are of no service for anything else—the refuse of sin, Satan, and the world? Does not your fear tremble at such a thought, your generosity scorn it, and your sense of gratitude recoil from it?

Seriously attend to the following motives by which early piety may be enforced upon you. Alas, that you should need them! Think of its being told to the angels in heaven that mortals upon earth need to be urged by inducements to love, serve, and glorify that God whose service is felt to be their bliss, their honor, and their reward. However, you do need them, and they are at hand.

There are motives which apply to you in common with the other sex, such as, for instance, the nature of religion itself. What, for dignity, for happiness, or for honor, can be compared with it? What constituted the glory of unfallen woman in Paradise? Religion. It was her piety towards God that invested Eve, before she had spoiled the beauty of her soul, with her brightest charms. Conceive of her, bending in lowly reverence, in ardent affection, and with inexpressible gratitude before the throne of God; passing with holy dread and averted eye the tree of knowledge, to feed upon the fruit which grew upon the tree of life, and to hold communion with her husband in that sacramental type and pledge of immortality. Not a thought, feeling, or volition was then in opposition to God. She heard His voice in the garden and hastened to meet Him.

Now religion is intended to bring you back as near to that state as our fallen nature in this sinful world will admit. Yes, religion was the repose of her happy and holy spirit, of which the Fall deprived her, and which it is the design of the whole scheme of redemption to restore to her daughters as well as to her sons. True, your religion must have some ingredients which hers, before her lapse, had not: but insofar as it consists in the service of God, it is the same in substance. Look up into heaven, and what constitutes the felicity and glory of the blessed inhabitants of that happy world? Is not religion the beauty of every spirit made perfect, the ephod in which every seraph ministers before the throne of the Eternal?

But to judge of the real dignity, honor, and felicity of true religion, hear what our divine Lord said. On one occasion, "A certain woman of the company lifted up her voice and said unto Him, 'Blessed is the womb that bare Thee, and the paps which Thou hast sucked.' " And who does not admit the justice of addressing this congratulation to that distinguished woman to whom was granted the honor of being the mother of the Savior of the world? What woman on earth would not have esteemed such an honor infinitely higher than to have been the queen of the whole earth? Yet what was the reply of Christ? "Yea, rather, blessed are they that hear the Word of God, and keep it." It is as if Christ had said, "Yea, she is to be congratulated; but still higher is the honor of being a child of God by true piety than the honor of being the mother of Christ without it."

Beautiful is the language of Quesnel, the pious Jansenist, on this passage: "The Holy Virgin is not blessed in having borne Christ, or on any other account, but only because He, being much more holy than the holiest of saints, made her worthy to be His mother by sanctifying her. Christ does not blame the woman for praising His mother, but completes it by intimating that her blessedness proceeded from her having borne the Son of God in her heart even before she bore Him in her womb." In other words, He declares that her honor as a woman would have been of no account to her but for her religion as a saint.

(By way of application, could any language of our Lord have tended more effectually to rebuke the preposterous and blasphemous honors which are paid to the Virgin by the Papists? It would seem that, foreseeing all that the church of Rome has accumulated of error and impiety in this way, He had determined in the most effectual and impressive manner to furnish the antidote and refutation in this impressive language. Let anyone study the spirit of this reply of Christ to the congratulation of the woman who blessed His mother, and see if it is not the most convincing answer which could be given to the dreadful system of Mariolatry, which prevails so extensively in that corrupt and apostate church.)

Is it possible, my young female friends, to find a richer, loftier commendation of the dignity and felicity of true religion than this, which places those who possess it above the honor of giving birth to the humanity of Christ? I ask you most intently to ponder this passage of the gospel history.

In common with the other sex, you also are liable to the stroke of death, and therefore youth may be the only time given you to attend to this high concern; if neglected then, it may be neglected forever. In the pathetic and poetical language of Job it is said, "Man cometh forth like a flower and is cut down." How impressive is this figure of the frailty of humanity. Man is not like the cedar of Lebanon, or the oak of the forest, which defies and outlives the storms of centuries; no, nor the shrub of the mountainside, or even the flower watched by the gardener's care and protected by the greenhouse from the frost and hail, the storm and rain, but the flower exposed to the force of the elements and the vicissitudes of the weather, soon and easily destroyed by adverse influences. Such is humanity: tender, frail, and fragile.

How often have we seen some lovely flower in our garden, prepared by nature to live in full-blown beauty through a long summer, suddenly pierced by the arrows of frost, just when its bud was bursting and opening its beauties to the sun and the eyes of the beholder, and then drooping its head upon its stalk and gradually withering away. So also have we often seen an amiable girl, apparently destined to live long upon earth, smitten by tuberculosis, at a time when all her powers of body and of mind were developing into womanhood, and then wasting away by incurable disease till death closed the scene and left us weeping over the lovely flower cut down in spring. What multitudes of such faded, withering flowers do we see every year! Could we from some high place in the air look down into all the chambers of sickness only of one town, how many estimable young females should we see sinking under disease, amidst the tears of parents sorrowfully beholding their pride and hope thus incurably diseased, and others amidst the anguish of heart-stricken lovers thus witnessing the flower cut down just when they expected to transplant it into their own garden of domestic delights. Oh, painful reverse, to sigh out the last adieu at such a time and under such circumstances; to put on the shroud instead of the bridal attire; to go down to the tomb instead of taking possession of the elegantly furnished house; and to be gathered to the "congregation of the dead" instead of going into the happy circle of the living! Does this never happen? Alas, you mourners, your sighs and tears answer in the affirmative. Yes, and you, my young friends, may add to the number. Would you die without religion? No, you answer, not for a thousand worlds. They why live another hour without it? To have it in a dying hour, you must seek it in living ones. Few find it on the bed of death. With religion shedding its luster on the tomb, and pouring its consolations into your bosom; with the attractions of heaven drawing up your soul to its glories; with a hope full of immortality surveying the mansions of the just men made perfect—you will be able to turn away from earth when it is holding out its brightest scenes to your view, and scarcely cast one longing, lingering look behind.

But should you live, as in all probability you will, still, if you neglect religion in youth, you will most likely neglect it forever. There is nothing more likely to perpetuate itself than neglect, in every case and in reference to everything. Procrastination grows, like other things, with indulgence. Nothing in all the world requires prompt decision so much as religion. Nothing is more likely to be postponed forever, if postponed from the present moment. I have no doubt you intend to be pious. You would shudder at the idea of deliberately purposing and determining to abandon religion forever. It would appear to you the height of impiety, a species of blasphemy, to say, "I will never become a Christian." Yes, and it is thus that Satan would cheat you out of your salvation. He will allow you to be as solemn, serious, and even sincere in your intentions as you please, to be religious at some future time, if he can persuade you to put it off from the present moment to a more convenient season. But you must be told that not one in a thousand of those who go through the period of youth amidst evangelical advantages of religion, and with a deliberate postponement of the matter to futurity, ever fulfill their purposes. Those who come to womanhood, and collect around them the cares and anxieties of a wife, mother, and mistress, without religion rarely ever find leisure or inclination for it in such circumstances.

But I now go on to dwell on some other motives and persuasive arguments to early piety, which appertain with greater force to your sex than to the other, or, at any rate, to a large proportion of it. Consider your natural temperament. There can be no doubt that though religion is not exclusively, nor principally, it is partially a matter of emotion. In many affairs of human conduct we are moved to action partly by our feelings, even before the decisions of the judgment are made and deliberated upon. The head should always move and lead the heart, but oftentimes the heart rouses and moves the head. The feelings are excited even when the judgment is only half-awake and half-informed.

This is no doubt the case in religion. Your quick sensibility, your soft nature, your tender heart, your great imaginativeness, all render you naturally susceptible of pious impressions. Religion contains not only much that is stern, bold, and sublime, and much that is truly logical and truly philosophical, which addresses itself to the judgment, but also much that is pathetic, tender, and touching, which appeals to the heart. You are easily moved to fear, and therefore the terrors of the divine law have greater power to cause you to tremble. You are readily excited to pity, sorrow, and love; and therefore the gospel, that wondrous mixture of suffering, grief, and mercy, powerfully stirs up your tender emotions and calls into exercise your gentle affections. I do not forget that you partake of the common corruption of our nature, and that you also need the grace of the Holy Spirit for your conversion; but still I contend that, so far as natural advantages are to be taken into consideration, the very temperament of your minds is in your favor. Hence it is that so many more women are truly pious than men. It is not that the gospel is unworthy of the more robust intellect of the other sex, but that it falls in more with the softer nature of yours. In most things the God of grace seems to follow the order established by the God of nature.

I may mention, in reference to many of you, your sheltered condition at home and the protection you there enjoy. Your brothers must go out into the world, encounter its temptations, and be exposed to its moral dangers. While they are in peril of making shipwreck of faith and a good conscience on the troubled ocean of human life, you are in the quiet haven of a pleasant domicile. Or, to change the metaphor, you are nestling under cover of a mother's wing while they are left in all their inexperience and moral feebleness to the attacks of birds of prey.

Besides this, at home you enjoy, if you are the children of the godly, many religious advantages. There you are called to join in offering the morning and evening sacrifice at the altar of family devotion. There you regularly accompany your parents to the house of God, keep holy the Sabbath, and enjoy the other ordinances of social worship. There you are guarded from the withering influence of evil companionship. How favorable is all this to the cultivation of piety! Should your heart be inclined to serve the Lord, you do not have to encounter the jeers of scoffing associates, the poisoned arrows of infidel wit, or the sharp spear of profane humor. No heroic or martyr-like moral courage is requisite to enable you to persevere in a religious course, as is sometimes the case with your brothers; on the contrary, every advantage will be afforded you; every stone will be gathered out of your path.

Nor is this all, for, independent of parental vigilance and home protection, your sex is less exposed to the assaults of those temptations which, assailing young men and conquering the virtue of so many, harden their hearts against the impressions of religion. A keen sense of female decorum has thrown a covering over you. By common consent, a vicious woman is a more vicious character than a profligate man, and hence is a more rare one. The prodigal son is, alas, no infrequent character, but the profligate daughter does not often occur. A tenth part of the criminality which some men commit and yet retain their place in society would banish a woman from it forever. It is the high sense of female honor, the moral delicacy, and the fastidious modesty which are at once your glory and your protection. But then this very circumstance increases your responsibility. You are not hardened by crime into insensibility, nor confirmed in guilty habits by repeated acts of sin, nor petrified by infidelity into a stone-like indifference to religious impressions. Your moral susceptibilities are not so blunted by long-continued vicious courses as to leave no avenue to your hearts open for the voice of warning.

And then consider one thing more, your leisure. I now speak of females living at home with their parents, who are not required to earn their own support by their own labor. Your time, except that which is put under requisition by a judicious mother for her assistance in household matters, is all your own. Your brothers, whether at home or abroad, must of necessity be much engaged in business. Their time is scarcely at their own command; and too often this is felt, or at any rate pleaded, as an excuse for neglecting the claims of religion and the salvation of the soul. You have no such excuse. Your time is so much at command that you can walk, read, work, or visit at will. You have so much leisure that to get rid of time, which sometimes hangs heavy on your hand, some of you I fear squander hours every day upon useless labors of fancy and taste. You, of all persons in our world, can with the least truth say you have no time to think of eternity, no opportunity to seek for salvation. Is it possible you should overlook your present happy freedom from solicitude of almost every kind? You will perhaps at once think of the apostle's words: "There is a difference between a wife and a virgin: the unmarried woman careth for the things of the Lord, that she may be holy both in body and in spirit: but she that is married careth for the things of the world, how she may please her husband." How much of instruction, warning, and advice is there in these few words. The apostle did not intend to say that all unmarried females actually do (alas, we know that too many of them do not) care to please the Lord; but his meaning is that in the absence of all the solicitudes of a wife, a mother, and the mistress of a house, they have the most opportunity to attend to the things that belong to the soul.

Ah, young women, you can perhaps form some idea of what awaits you by seeing what has come upon the head, the heart, and the hands of your mother. Even with the most judicious domestic arrangements, and a mind happily freed from excessive care and troubling thoughts, how incessant are her cares, and how exhausting of time, strength, and spirits are her duties! She has no resting hours, no holiday seasons, no sabbath leisure; but care, incessant care, is often her lot. Is this the time, and are these the circumstances, to which you would postpone the consideration of the high concern of religion? Is it amidst such distractions of thought, such perturbation of feeling, and such occupancy of time that you would begin the momentous pursuit of salvation and the sacred duties of religion? Why, the real, yea, the established and eminent Christian woman finds it as much as she can do to keep her piety alive amidst so many perplexities and demands. And will you begin it then? These remarks apply to all, even to those who have servants at command, but especially to those who have no such help. Females of the laboring class, how with a mother's duties will you be able to commence a religious life, with your unshared and unalleviated anxieties? Oh, let me say, with an emphasis borrowed from what I have witnessed myself, "Remember your Creator in the days of your youth." Halcyon season, did you but know it! Take advantage of it while it lasts.

Dwell, my female friends, upon the rich advantages placed by the order of Providence within your reach. Their practical value and tendency are evident in their results. How else shall we account for it that so much larger a number of the disciples of Christ are found among your sex than among the other? It is not, I repeat, that religion, as some say, better suits the weaker intellect. This is a double insult, first of all to religion itself, as if it were adapted only to imbecility, and to you, as if that imbecility were yours. The circumstances I have just stated will account for it without supposing that either your minds or the proofs of revealed religion are weak. Religion, which is the glory of an archangel and the very image of God, can never be below the dignity of man, or unworthy of the attention of the mightiest intellect. If religion depended upon authority, a thousand times more authority of lofty intellect has been arrayed on the side of Christianity than has been marshaled against it. In addition to the circumstances mentioned above to account for the prevalence of piety among your sex, I might remark that it would seem as if God had intended it for the greater humiliation of Satan that, as he triumphed over man by woman, so God would triumph over him by woman; that as she was the instrument of his success in the Fall, she should be the instrument of his humiliation in redemption; that she who was the first to come under his yoke should be the most eager to throw it off, and thus his trophy should be snatched from his hand, and his boast rendered nugatory by the power of Him who came to bruise the serpent's head and to destroy the works of the devil. But there is another mark of the wisdom of God in this arrangement, which is that as religion is so momentous to the interests of society and the welfare of immortal souls, that sex should be most inclined to it to which is consigned the first formation of the human character.

I will now set before you the benefits which will accrue to you from early piety.

Are the blessings of religion itself nothing? Remember, piety is not merely the performance of duties, but also the enjoyment of benefits. This is too much forgotten, and the whole business of a holy life is regarded by many in something of the light of penance, or, at any rate, of a service somewhat rigid and severe. If it were so, it would still be our wisdom to attend to it, since it is the only thing that can prepare us for heaven and eternity. That it is service is very true; but it is also a state of privilege. It is the service not of a slave, but of a child; and with the duties of a child it brings also the privileges of a child. Dwell upon that one thought: a child of God! Can you conceive of anything higher, greater, or nobler? Does an angel stand in any higher relation to God? To be able to say in the fullest, richest sense of the language, "Our Father which art in heaven"; to be an object of the love, care, and interest of the one Infinite Being; to be interested in all the privileges of the divine, redeemed, and heavenly family! Oh, my young friends, is this nothing? Is it not everything? Many of you are orphans, and is it not blissful to say, "When my father and my mother forsake me, then the Lord will take me up"? Is it not a blessed thing to have Him as the guide of your youth? Hear what God says: " 'Wherefore come out from among them, and I will be a Father to you, and ye shall be My sons and My daughters,' saith the Lord Almighty." Oh, hear His voice, accept His invitation, and come into His family. Hence it is that we propose religion to you not simply in the shape of duty, but of bliss. Yes, it is another name for happiness; and can you be happy too soon? You want to be happy. You are made for happiness, and are capable of it; and where will you find it? Pleasure says, "It is not in me"; and knowledge says, "It is not in me." Rank, fashion, and wealth affirm, "We have heard the fame thereof with our ears." But religion says, "Ho, every one that thirsteth, come ye to the fountain and take of the water of life freely." Universal experience attests that pure and full satisfaction is not to be found for the soul of man in any of the possessions of this world; and if they are satisfying, they are all uncertain, mere unsubstantial shadows which flit before us and are lost.

You have perhaps formed totally wrong conceptions of religion. "Happiness," you say, "in religion? I can conceive of it as duty, somewhat severe, though incumbent duty; but to speak of religion yielding pleasure is like supposing that the entrance of a ghost would increase the delights of a ballroom!" Yes, I know it is, in the imagination of some of you at least, a spectral form, muffled, sullen, and gloomy; frightening the young by its awful look, petrifying them by its icy touch, and casting over them its gloomy shadow. But you mistake it. It is, on the contrary, a seraph from the presence of God, lighting on our orb, clad in robes of celestial beauty, radiant with beams of glory, shedding smiles of joy on this dark scene, and echoing the angels' song, "Glory to God in the highest, and on earth peace and good will to men."

That ministering spirit meets you, my female friends just setting out in life, and offers to be your guide, protector, and comforter through all your perilous journey to eternity. Hear her voice as she beckons you to follow her: "If you are in danger I will shield you; if you are desolate I will befriend you; if you are poor I will enrich you; if you are sorrowful I will comfort you; if you are sick I will visit you; in the dangerous walks of life I will protect you; in the agonies of death I will sustain you; and when your spirit quits its clay tabernacle I will conduct you into the presence of God, where there is fullness of joy, and place you at His right hand where there are pleasures forevermore." And will you refuse such a friend? Will you turn away from such bliss?

Is religion all gloom and melancholy? Yes, if Eden was a gloomy place. Yes, if heaven is a region of sighs and tears. Yes, if saints made perfect and holy angels are clad in sackcloth, and the song of the seraphim is changed into the groan of despair. Oh, no, "her ways are ways of pleasantness, and all her paths are peace." Her duties are pleasant; her very sorrows are mixed with joys, to say nothing of her privileges. To exhort you, therefore, to be pious is only, in other words, to invite you to take your pleasure—pleasure high, rational, holy, and angelic; a pleasure accompanied by no venomous sting, no subsequent loathing, no remorseful recollections, no bitter farewells. Honey in the mouth never turns to gall in the stomach. It is a pleasure made for the soul and the soul for it; adapted to its nature because suited to its spirituality; adequate to its capacities because the enjoyment of an infinite good; and lasting in its duration because itself eternal. It is such a pleasure as grows fresher instead of becoming wearisome by enjoyment; a pleasure which a man may truly call his own because it is seated in his heart, and carried with him into all places and all circumstances, and therefore neither liable to accident nor exposed to injury. It is the foretaste of heaven and the earnest of eternity. In a word, beginning in grace, it passes into glory and immortality, and those joys which neither eye has seen, nor ear heard, nor the heart of man conceived.

Perhaps I may suggest, without at all intending to utter a suspicion of your regard to virtue, or a reflection upon your firm attachment to its rules, that you may need religion in youth to protect you from the moral dangers to which even females are exposed. A vicious woman, I have already admitted, is a much rarer character than a vicious man; but still it sometimes occurs. What instances the records of some institutions could reveal! How many victims of the tempter's wiles could there be found who would have been preserved from degradation and misery had they been found under the protecting influence of religion when the assault was made upon their purity or honesty! I know that multitudes are kept strictly chaste and upright without religion; but I know that, of the numbers who have fallen, not one would have lapsed if they had been living in the fear of God. After Eve's fall from perfect innocence in Paradise, no woman should feel offended by the admonition to be cautious and vigilant, nor suppose that her circumstances, feelings, or principles place her so far beyond the reach of temptation that her safety is guaranteed with absolute certainty. "Pride goeth before destruction, and a haughty spirit before a fall." To many a once high-minded woman, proud of her reputation, the taunt has been uttered by the victims of frailty, "Art thou also become weak as we?" "Be not high-minded, then, but fear."

But you need religion for your consolation amidst the sorrows of your lot. If it is truly said of man that he "is born to trouble as the sparks fly upwards," it may with greater emphasis be so said of woman. As if in the way of righteous retribution, she who mixed the bitter cup of human woe is called to drink the deepest of its dregs. Sorrows are apportioned to her sex in common with ours, and there is scarcely an affliction to which humanity is incident to which she is not herself exposed. In addition, how many has she peculiar to herself! The weaker vessel, she is liable to be oppressed by the stronger; and to what an extent is this oppression carried on! How is she trodden down, not only in countries where the protective influence of Christianity is not known, but in this one where it is! To how much greater bodily infirmity is her more delicately wrought and more sensitive frame subjected than ours! Dwell upon her dependence and her helplessness in many cases. To me, some single friendless women are the very types of desolation. Then think of her privations, sufferings, cares, and labors as a mother. I admire the patience, contentment, and submission which enable her to say, "I am a woman," without repining or complaining of the hardness of her lot; for certain it is that her groans are the loudest in creation. Think not, my young friends, that I am scaring you into religion by filling your minds with these gloomy forebodings. By no means; but I am anxious to prepare you, by its sweet, soothing, tranquilizing, and alleviating power, to meet a woman's trials with a woman's piety.

Early piety is at once the most secure basis and the most complete finish of all female excellence. Look over what is said in the previous chapter on "Woman's Mission," and the virtues and tenderness that qualify her to fulfill it, and think what a support to all these is furnished by sincere piety. The surest basis of all moral excellence will be found in it. What is so productive of humility, of meekness and gentleness, of contentment and submission, and of self-denial and fortitude? In what soil will these mild and yet heroic dispositions grow and flourish so luxuriantly as in that of piety?

We have stated that woman is created to love and be loved. To love is natural to her; and what cherishes this state of mind like religion, which, both in its doctrines and duties, is one bright and glorious manifestation of love to the universe? To all these varied excellences religion adds the firmness and consistency of principle, and the power and government of conscience, and takes them out of the region of mere taste. And what a holy and ineffable loveliness does it throw over the female character! Beauty is woman's attribute, and her form is the most perfect type of exquisite symmetry to be found in the whole material universe. And if woman's form is the finest specimen of material beauty, woman's piety is the most attractive instance of moral beauty. Who can look upon any well-executed pictorial representation of it without admiration? Where does woman look so altogether lovely as when seen lifting the eye of devotion to heaven, that eye which expresses the mingled emotions of faith, hope, and love? The Church of Rome has known the power of this, and has maintained its dominion in some measure over its votaries by the power of the painter's art in depicting female beauty associated with female piety. In a religious female, the beauty of heaven and earth combine. The graces of the seraph and those of the daughters of Adam are united, just as in a holy man the sublimer grandeur of mortals and immortals is found associated.

Yet, notwithstanding all this, many of you are not pious. Consider what a chasm in excellence remains to be filled up, what a defect to be supplied, while religion is wanting in the female character. There are few men, however irreligious, but would shrink from impiety in a woman; it involves a coldness and hardness of character offensive to both taste and feeling. "Even when infidelity was more in vogue than at present, when it had almost monopolized talent, and identified itself with enlightened sentiment, the few women who volunteered under its banner were treated with the contempt they deserved. The female Quixote broke her lance in vindicating the 'Rights of Woman'; and no one sympathized with her in her defeat. And depend upon it, whatever other female follows Mary Wolstencroft, and essays the emancipation of her sex from the obligations of piety, will, like her, be consigned to abhorrence by the verdict of society. The mere suspicion of irreligion lowers a woman in general esteem. Religion is indeed woman's panoply, and no one who wishes her happiness would divest her of it; no one who appreciates her virtues would weaken their best security" (*Woman in Her Social and Domestic Character* by Mrs. John Sandford).

What is it, then, that prevents your giving to the subject of religion that attention which its infinite and eternal importance demands and deserves? Let me ask you with a beseeching importunity, as the apostle did the Galatians, "Who (or what) did hinder you that you should not obey the truth?" Ah! what? Let me speak to you of the hindrances that are in the way of your obtaining life eternal. Hindrances! Should anything but absolute impossibilities prevent you?

It is not infidelity, you say? No, you are not infidels. You shudder at the idea. A female infidel is a character as rare as it is odious. Nor is it absolute irreligion, but the negative character of no religion, that we have most to complain of—not direct opposition to its claims, but the neglect of them for other things. It is a guilty apathy to the most momentous subject in the universe, a careless indifference to the most valuable interests of time and eternity, and a fatal oblivion of all that belongs to another world, which we regret; it is a contentment with things seen and temporal, without any solicitude about things unseen and eternal, which we deplore. Your minds are preoccupied. You are taken up with other things, and say to religion when it appeals to you, "Go your way for this time, and when I have a convenient season I will call for you."

There is, I know, a repugnance to true, spiritual, vital, and earnest piety, which is the natural working of an unrenewed heart. You can observe Sabbath day forms of godliness by attending the house of God; but even this is more from custom than from choice, a kind of weekly compromise with piety, that you may for so much Sabbath occupation be left to yourselves and other pursuits all the rest of the week. Your religion is nothing more than a Sunday dress, worn for the place and the season. But this is not religion, but merely a substitute and an apology for it.

Some of you are bent upon present worldly enjoyment. The apostle has described your taste and your pursuits when he speaks of those who are "lovers of pleasure more than lovers of God." Ponder that description. Does it not startle and horrify you? Lovers of parties, of the dance and the song, of the party scene and frivolous discourse more than God! Just look at this thought in all its naked deformity. A ball, a concert, a rout, a party, loved more than God! Not to love God at all for higher objects than these—for science, literature, fame, rank, and wealth—is a dreadful state of mind; but to neglect and despise God for scenes of frivolity, mirth, and conviviality, is it not shocking? Did you ever yet seriously reflect thus: "What a soul I must have that can love pleasure, but cannot love God!" Consider, what will this taste for pleasure do for you in the hour of sickness, in the scenes of poverty, in the season of calamity, and in the agonies of death?

In the case of some of those who possess a more than ordinary degree of personal attraction, the consciousness of beauty fills the mind with complacency and constant thirst for the admiration and attention of others. No really elegant woman can be ignorant of her natural accomplishments; and too rarely is a beautiful mind the lovely tenant of a beautiful body. What an odious spectacle is presented when mind and matter are thus exhibited in contrast. What beauty can be compared with that of the soul, and what beauty of the soul can be compared with holiness? This is the beauty of angels, yea, of God Himself. How foolish is it to be vain regarding that which a cutaneous eruption may turn into loathsome deformity, and which, if sickness does not destroy it at once, advancing age must obliterate and the grave consume. Many a woman, even in this world, has had to rue the possession of a captivating face or form, and to deplore it forever in the world to come. Beauty has lost body and soul, character and happiness, in thousands of instances.

Vanity displays itself also in attention to personal decoration, even where there is no pretension to beauty, and not infrequently attempts to supply the want of it. How many are a thousand times more concerned about jewelry than religion, the pearl of great price, and about millinery than about the robe of righteousness and the garments of salvation. A love of dress is not only a foible and a fault, but almost a sin, and in innumerable cases has led to confirmed vice. Is it not lamentable to conceive of a rational and immortal being spending her time and exhausting her solicitude in adorning her body, and caring nothing about the ornaments of her soul—thinking only how she shall appear in the eyes of man, and caring nothing how she shall appear in the sight of God? With this is too often associated a levity and a frivolity of disposition which are the very opposite of that seriousness and sobriety of mind which a real regard for spiritual religion requires.

There is no sin in cheerfulness, and no piety in gloom. Religion is the happiest thing in the world, for it is in fact the beginning of heaven upon earth. Religion gives a peace that passes all understanding, and yields a joy that is unspeakable and full of glory. So I wish you to understand, my young friends, that I do not require you in becoming Christians to put on a veil, cut off your tresses, put aside every elegant dress, part with your smiles, and clothe yourself like a specter in the gloom and sullen silence of the convent. But religion is still a serious thing, a thing that deals with God, salvation, heaven, and eternity. And surely the frivolity and the levity that can do nothing but laugh, rattle, and court attention by studied airs, empty loquacity, and personal display are utterly incompatible with that dignified and chastened (yet by no means formal, much less gloomy) sobriety of mind which religion requires.

Companionship hinders many from giving their attention to this momentous subject. They are surrounded by associates who have no taste for religion; and they have, perhaps, formed a still closer friendship with one or more people who unhappily do not conceal their distaste for this high and holy concern. From the spell of such a circle, it is difficult indeed to break away. It has been thought and said by some that the influence of companionship, both for good and for evil, is greater with women than with the other sex, on the ground that there is less of robust independence and of self-reliance in woman than in man. If so, how much does it become every female to take care what companions she selects! How difficult it is to oppose the spirit and conduct of those with whom we act! Generally speaking, we must conform to them or give up their friendship. Even if a solicitude about religion is in some degree awakened, it will soon be checked and extinguished in the society of those who have no sympathy with such anxiety. Shall the dearest friends you have on earth keep you from salvation? Will you sacrifice your soul, your immortal soul, at the shrine of friendship? Will you refuse to go to heaven because others will not accompany you? And will you go with them to perdition rather than part company on earth? Will you carry your friendship so far as to be willing to be friends even in the bottomless pit?

You are perhaps prejudiced against religion by the conduct of some of its professors. And it may be that some of your own age and sex are included in this number. I am sorry there is any ground for this. I admit that much you see in many of them has but little in it to recommend religion to your favor. But all this was foretold by Christ, must be expected considering what human nature is, and ought not to be allowed to prejudice your minds against piety. If you saw a number of persons under a course of medical treatment which required them to observe a particular regimen, but which they constantly violated, and were of course no better for the medicines they took, you would not reject the system because it did not cure them. Just so it is with religion. These persons, though they profess to be under it, are constantly violating its rules, and are no better than those who do not profess it. But is this a valid reason for rejecting the system? You are to try religion by its own nature as set forth in the Bible, and not by the conduct of its professors. If your soul should be lost, it will be no excuse before the bar of God, nor any comfort to yourselves in the

world of despair, that you suffered your mind to be prejudiced
against religion by the misconduct of some who professed it.

And now, in concluding this chapter, let me, young
women, abjure you at the outset of life to consider the great
end and purpose for which, as regards yourselves, your great
Creator placed you in this world. Think not too highly of
yourselves, for you are sinners as well as others, and need, and
may obtain, the salvation that is in Jesus Christ, with eternal
glory. Think not too lowly of yourselves, for you are immortal
creatures and may inherit everlasting life. Rise to the true
dignity of your nature by rising into the region of true religion.
Consume not your life in pursuits, innocent though they may
be, but frivolous and unworthy of your powers, your destiny,
and your duty. Along with a clear and right understanding of
your mission as regards this world, connect as clear a perception
of your mission as regards the world to come. Behold an existence opening before you which you may fill with the sanctity,
bliss, and honor of a Christian as well as with all the virtues of
a woman. Withdraw your heart from vanity and consecrate it
to piety. Give the morning of your day to God, and then,
whether it is long or short, whether it is passed in wedded or
single life, whether it is bright with the sun of prosperity or
dark with the clouds and stormy with the winds of adversity, if
it shall close suddenly by one of those visitations to which your
sex is peculiarly exposed, or if it shall include a long and gloomy
evening—it shall usher in for your happy spirit, delivered from
the burden of the flesh, that cloudless and eternal morning to
which there shall be no night. Then shall it be found that the
chief end of woman, as well as man, was to glorify God and
enjoy Him forever.

Chapter 5

Religious Zeal

"Those women which labored with me in the gospel . . ."
Philippians 4:3

The subject of this chapter harmonizes with the scenes which we often witness in the metropolis of our country; I mean the missionary and other religious meetings which are held annually in that great center of the world's family. The month of May is wisely selected as the time of holding the anniversaries of these organizations of Christian zeal. Then, when the principle of fertility, after the dreariness of another winter, is flowing in a thousand channels, and when all nature in this country is verdant and blossoming with the hopes of another year, it is well for the Church of Christ to exhibit those institutions which are, in the moral world, the vernal signs of retiring frosts and approaching summer. It is a glorious sight to behold the trooping multitudes hastening with willing feet, joyful countenances, and beating hearts to the place of convocation, and blending all the joys of friendly greetings with all the sublimer delights of Christian zeal. We feel called upon there to bless God that we live not only in a world which He has visited in mercy by the Person and work of His incarnate Son, but in an age and country in which so much is done for the spread of the knowledge of this great fact to the ends of the earth.

At these meetings all is matter of delight. The crowded platforms containing the pastors, deacons, and members of our

113

churches who have connected themselves with the Missionary Society; the presence of missionaries from the fields of holy labor; the eloquent addresses of the speakers; the vast crowd of listening hearers; the thunders of eloquence reverberating in other thunders of applause—all are calculated to make one feel how happy an exchange we have made in giving up the pleasures of sin and the world for those of religion.

But there is one other sight on these occasions which is as delightful as it is common, and that is the number of women, and especially of young women, who are always present. This reminds us how deep an interest they have in these proceedings, and how large a share they bear in them. And, indeed, without going to the metropolis in the month of May, or witnessing the scenes of Exeter Hall, what public meeting for any religious object is ever held in our own or any other town, of which women do not form by far the larger portion? But I do not adopt the world's vocabulary and talk of the beautiful and elegantly dressed females who are there. I would rather speak of "the holy women," like one apostle, and refer to them, as another apostle does, as "those women which labor in the gospel."

Let us attend to what the passage at this head of the chapter says: "Help those women that labored with me in the gospel." Clearly women may labor in the gospel, for they did so in apostolic times, and received the commendation of the apostle for it. If they did then, they may now; and if they *may* do so, they *ought* to do so. Hard would be woman's lot, bitter her privation, and degraded her condition if, on account of her sex, she were excluded from all participation, beyond her own personal religion in the sublimest enterprise in the universe. She might well deplore her misfortune if, while man was permitted the exercise of religious zeal, she were denied all service at the altar of God. "Even heathenism," she would mournfully exclaim, "honored our sex, as it was represented by the Vestals, to whose vigilance was committed the guardianship of the sacred fire, and also by its priestesses, to whose inspiration was entrusted the responses of the oracles. And does the religion of Jesus exclude us?" No, it does not, and I refer you back to the first two chapters for proof that it does not. I now call your attention in the present one to learn how you may avail yourselves of the honor placed within your reach, and discharge the obligations which you are under to promote the interests of religion in this dark and disordered world.

To be useful in the cause of God! How noble, how vast, how sublime, how godlike an idea! Dwell for a moment upon it. Did you ever weigh the import of that very common but very delightful word, "usefulness"? Did you ever ponder in sober seriousness of thought the kindred phrase "to be useful"? Have you never had your admiration excited by hearing it said of anyone, "She is a useful woman"? I cannot let you read another syllable till I have endeavored to fascinate you, if possible, by the beauty, and to captivate you by the force, of that glorious word "usefulness." Look at its opposite, "uselessness." How low and dull and mean a sound, and how despicable the character it represents! A rational, social, and immortal being, useless; doing no good, carrying on no benevolent activity, exerting no beneficial influence; a worthless weed, and not a flower; a pebble, and not a gem; a piece of dead wood floating down the stream, instead of a living fruit tree growing on its bank! Yes, worse than all these, for the weeds, stones, and wood may be converted to some good purpose; but to what purpose can one who does no good be turned, except to serve as a warning to others? Let your young hearts, then, beat with a desire to do good. Aspire to the honor of doing good. Contract not, shrivel not into a despicable selfishness. Cherish a yearning after benevolent activity, and feel as if it were but half-living to live only for yourselves.

In this cause I want you to be ever zealous. The apostle says, "It is good to be zealously affected always in a good thing." Zeal, as you know, means an earnest, ardent desire, giving rise to a correspondent energy of action to obtain some favorite object; and, when directed to a right object, it is a noble and elevated state of mind. It is, however, a state of mind that requires great caution in its exercise, especially in the young, and most of all in young females. It is like fire, which may be applied to many useful purposes when under wise direction, but which, if not kept in its proper place and under proper restraint, may cause a conflagration. Or, to change the illustration, it may be only as the healthful, vital heat which keeps the body in comfort and in action, or it may become a fever of the soul, to consume its strength and destroy its life. Or, to venture for the sake of emphasis even upon a third comparison, many a zealous mind is set on fire by the speed of its own action, and for want of some regulator to check its speed, and of some lubricator to lessen its friction, bursts into a flame and consumes the whole machine, and does mischief to others as well as to itself. A warm heart requires a cool judgment to prevent these consequences of a misguided zeal.

The female mind, being so susceptible, is far more liable to incautious action than that of the other sex, and is less disposed to reflection. In man the judgment more generally keeps the heart in check till it is itself enlightened and convinced. In woman the heart is often engaged before the judgment, and hence the danger of female zeal is sometimes wrong in its object, excessive in its degree, and impetuous in its action. Almost all new theories, whether relating to medicine, theology, or any other practical matters, find favor first of all chiefly with women. Too often led more by their feelings than by their reason, they get entangled, like their first mother, by appeals to their passions and affections, and allow their hearts to lead astray their judgment. The Greek philosophers classified zeal under three headings: the zeal of envy, the zeal of emulation, and the zeal of piety. Extinguish all feelings of the first as so many sparks thrown off from a flame kindled by the fire of the bottomless pit. Have very little to do with the second beyond an unenvious imitation of what is good; and let the third be put under the guardianship of sound judgment and the guidance of holy Scripture.

I will first of all advert to the objects of your zealous activity. You dwell in a vale of tears and amidst the groans of creation, occasioned by poverty, disease, misfortune, and death, and are not to be insensible to the sights and sounds of affliction by which you are surrounded. The female heart is supposed to be the very dwelling-place of mercy, and an unfeeling woman is a libel upon her sex; formed by nature to weep with those who weep and to minister to the bodily woes of humanity, she should enter into the design of Providence and become a ministering angel in the chamber of sickness. You have seen those cloaked and demure women who issue from conventual establishments on errands of mercy to the abodes of sickness and poverty, deeming no office too menial, no service too self-denying, which can alleviate the pains or promote the comfort of the sufferer. I would not question the purity of their motives, or the tenderness of the offices which they perform for the children of want and woe; but they look, after all, like a device of the church which employs them to obtrude itself on public notice and to win converts to itself. I call upon you, without cutting the ties of your connection with society and abjuring the characters of wives and mothers, to be our Sisters of Mercy, and to make it your business and your pleasure to visit the scenes of sickness and the abodes of poverty. Even in youth, acquire the habits, the tenderness, the delicate tact of a nurse. Loathe that spurious sentimentality which can weep over the imaginary woes of a novel, but turns away, with either a calloused or a cowardly heart, from the real sufferings which abound on every hand.

But I now more particularly refer to zeal for religion, or for matters connected with it. Religion is everyone's business, not only as regards the possession and practice of it as a personal concern, but also as regards its diffusion. Everyone cannot only be truly pious, but, by the blessing of God, can do something to help make others so. To spread religion in our world is not merely the work and duty of its ministers, but of all without exception, whether young or old, rich or poor, learned or illiterate, male or female. Everyone who understands the nature, feels the influence, and values the privileges of the gospel of Christ can do something to bring others into the same happy condition. Where there is no desire and no effort to do this, there can be no real piety. Those who have no concern for the salvation of others have no right to conclude that they are in a state of salvation themselves. There is room, opportunity, and obligation for all to work in this cause. Even children can do something here, and have done it. A little girl, being deeply affected by the notorious violation of the Sabbath in the neighborhood where she lived, by the number of shops open on the Lord's day, went to her minister and solicited some tracts on the subject. She enclosed them in envelopes, took them around and modestly left them at the different houses without saying a word. And as the result of this humble and unostentatious effort, seven shops from that time on were closed on the Sabbath. God sometimes employs the humblest instruments for accomplishing great purposes, as I observed when remarking upon the conduct of the little Hebrew maid in Naaman's family.

Paganism teaches us something here; for what did Jehovah

say to the prophet when referring to the heathen practices
which the Jews had imitated? "Seest thou not what they do in
the cities of Judah, and in the streets of Jerusalem? The
children gather wood, and the fathers kindle the fire, and the
women knead their dough, to make cakes to the queen of
heaven, and to pour out drink offerings unto other gods."
What a busy scene: all minds engaged, all hands employed,
men, women, and children! Let us be instructed by this bad example, and show a zeal for the true God equal to that which
the apostate Jews did for false ones. Christianity can find work
for women and children as well as paganism; and how solemn
are the obligations to propagate it which it imposes on all who
profess it!

As no service can be well performed by those who are not
qualified for it, I will here enumerate the chief prerequisites for
a course of female activity in the cause of religion.

Religious zeal should in every case be the offspring of personal piety. Without this there can be no intelligent, well-
sustained, or very efficient effort. Something, no doubt, may be
accomplished without it. God may make use of labors which
were not directed to His glory. But it is only the truly pious
mind that can understand the object of religious zeal, be actu-
ated by right motives, and be likely long to continue the work,
or to bring down the blessing of God upon what is done. Your
own heart must be right with God or you will know little
about the way of making others so. Example must support exhortation, or the latter will have little effect. Much of the
effort of the present day is sadly wanting in devout seriousness,
spiritual earnestness, and holy solemnity. It is a bustling,
prayerless, unsanctified activity. There is in too many a frivolity
about it that looks as if those who are engaged in it know not
or forget that they are doing the work of the Lord; all is so
light and trifling that it is evident in this case that zeal is only

another species of amusement. The zeal that is likely to be continuous, to honor God, and to do good to our fellow creatures is that which is cherished in the closet of devotion, fed by the oil of Scripture, and fanned by the breath of prayer. There is upon the minds of those who manifest it that awe which warns them how they touch a holy thing.

Religious knowledge is essential to well-directed efforts to do good. I now more particularly refer to a knowledge of the object to be accomplished, and of the means of accomplishing it. A young person anxious to do spiritual good should well understand three great principles in religion: the ruin of human nature by sin, its redemption by Christ, and its regeneration by the Spirit. That person should consider that all efforts of zeal must be directed to the accomplishment of the two latter. To fit her for this work, she should study well the Word of God, read some of the many treatises on the subject of religion with which the press teems, and make herself acquainted with some of the best tracts and books for putting into the hands of those who become anxious about religion.

An intense and longing desire to be useful must lie at the bottom of all her efforts. It is not a mere love of activity, a taste for social union and occupation, a desire for power and influence over others, and an ambition for distinction which are the impulsive causes of religious activity, but a tender pity for the immortal souls of our fellow creatures, and an earnest solicitude for their salvation, coupled with an enlightened and fervent zeal for the glory of God. It is that piety which melted the heart of David when he said, "Rivers of waters run down mine eyes because they keep not Thy law"; which agitated the soul of Paul when, amidst the splendors of Athenian architecture and sculpture, he was insensible of all the glory that surrounded him in consequence of the sin with which it was associated, and felt his spirit moved within him at seeing the city wholly given to idolatry, and which, indeed, is taught in the first three petitions of our Lord's prayer: "Hallowed be Thy name; Thy kingdom come; Thy will be done on earth, as it is in heaven."

Understand, my young friends, then, what you have to do: not the work of a low and narrow sectarianism, in proselytizing persons from one denomination to another; nothing resembling the operations of female Jesuitism; nothing of zeal to establish one denomination upon the ruins of another; no, but the nobler and holier work of saving the souls of your fellow creatures, especially those of your own sex, from the dominion of sin here, and from the wrath to come hereafter. Begin life with an abhorrence of bigotry, and never let your zeal degenerate into the meanness and malignity of that earth-born spirit; let it be a fire kindled by a coal taken by the seraphim from the altar of God, and not a flame lighted by a spark from the bottomless pit. Let it be your aim to spread that religion which consists not in forms of government and religious ceremonies, but in faith in Christ, love to God, and love to man. To accomplish this, let there be a real engagement of your heart. Give up your soul to a passion for being useful. Cherish the most expansive benevolence. Feel as if you will not understand, secure, or enjoy the end of life unless you live to be useful. Account usefulness the charm of existence, the sugar that sweetens the cup of life. Ever feel as if you heard a voice saying to you, "Do something; do it at once; do it heartily; do good, this good, good to the soul."

A habit of self-denial is essential to the exercise of religious zeal and Christian benevolence. Our Lord said, "If any man will come after Me, let him deny himself, and take up his cross and follow Me." This is true of the way of holiness, but it is especially so of that of benevolent activity. Christ could do us no good without His cross, nor can we do others much good without ours. I would not deceive you, and endeavor to lure you into the career of holy activity by representing it as leading through a garden of Eden where all is blooming and beautiful, ease and enjoyment. No such thing. The course of religious zeal is often a wilderness, over sharp stones and bare rocks, and amidst thorns and nettles. You must make sacrifices of time, ease, enjoyment, feeling, perhaps of friendship; you must bear hardships, and encounter many disagreeable things; you must be prepared to give up self-will, pertinacity, and claims to pre-eminence. Can you be zealous for good works on such terms? If so, come on; if not, go back; for the career of mercy is not for such tender feet as yours to tread.

But, my young friends, can you allow yourselves to sink into such effeminacy and feebleness of character? Can you be content to degenerate into littleness, and pass through life as a species of nonentity because you cannot endure noble self-denial? I do not appeal to your love of romance. I would not set your imagination on fire in order that you may offer your-selves up as a burnt offering to benevolence in the flames of enthusiasm. I do not stimulate you to become heroines of mercy, and to set all the comforts of life at defiance. There are some who love the adventures of a career of active mercy. There may be romance in everything, even in pity. I do not desire this, but I want to see young women practicing a sober self-denial, a judicious disregard of ease and comfort, in order to do good. Unite a masculine hardihood of endurance with a feminine tenderness of feeling and delicacy of manner. Passive fortitude belongs to you.

Patience is another qualification for doing good. Those who would accomplish this must not be weary in well-doing. There are many things to make them so: the neglect of others, opposition, disappointment, ingratitude, perhaps censure. Those who expect to benefit their fellow creatures with as much ease and as speedily as some do them injury had better not make the attempt, for they are sure to fail. Scarcely any people in the world have more need of patience than those who set themselves to instruct the ignorance, relieve the wants, alleviate the sorrows, and reform the vices of their fellow creatures.

See how this was illustrated in the history of our Lord. Consider how His benevolence was ever resisted by the malignity of those whom He sought to benefit. He lavished upon them His mercy, and it was equaled by their ingratitude. They refused His offers, rejected His invitations, misrepresented His actions, disbelieved His words, and misconstrued His motives. Never was so much goodness met by so much venomous opposition. Yet behold His patience. A thousandth part of the opposition which He met with would have exhausted the forbearance of an archangel; and yet "He endured the contradiction of sinners against Himself," gave them His tears when they had refused His miracles, shed for them His blood when they despised His tears, and bade His disciples to make to them the first proclamation of His grace when they had even scoffed at His death.

Study the history of Christ, my young friends, for the purpose of seeing an example for you to imitate in the career of mercy. Follow Him who went about doing good, in order to teach you with what patience you should go and do likewise. Many who are all ardor at the start soon grow tired because they do not find the course easy to complete in a single bound, or are opposed in the way. It is a despicable as well as a pitiable sight to behold a young person entering into the work of benevolence as confident and eager as if she would surpass all others, and then almost at the first stage, when the novelty is over and difficulties arise, and the expected flowers do not appear in the path, giving all up and turning back to indolence, ease, and uselessness. On the contrary, it is a sight on which angels and God Himself look down with delight, to see another holding fast to her way in her humble career of benevolence, amidst disappointment and opposition, persevering in her attempts to do good, and finding in the consciousness of her aims and motives, and her knowledge of the excellence of her object, a sufficient inducement to persevere, though at present she reaps little else but discouragement and defeat.

A spirit of dependence upon God for success, united with a high sense of the importance and necessity of human effort, is essential to religious zeal. This gives a twofold boldness of mind and firmness of step, and makes us strong not only as instruments in ourselves, but also in the Lord and in the power of His might. What courage is derived in the career of benevolence from such a consideration as this: "I know I am seeking a good object by right means, and I will go in the strength of the Lord!" Young women, even in your humble sphere and feeble efforts to do good, a spirit of believing prayer (which, indeed, is the spirit in which everything should be done) will bring the God of angels to your help, the Lord of hosts to your aid. Go forth with the consciousness that you are doing right, and with a belief that Omnipotence is by your side. It does not show pride nor self-conceit, but only that proper sense of capability which everyone should cherish, to say, "I feel I am something, and can do something. I need not be a cipher, for God has not made me one. I have a mind, a heart, a will, and a tongue, and with these I may do something for God and my fellow creatures. Others of my own age and sex, feeble and humble as I am, have done something, and so may I; and by God's help and blessing, I will." You are right; it is all true. This is self-knowledge and right self-esteem. Cherish these thoughts; act upon them, and you will do something. With such qualifications you may go to the work of religious zeal.

Permit me now to point out to you the ways in which your

zeal may be employed appropriate to your sex, age, and circumstances. "As we have opportunity," said the apostle, "let us
do good." Opportunities are more precious than rubies, and
should never be lost by neglect. There are three things which,
if lost, can never be recovered: time, the soul, and an opportunity. And it is of importance for you to ponder this. It become us all to remember the advice of the sage to his disciples,
"Be mindful of opportunities." Youth is your opportunity for
doing good—not your only one, but it is a very precious one.
The remarks made in the last chapter on the subject of the
leisure afforded by your present situation for the cultivation of
piety apply with equal force to the opportunities it affords for
usefulness. In married life, with a family around you, and all
the cares it brings with it, you will have comparatively little opportunity, at least for some of those activities which you can
now carry forward.

Among the ways in which female activity could be appropriately carried on, I must begin of course with the education
of children in our Sunday schools. The instruction of the girls
is entrusted to females, and what an honor is thus assigned to
them! It is strange how any young woman pretending to religion can satisfy herself that she is doing all she can, or all she
ought, for God's glory and the good of her fellow creatures if
she is not devoting her youthful energies to this blessed work.
And yet it is painful to observe how many of the young
women of the more respectable families of our congregations
withhold their services from this useful and valuable sphere of
female activity. I am not unaware of some difficulties and objections to this engagement of her daughters which present
themselves to the mind of a careful, judicious, and anxious
mother. But surely the proper exercise of maternal influence
and authority would, in most cases, be sufficient to counterbalance those contingent evils to which the mixed society of the

Sunday school community might expose young females (I mean, in the way of forming acquaintances and unsuitable connections). A well-taught and wisely trained girl will know, and ought to know, how to avoid general and undesirable familiarity without being suspected of haughty disdain or proud neglect of those who are not upon her level in the ranks of social life. It does require care, I admit, but care will be sufficient to avoid the evils alluded to. And I freely confess that the frequent and mixed meetings of teachers of both sexes which are held in some schools are by no means necessary for the good working of the system, and are very undesirable on other accounts; and it is not to be wondered at that, for this reason, many mothers do not allow their daughters to become teachers, and that daughters themselves do not wish to engage in the work. Acquaintances, by no means suitable, have, no doubt, in some cases been formed. It is therefore incumbent upon all who are thus engaged to be anxiously watchful that no part of their conduct gives, to those who seek it, occasion to speak ill of the effect of Sunday school teaching upon the character and conduct of the females who devote themselves to it.

District visiting societies and benevolent institutions for affording temporal relief and spiritual instruction to the sick poor, conducted by female agencies, have become very common both in the Church of England and among Dissenters. It would not be desirable, of course, that these should be chiefly conducted by young women. Matronly age, experience, and weight are necessary to give propriety and effect to such a labor of love, but surely there is no impropriety in associating, even in these good works, a youthful female with an elderly one.

The Bible and Missionary Societies, and other religious institutions, have called into operation a large number of fe-

males who are employed in collecting money for those important organizations, and for supplying the poor with copies of
the Word of God. There can be no objection to this, provided
that the more youthful portion of the sex so employed is associated with those who are older, and also that very young girls
are not employed at all in the work. Nothing can be more re-
pugnant to my sense of propriety than for young females to be
sent out with what are called "collecting cards," to wander over
a town knocking at the doors of anybody and everybody for the
purpose of begging money, and sometimes even entering
counting-houses and assailing young men with their impor-
tunities.

The distribution of religious tracts is another line of female
activity in which many may be eminently useful. This is a
means of doing good universally characteristic of the age. The
press was never so active either for good or for evil as it is now.
Its productions are instruments which every hand can wield,
not excepting that of a young (and even comparatively illiterate) female. But the same caution must be applied here also, so
that nothing is done to break down the barriers of female
modesty.

Perhaps it will be thought that I ought not to overlook one
line of female usefulness peculiar to the sex, and especially to
the youthful portion of it, and that is furnishing articles of the
pencil and needle, the products of which, when sold, shall go
to the support of the cause of Christ. There is one way of doing this about which, I confess, I have serious doubt. I mean
the modern practice of bazaars, or, as they are now called,
"fancy sales." I am aware of all the arguments that are employed in favor of them, such as their gainfulness, and their
calling forth contributions from those who would give or could
give in no other way. A very beautiful little tract entitled "The
Bazaar" was published two years ago, in which the writer, not

without a show of argument, endeavored to prove that these means for the support of religion hardly comport with the sanctity of the object. A certain air of frivolity and worldliness at these sales is thrown over the whole matter, so that such a scene looks like piety keeping a stall at "Vanity Fair."

"Recall," says this writer, "the scene itself, the gay dress, the music and the raffle, flattery and compliment instead of truth. Purchases made from regard to man, and not free-will offerings to God. Mortification and disappointment in place of the approving consciousness of her who 'had done what she could.' Skill exercised in making that which is worthless pass for much. Arts practiced and advantages taken, with the excuse that it is for a religious purpose, that would be thought dishonorable in the common business transactions of the world. Then follows ennui after excitement; the gaze at the heap of left things to be disposed of, or that will do for other bazaars, with the false estimate of the result of this. There is another fact in the history of such sales: some who shun the ballroom and the concert, and never entered a theatre, act there the shopwoman, talk the nonsense befitting the bazaar room, and are as worldly, vain, and foolish as she who seldom dreams of anything but pleasure, earth, and time."

Now this, I admit, is rather severe, and is perhaps a little exaggerated. Still there is much truth in it, and it may serve as a corrective, if not as a dissuasion. To the pure, all things are pure; and there may be those who can enter, pass through, and leave such scenes without receiving the smallest injury to the devout and happy seriousness of their religious character. At any rate, it comes near the appearance of evil, and should excite caution and prayer on the part of those who consider the matter as innocent and, therefore, lawful. Bazaars, however, are not the only way in which the needle is employed by pious females for works of charity. Working parties are very common; one meets periodically in my vestry, at which articles of utility are made and shipped for sale in India, the produce of which, amounting sometimes for one year's labor to eighty pounds, is devoted to the support of orphan schools connected with our missionary stations abroad. At these meetings, piety, friendship, and zeal all blend their feelings of enjoyment, and furnish happy seasons for those who attend them.

I knew a most accomplished woman, long since in heaven, who was called by grace, and who, after her conversion, felt an irresistible desire to do something for the spiritual welfare of her fellow creatures and the glory of God; but her means were more limited than her aspirations. She thoroughly understood the science of music, and her most exquisite singing had been the delight of many in fashionable circles. Her taste in drawing and painting was equal to her skill in music. After her conversion to God she turned these accomplishments to the purpose of glorifying God, "who doth instruct man to discretion," by setting some of the most admired Italian and German airs to sacred words, as well as painting Scripture subjects, and selling the music and pictures in the circle of her friends (the paintings often for large sums), and consecrating all, like the woman who broke her alabaster box of ointment, to the honor of the Savior whom she intensely loved. Perhaps there may range over these pages the eye of some similarly gifted woman with a heart for Christ and His cause, but with as scanty property to serve Him as the female above alluded to. To her I would say, "Go thou and do likewise."

There is another way in which young females, unable to do much in producing tasteful works, may be occupied in doing good for God and their fellow creatures, without in the smallest degree violating the rule of decorum or infringing on the delicacy of female modesty. I refer to visiting the chamber of sickness, or the cottage of poverty, to read to the invalid, or to ignorant persons of their own sex, the Word of God and religious tracts. Surely it is no invasion of either the rights of man or the duties of the minister for a pious, modest female, though young (of course I do not mean a child), to go to the bedside of a sufferer and pour into her ears the words, and into her heart the sacred truths, of that precious volume, which is the best balm for a wounded spirit, and the only consolation for a broken heart. Nor can it be improper for her to take her chair by the side of a poor mother who, while she is plying her needle or watching the cradle, is ready to hear words whereby she may be saved. What a field of usefulness, almost unoccupied, is here opened to the ambition and the energies of our pious young women who have leisure for such occupation! How many thousands of women of the laboring classes are there in every large town who are so occupied by the cares of their families and the demands of their husbands as never to join the public assemblies for worship, or to hear the joyful sound of the sermon or the psalm, who would hail as a ministering angel a female coming to their scene of constant monotonous care and labor, and causing their dreary abode to echo with the music that tells of a present salvation even for them, and of a land hereafter where the "wicked cease from troubling, and the weary are forever at rest." Oh, you devout women, if you have hearts of pity for the poor, or compassion for the souls who are likely to be lost amidst their being careful and troubled about many things and their much serving, or if you have any zeal for the glory of God, employ your leisure hours in paying these visits of mercy to the houses of poverty, ignorance, sickness, and misery! Here there can be nothing in opposition to female modesty, nothing that can minister to female vanity. The seclusion of the scene prevents all this. No rude or inquisitive gaze follows a young woman there; no language of fulsome compliment or sickly adulation is addressed to her there; she is alone with sorrow, or witnessed only by her conscience and her God. Oh, what compared with a young female so occupied is the most elegant and beautiful woman glittering in the gay scene of fashionable folly, the admiration of many eyes and the envy of more? What is all the adulation poured by the lip of flattery into the ear of beauty, when compared with the blessing of her who was ready to perish, so gratefully bestowed on that sister of mercy who has thus caused the widow's heart to sing for joy?

Companionship affords a means of usefulness of which you ought not to be slow in availing yourself. It may be that you have formed friendships in the days of your thoughtlessness with some as thoughtless as yourselves. But you have been awakened to solemn and holy reflection. You have, through the work of divine grace, passed from death unto life; but your friends still remain under the power of the world and far from God. Here, then, is a most legitimate object of pious zeal: to seek by all affectionate and judicious means their conversion to Christ. What an honor and felicity would it be should you be the means of saving the soul of your companion! How close and tender would be your friendship from that hour, when the tie of affection was doubled and sanctified by the bond of religion! How happy would be your intercourse, how sweet your communion! A covenant is made between you which will go with you to heaven; for all friendships formed on the basis of religion will last forever. Take with you then if you can, to that happy world, the friend of your heart, there to renew, perfect, and perpetuate the intercourse which you have commenced on earth, and realize the idea that the closest and happiest friendship commenced below is but the bud, and scarcely even that, which will blossom with amaranthine freshness through eternity in heaven.

Women's talent for a flowing, easy, tender style of correspondence is generally acknowledged; and ought they not to employ this as a means for serving God and their fellow creatures? How many have been thus led to an acquaintance with religion! There is a great moral power in a well-written religious letter. It is known and felt to be an effusion of love from one heart to another. It is read alone, when no one is a witness of the effect. There is not the reproving or monitoring presence of the writer. There is no disposition to feel offended and to resent the intrusive advice or warning. Young women, employ your pen, and let your affection in this manner breathe from your letters.

I shall now lay down some rules for the direction of female activity, which must be very rigidly observed in order to prevent it from doing harm in one way as well as good in another.

The zeal of young women must ever be exercised with the strictest regard to the modesty of youth, and especially of youthful females. It must never be forgotten that bashfulness is the beauty of female character; like the violet which seems to court seclusion, and indicates its retreat only by its fragrance, retiringness in her adds to her attractions. Anything that would destroy this, that would strip off this delicate veil of modesty and make her bold and obtrusive, that would thrust her by the impulsive ambition of her own mind upon the public notice instead of being sought out for usefulness, that would make her clamorous in her complaints of neglect and imperious in her demands for employment—such things would inflict an irreparable injury on society by depriving her of that passive power of gentleness by which her influence can be most effectually exerted in society.

I confess that with all my desires for female activity within its proper sphere, and for the legitimate exercise of woman's zeal, the extent to which in the active spirit of the age the sex is employed makes me not a little jealous for the delicate beauties and excellences of the female character. Money might flow into the treasury of our societies, numbers might be added to their friends, spirit might be given to our operations, and the triumphs of the cause might seem to be multiplied, but if any injury were sustained by the female character, all that was otherwise achieved would be accomplished at a dreadful cost and a fearful loss. Therefore I entreat you, my young friends, to guard against this evil. Cultivate the meekness, gentleness, and retiringness which are your brightest ornaments. Make it appear that in what you are doing for God and His cause you neither seek publicity, nor aim to attract attention or court applause. Avoid all that undue familiarity, flippancy, and trifling with the other sex which would look as if your object was rather to attract notice from them than really to do good. I ask for nothing prim, prudish, or repulsive, for no dread of conversation with men or for flight from their company, as if there were moral contamination in their presence and pollution in their words. Excessive prudery has not always been associated with the highest-toned purity; nor has an easy, artless frankness of manner ever been the indication of a bold and forward disposition. Still, be reserved, without pride or coldness; be frank, easy, and ingenuous without familiarity and obtrusiveness. In this age your danger lies in the latter extreme rather than in the former. Be content that your influence should flow through society like the blood in the human frame, carrying life and energy with it, but by channels where it is neither heard nor seen.

Female zeal in religious matters must ever be carried forward with due regard to the duties of home. If, as I have stated, home is the sphere of woman's mission, and the first and chief place of her duty, no public objects of any kind must be allowed to interfere with them. This I have already alluded to, but on account of its importance I refer to it again. It is not

to the honor of religion nor to the credit of a wife and mother
for a husband to come home at the dinner hour, expecting to
see everything ready and in order, and to find all in confusion,
nothing properly arranged, and have his time wasted by waiting for his wife, who has not finished her benevolent rambles
or her morning's attendance at some females' meeting. Nor is
it much for his happiness on coming home in the evening,
suffering from the fatigue and vexation of the world's rough
business, and when wanting the soothing influence of a wife's
sweet voice, to have to sit hours in sadness and solitude because
she is away at some public service. This is not the way to promote connubial felicity, or to interest his mind on behalf of the
objects of his wife's zeal. It will never do to serve the Lord with
time taken from domestic order, comfort, and family duty. A
neglected husband and family are a sad comment upon some
women's religious activity; and it is a comment not infrequently expressed by those who see it in the appearance of the
children and the house. These are the instances of which some
(who could do much without infringing on domestic claims,
but who will do nothing) avail themselves to justify their own
selfishness and indolence, and I am sorry that such instances
should ever be afforded to them.

Still a woman may look well to the ways of her household
and yet have time to devote to the cause of religion and humanity; and some do so who, by method, diligence, and
thoroughness, set their house in order. The description of the
virtuous woman comprehends both of these: "She looketh well
to the ways of her household. The heart of her husband doth
safely trust her, so that he shall have no need of spoil. Her
children rise up and call her blessed. She giveth meat to her
household, and her portion to her maidens. She eateth not the
bread of idleness." Here is domestic order, management, and
economy in perfection. Yet with all this is associated, "She

stretcheth out her hands to the poor; yea, she reacheth forth her hands to the needy, and in her tongue is the law of kindness." There the good housewife is supposed to find time for works of mercy abroad as well as of industry at home. When the comfort of a husband is never neglected, and he has no reason to complain, and does not complain, of the want of his wife's society; and when the supervision of the children, as to their general well-being, education, and home training are properly attended to, and the whole course of domestic order is maintained with regularity and precision—it is to a Christian woman's honor that her method of dispatch and order in the regulation of her household affairs is such as to leave her ample time for usefulness, without infringing on her duties as a wife, mother, or mistress. Except in the case of a large family, a destitution of all public spirit is no credit to any female. She cannot be educating her family as she ought to do if she is not, by her example as well as by her precept, training them in habits of benevolence.

These two extremes, then, are to be avoided by a married woman: allowing, on the one hand, the duties of home so entirely to engross her heart that she should feel no interest in anything that is going on in the world for the alleviation of its sorrows or the reformation of its vices, and to cherish no desire to promote the great objects of Christian zeal; or, on the other hand, allowing them to occupy her attention so far that she should neglect the claims of her husband, children, and servants. The chief danger in this age lies in giving too much attention to public duties, especially in the metropolis, the seat and center of all our great societies, and the place of their annual convocation. It is not much to the credit of a mother, nor for the advantage of her daughters, to be fond of taking them to many of these public gatherings. The month of May affords a strong temptation to this, and it should be most assiduously guarded against. It is not only lawful, but proper and desirable that our wives and daughters should be present at such meetings. Who would bar them from all these assemblies, shut them out from all these feasts of holy charity, or exclude them from all these scenes in which they take as deep an interest, and to which they have contributed equally with ourselves? Their sex is more benefited by them even than the other. Let woman's heart there bleed over the woes of humanity, and especially of her downtrodden sisters in the lands of darkness. Let woman's hand be there stretched out to lift them up from their degradation, and let woman's eye there sparkle with a brighter luster as it rejoices over the records of our missions and the triumphs of Christianity. But let not this rise into such a passion as shall spoil her for scenes partaking of less fascination in some respects, but to her of more importance in others.

In order to attain a proper balance, let younger women in these days of general benevolence guard against acquiring in youth that taste for public activity which, though it will not prevent them from entering into domestic life, will to a very considerable extent disqualify them for its duties. A love of activity is good; a passion for it is evil. There is such a thing as well-regulated, temperate, religious zeal, and there is also such a thing as a species of religious dissipation. When a young person loves home and home duties, but is ever willing and ready on suitable occasions, and for a proper object, to leave them for works of religious and common benevolence, she has a right disposition. But when home and home duties are irksome, and she is ever longing for the excitement of public services, her taste has been corrupted, her character damaged, and her prospects for future life have become somewhat clouded. If she has abjured the intention or wish ever to become a wife, and has, without entering a convent, determined to be a sister of charity, it may be all very well to desire to give herself wholly to works of benevolent activity; but if not, let her beware how she acquires predilections and forms habits which would make her unfit and indisposed for the duties of wedded life.

Young females while at home should be generally regulated by the wishes of their parents, and especially by their mothers. They are not, and should neither wish nor attempt to be, independent of parental control. A good and wise daughter will ever look up with affectionate deference to a good and wise mother, and will not therefore enter on any career of religious activity without consulting her. It may be that the wishes of the child and the opinions of the parent on this point are sometimes in opposition to each other; and it requires little argument to prove which in this case ought to give way. Perhaps some zealous, ardent, young female will put such a question as this: "I feel it is my duty to God to attempt to spread religion, and to do good to my fellow creatures, especially in the way of saving their souls; but my parents, not being themselves religious, oppose it, and will not allow me either to engage in Sunday school instruction, to collect for missionary or Bible societies, to distribute tracts, or to read the Scriptures to the poor. Is it my duty to follow my own convictions, or yield up my wishes to my parents?" It would be very proper for you, in a respectful and deferential manner, to state your wishes, and use every argument to obtain their compliance; but if this should prove ineffectual, you must then submit and bear the privation without resentful sullenness. To be moody, ill-tempered, and petulant under the refusal would too plainly indicate that you have much yet to do in your own heart to foster religion there before you seek to communicate it to others. You are under no such obligation to exercise your religious zeal in any particular way as you are to seek your own salvation. It is manifestly your duty to do good, and you can do it even under such restrictions as those I am now supposing; for you can set a holy example, and you can pray for the spiritual welfare of others, and correspond with absent friends, and perhaps influence by conversation your companions. Thus you are not, and cannot be, shut out from all methods of doing good; and as for those from which you are barred by parental authority, God will take the will for the deed, and reward the intention as He would have done the action had you been permitted to perform it.

Consider also that as your parents do not enter into your views of religion, they will regard your conduct, if you persist, in no other light than that of a refractory spirit, and will thus receive a prejudice against religion on account of your conduct. In contrast, a meek and good-natured yielding to their wishes, and sacrificing an object which they perceive to have been near your heart, will dispose them to think favorably of the religious principle which could produce such a spirit of unresisting and uncomplaining self-denial.

In order to be useful, it is necessary to cultivate habits of order, punctuality, and the right employment of time. These remarks apply, of course, to such as move in the wealthier circles of life, and whose opportunities of doing good are not confined to the Sabbath. Weekdays with them should be working days for God and man, by the offices of religion and humanity. There is no doing good without time. Two things cannot be done at once. Benevolence requires leisure. And how much time is wasted, which the miseries and wants of society require!

"Redeem the time" is a warning that should ever be sounding in our ears. We want it for our own improvement, and we want it for the good of others. We can do much with it and nothing without it. There is scarcely anything to which the injunction of our Lord ("Gather up the fragments that nothing be lost") more strictly applies than to this. Order redeems time, and so does punctuality; therefore order and punctuality are among the means of mercy and zeal, by supplying the time necessary for their exercise. Redeem time from useless reading, and also from that excessive addictedness to the accomplishments of music, drawing, and fancy work which is so characteristic of the present day. That some portion of time may be given by females in wealthy circles to these things is admitted. I am not for parting with the exquisite polish which skill in these matters imparts to female elegance. I love to see the decorations of female mind and manners. Of this I may have to speak again in a future chapter, and therefore shall merely now inquire: when the cries of misery are entering into her ears, and the groans of creation are arising all around her; when countless millions abroad are living and dying without the light of the gospel and the hope of salvation; when at our own doors will be found so many passing in ignorance and wickedness to their great judgment—is it for a humane, and especially for a religious, young woman to spend so much precious time each day over her knitting, crotchet, or embroidery work? As she sits plying those needles, and bringing out, it may be, the tasteful device hour after hour, does she never hear the cry of human woe, "Come over and help us"? Does it never occur to her how many souls have gone into eternity, unprepared to meet their God, since she took her chair and commenced her daily task? Or, even leaving out of view the employment of her time for deeds of religious zeal, is it not an afflicting sight to behold so much time thrown away on these elegant trifles, which might be employed in cultivating the mind by useful reading? You cannot, systematically, do good without redeeming time for the purpose.

Permit me now to remind you that all your efforts of religious zeal should be carried on in a spirit of faith and prayer. It should not be merely the love of activity, much less an ambitious fondness for publicity and display, that moves you, but the

overpowering feelings of love to God and love to man. It must
not be a substitute for religion, but the impulse and the constraining power of it. Instead of weakening your own piety, it
must strengthen it. Emanating from your own holy mind, it
must, like the newly kindled flame, react upon and increase the
fervor of its source. You must be watchful over your spirit, and
take care that your humility and spirituality are not impaired by
a spirit of vanity. You should look well to your motives, and
subject your heart to a most rigid self-scrutiny. In the
retirement of the closet you should cultivate that spirit of dependence which expresses itself in prayer, and is cherished by
prayer. The more you do for the spiritual welfare of others, the
more you must do for your own. You should take alarm if you
find that the excitements of zeal produce indisposedness for the
more retired and quiet exercises of devotion. A renewed consecration to your work should often taken place, preceded by a
renewed consecration of yourselves to God.

To encourage you in your career of holy activity, I may call
you, in conclusion, to consider the nature of your work, and
the consequences that will follow even your humble endeavors
to carry it on. It is religion, the gift of God to man, which
Jesus Christ came to our world to produce, and the Scriptures
are written to describe and impart; it is religion, the balm of
man's wounded heart, the renovator of his corrupt nature, the
means of his happiness, his preparation for immortal glory; it is
religion, the source of individual comfort, domestic peace, social order, national prosperity, and the whole world's restoration; it is religion which shall cover our earth with the glories
of the millennium, and raise up countless millions of our race
from the ruins of the Fall to the heavens of the eternal God; it
is religion which shall be the glory and the bliss of the redeemed Church throughout eternity; it is religion, the cause
for which prophets testified, apostles labored, martyrs bled,

ministers toil at home and missionaries abroad; it is this that you are promoting by all your efforts of religious zeal. In this cause you shall not labor in vain, nor without your reward, for "the earth shall be full of the knowledge of the Lord, as the waters cover the sea"; and your humble labors, though as drops in that mighty ocean, shall help to swell and impel the mighty mass. And after this shall come the world where you shall be gathered unto those holy women whose lives were briefly recorded in a past chapter, and to all those chaste virgins and holy matrons who have sought to weave by their labors the crown of glory, which shall ever flourish on the head of our Emmanuel.

Chapter 6

The Parental Home

"Children, obey your parents in the Lord; for this is right.
Honor thy father and mother—which is the first
commandment with a promise." Ephesians 6:1-2

"It is better to dwell in the wilderness, than with a
contentious and an angry woman." Proverbs 21:19

"Be kindly affectioned one to another." Romans 12:10

It was the saying of a judicious governess to a pupil on
leaving her establishment, "Be assured, my young friend, that
the order, comfort and happiness of a family very greatly depend upon the temper and conduct of the younger members of
it, when they cease to be children. I have seen the declining
years of some kind parents completely embittered by the pride,
self-will, and inconsiderate conduct of their young people.
When a young lady returns home, if she is not so good a
daughter as she was before, whatever acquisitions she may have
made at school, she had better not have been there."

This advice, so sensible and so appropriate, not only shows
how well-qualified was the admirable woman who proffered it
for the discharge of her duties, but is well worth being written
on the first page of every young woman's album, yea, upon the
tablet of her heart, and of being read by her every day of her
residence in her father's house.

It has been said that we are all *really* what we are *relatively*.

Akin to this, I may add, everyone is best known at home. Many not only dress their persons, but their characters, when they go into company, till it has become almost a current saying: "Tell me not what people are in company, but what they are in the family circle."

Home, as I have already said, is one of the sweetest words in our language, and nowhere better understood than in our own country. But it involves as many duties as it does enjoyments. It is not only a paradise of delights, but a school of virtue. A family is a little world within doors, the miniature resemblance of the great world without. It is in the home of her parents that a young female is trained for a home of her own; and, generally speaking, what she was in the former, that, in full maturity and expansion, she will be in the latter: the good wife and judicious mother, looking well to the ways of her household, being the full-blown rose of which the good girl at home was the bud of promise and of hope. And it may be depended upon as a principle suggested by reason, as well as a fact corroborated by observation, that she who contributes nothing to the happiness of her early home as a daughter is not likely to find others contributing to her later one as a wife, mother, and mistress. It is therefore of immense importance that you should at once, at the very commencement of this chapter, pause and ponder this momentous truth: that you are preparing your own future home by the manner in which you conduct yourself in that of your father. And because of its importance it is thus dwelt upon with such repetition.

In one aspect the subject of this chapter is of more consequence in reference to you than it is in reference to your brothers; you remain longer at home than they. It is the usual order of things for them to remove early from beneath the parental roof, first to learn, and then to pursue, their avocations in life. Thus, if their temper is unamiable and their habits unfriendly to domestic peace, they soon depart and the annoyance goes with them. But you, if not required to go out and earn your own support, remain with your parents until you are married; and if not wedded, you are with them continually. In the latter case, being a fixture in the household, you are under the greater obligation to increase its happiness. Of how much comfort or disquiet, according to her character and conduct, may a daughter be to a family through a period of ten or twenty years, dating from the period of her return from school! Hence it is always a source not of unmixed delight, but of some anxiety, to a considerate mother what kind of home character her child will prove to exhibit when she has finished her education, and when she exchanges the company of her governess and fellow pupils for that of the family circle.

Here, then, is the first thing, the great thing, to be determined by the young woman on her return home: to be largely a contributor to the happiness of the domestic circle. You cannot be a cipher in the house or a negative character. The other members of the little community must be affected by your conduct. You are ever in the midst of them, and your actions, words, and even your looks exert an influence upon them. Behold, then, your starting point in the career of home duties. Take up this resolution, intelligently, deliberately, determinately: "I will, by God's grace, do all I can to make my home happy to others, and thus comfortable to myself." Look at this resolution, ponder it, and imprint it on your memory, heart, and conscience. Is it not wise, virtuous, and right? Do not reason, conscience, and self-love approve it? Let it be a serious matter of consideration with you, not merely a thought passing through the mind and leaving no trace behind. Let it be a deep, abiding, influential consideration. Have not your parents a right to expect it? Is it not the most reasonable thing in the world that, enjoying the protection and comforts of home, you should in return make home happy?

To diffuse happiness anywhere is a blissful enjoyment, but most of all at home. To light up any countenances with joy is, to a benevolent mind, a desirable thing; but most of all the countenances of parents, brothers, and sisters. Set out with an intense ambition to compel from the whole family circle the testimony that it was a happy era in its history when you came permanently to reside at home. Oh, to hear a mother say, "Your coming, my daughter, was as the settlement of a ministering angel among us; your amenable temper, your constant efforts to please, your sweet and gentle self-sacrificing disposition have been a lamp in our dwelling, in the light of which we have all rejoiced. What a large increase, my beloved child, you have brought to our domestic felicity! Receive your mother's thanks and blessing." A harder heart than yours, my young friends, might be moved by such a hope as this.

Contemplate now the contrast to a situation where the conduct of the daughter extorts such a declaration as the following from sorrowful parents: "We looked forward with pleasure and with hope, not altogether unmixed with anxiety, to the time when we should receive her back from school to be our companion and our comfort. How bitter is our disappointment! Her unamiable disposition, her disregard for our happiness, her restlessness in the family circle, her craving for any company but ours, are painfully obvious. It was, we regret to say it, a sad increase of our domestic trouble when she became a permanent inmate of our house." Sighs and tears follow this sad confession. Which of these shall be the case with you? Can you hesitate?

Having then made up your mind to be a comfort at home, you should, and will, of course, inquire into the means of accomplishing your purpose. These will, if the purpose is fixed and the desire intense, almost without any enumeration suggest themselves. Those who really want to make others happy will find out their own means of doing so, and be ingenious in their devices to effectuate their end. Many things are difficult and require deep thought, but not so the desire to please. If our heart is set upon it, we can diffuse bliss almost without effort or contrivance. From a heart fully possessed with the desire to make others happy, kind acts and offices will perpetually flow off like the waters of a spring ever rising of themselves.

But I will lay down rules for your guidance so that your behavior at home may contribute to the happiness of your family circle.

Should your parents themselves be truly pious people who have trained you up in the fear of the Lord, their deepest solicitude and most earnest prayer for you is that you may "Remember your Creator in the days of your youth." You have been the witnesses of some of their anxiety on this ground, and for this object. You have heard a father's prayers, have seen, perhaps, a mother's tears for your salvation; but of the whole of their concern on this point you never can know. It is too deep for you to fathom. Till this great subject is determined, till they see you in earnest to lead a pious life, they cannot be happy. They value your love, your respect, your attentions to their comfort, your general good conduct, and the skills you have acquired, and not infrequently feel a parent's pride over you. But "Alas, alas," they say, "one thing you lack yet, and that is the one thing needful: true piety, the salvation of the soul. Oh, my daughter, that you were a real Christian, and that your love to Christ was as sincere as your love for me, so that all thy other excellences would be sanctified by the crowning one of true religion." What a check is such a reflection to the joy of a Christian parent! How many hours of bitterness such reflections occasion! What an interruption to the bliss of a family does it occasion when there is a difference of taste on this most momentous of all subjects! How is a mother's heart grieved to see her daughters, after all the pains she has taken to form their religious character, more taken up with fashion, company, and gaiety than with eternal realities! And that good man, their father, how is he distressed to see his counsels unheeded, his prayers unanswered, and they whom he had hoped to lead to the altar of God far more fond of the fair ceremonies of the world!

On the other hand, how happy are those parents whose children are one with them in this momentous concern. How sweet and sacred are the seasons of family worship when, not by constraint but willingly, the children assemble round the domestic altar and join in the sacrifice of prayer and praise. No jarring or discord now arises for the want of sympathy in these great subjects. No opposition of tastes occurs, no clashing of interests. Often does the mother exclaim in the fondness of her heart, "Thank God, that dear girl is a Christian, and to all her other excellences which endear her to my heart, she adds piety towards God. The beauties of holiness invest her charms with a loveliness that nothing else can impart."

In order to make home happy, there must be a proper consideration and right discharge of all the duties you owe to the various members of the little community of which it is composed.

First of all, there are your parents. That home cannot be a happy one where they are neglected, and where filial duty is wanting in the heart and conduct of the children. God has selected the most comprehensive term that could be employed on this subject, "Honor thy father and mother." This includes respect, love, and obedience. It is not necessary here to state the claims which parents have upon your gratitude, reverence, and regard. I can only remind you how much of the happiness of home depends upon a right understanding and discharge of the duties you owe to them. When the father's heart is wounded by disobedient conduct, or even disrespectful language; when the mother's comfort is neglected, and her burdens are unshared; when it is apparent that the children are much more intent upon their own gratification than that of their parents; when services are rendered to them tardily, reluctantly, and with ill nature; when complaint is uttered on one part, only to be answered by impertinence on the other—happiness must be a stranger in such a home.

Disobedience in young children, in whom reason and reflection are yet feeble, is bad enough; but it is far worse in those who are grown or growing to years of maturity. On the other hand, if it is beautiful to see the tender assiduities and affectionate attentions of childhood, which are rather the efforts of instinct than of reason, it is a far more attractive scene to witness the reverent regard, the studious desire to please, and the anxious effort to gratify, manifested towards her parents by a grown-up daughter. Here the intelligent mind is moved by the affectionate heart, and the affectionate heart is, in return, guided and impelled by the intelligent mind. If your parents have been less educated than you, and at the same time have spared no expense to afford you advantages which they did not possess, how ungrateful would it be in you, by any part of your conduct, to display your superiority and make them conscious of their ignorance!

Before a mother's infirmities reach the point of actual incompetence, a good daughter will feel solicitous to share with her the burden of domestic care, and to relieve her as far as possible from her load of maternal duty. This requires caution lest, by an officious obtrusion of help, it should be suspected that she was desirous of thrusting the mother from her superintendence, and of stepping into her place. It can never fail to wound a mother's heart to be supposed to be incompetent to fill her own situation as female head of the family. Even when imbecility is creeping on, she should be made to feel it as little as possible, and the forms and show of authority should be suffered to remain when the reality has passed away. Jealousy is one of the last passions that die in the human heart, and it should not be awakened by any part of filial conduct in the mind of a parent. A wife, mother, and mistress, deposed by her daughter, is a painful sight. She may have much weakness, but still enough reflection remains to make her feel her humiliation. Therefore, young women, in aiding a mother, do not attempt to wrest the keys from her keeping, but only employ them under her direction; for this be ever ready.

It is to me one of the most lovely scenes on earth to see a young woman risen up to be the companion and helper of her mother, placing herself by her side, and foregoing many an invitation and opportunity for personal enjoyment to relieve her solitude, to lighten her cares, or to minister to her comfort. Your object should be to share your mother's labors without superseding her authority, and to assist her in a way so tender and so delicate as shall neither awaken her suspicion that you wish to supplant her, nor make her feel that she is incapable of doing without you. To these duties all should be attentive, but especially those daughters who make a profession of religion.

Many who will read this work are happily in this state, and to them would I most earnestly and affectionately say, "Let your light shine" at home so that its inmates, "seeing your good works, may glorify God your Heavenly Father." Let it be most impressively and constantly felt by you, and let it be seen by others, that you feel that religion is no abstract matter of times, places, and occasions, but an element of the general character which is to enter into all relations, all duties, and all engagements. It must improve you in everything, spreading like a gilded surface over your whole selves and all your conduct, and shining like a beautiful polish on every other excellence. It must make you a better daughter in every respect, more respectful, more kind, more devoted to your parents, and compelling them to say, "Happy was the day when she became a Christian, for from that hour she became a lovelier and more loving child."

It may be that the parents of some of you are not truly converted to God. This places you in a difficult and delicate situation, and will require the utmost solicitude, care, and prayer, that you may be prevented from doing or being anything that would prejudice them against religion, and that you may be enabled on the contrary so to conduct yourself as to predispose them in its favor. You must affect no superiority, nor ever seem to say, "Stand by, I am holier than you." This is improper towards anyone, much more towards a parent. You can pray for them, and you can exhibit to them by your example, invested with all the beauties of holiness, what religion is; but direct efforts to bring them under its influence, though they should not be altogether withheld, should be conducted with the greatest tenderness, humility, modesty and delicacy. There must be no lecturing, much less any reproach or accusation. A deep, tender, loving solicitude for their spiritual welfare must be seen—veiled with modesty, but still seen—penetrating the transparent and graceful covering; a solicitude which only now and then presumes to speak, but, when it does, always speaks in love. Such a line of conduct may accomplish its purpose, and produce results like the following.

A female, who had been some years known and respected for her quiet, consistent, unobtrusive, Christian deportment, called on her minister to introduce her aged mother, who leaned on her arm and seemed to repose on her that tender dependence which is so soothing and delightful to an aged parent, and so heart-thrilling to a dutiful and grateful child. Both were overcome by their feelings, and it was some moments before either could speak. The minister desired them to be seated, and cheerfully said, "Well Hannah, I suppose this is your good mother. I am very happy to see her." "Yes," replied the mother in broken accents, "her mother and her daughter too. Twenty-five years ago I bore her in infancy; and now, through her instrumentality, I trust I am born to God."

Mr. [William] Jay relates a similar anecdote: "Well," said a mother one day, weeping (her daughter being proposed as a candidate for Christian communion), "I will resist no longer. How can I bear to see my dear child love and read the Scriptures, while I never look into the Bible; to see her retire and seek God, while I never pray; to see her going to the Lord's table, while His death is nothing to me? Ah," said she to the minister who called to inform her of her daughter's desire, wiping her eyes, "Yes, sir, I know she is right and I am wrong. I have seen her firm under reproach, and patient under provocation, and cheerful in all her sufferings. When, in her late illness, she was in danger of perishing, heaven stood in her face. Oh, that I was as fit to die! I ought to have taught her, but I am sure she has taught me. How can I bear to see her joining the church of God, and leaving me behind, perhaps forever?" From that hour she prayed in earnest that the God of her child would be her God, and was soon seen walking with her in the way everlasting.

But there are, in most cases, other members of the household besides parents, brothers and sisters, who also require attention and right conduct from a young woman at home. A loving, united, harmonious family, I repeat again, where the children all promote the comfort of their parents and of one another—where each is studious to please and to perform all kind offices for the rest, and all seek the happiness of each—is one of the loveliest scenes to be found in our divided and discordant world. Much, very much, depends upon the daughters for this domestic harmony. They can exert, if prudent, good-tempered, and obliging, a softening influence over the minds and manners of their brothers. Sisterly affection, judiciously displayed, is one of the sweetest and most powerful ingredients in the cup of domestic enjoyment. True it is that it will require occasionally some little self-denial, and sacrifice of personal gratification, predilection, and feeling, to conciliate the affection and secure the good will of brothers, who are apt to begin too soon to feel that they are the lords of the creation; but this is necessary to keep the peace of the family. And a girl of good sense and affectionate disposition will do a great deal towards it. Woman is made to yield, though not to be trampled upon. Her gentle nature is formed for submission, rather than for resistance. A good and wise sister will feel this, and her affection will, in most cases, be her protection. Let her put forth the thousand little ingenious arts of which she is or may be mistress, and throw the silken cords of love over her brother's hearts, and she may do much to attach, and in some cases even to subject, them to her, and make them fond of home. A husband is but too apt to run away from the home which is tenanted by an ill-natured wife; and brothers have been often driven away to company by cross, sullen, unaccommodating sisters. I am aware that it is but too frequently the case that young men are polite and attentive to every female but those they meet every day at home, and that scarcely anyone has to complain of a want of civility and complaisance but their sisters. At the same time it must be confessed that some young women have themselves to blame for this, for it requires more virtue than is ordinarily found to be much attached and very attentive to such an impersonation of peevishness, ill humor, and vanity as some silly girls present at home. How many parents' comfort is disturbed, and their hearts half-broken, by the jealousy, envy, and contention of their children!

To the elder daughter, especially if she is older than her brothers also, a larger share of responsibility attaches than to any other of the children, because her influence is greater. She does almost as much to form the character of the younger branches as the mother, and, when the latter is feeble or inefficient, perhaps more. It is a lovely sight to behold an intelligent and affectionate girl, exerting a plastic yet not authoritative or dictatorial power over her younger brothers or sisters, setting them a beautiful example of filial piety, and devoting all her efforts to uphold parental authority over them, conciliating their confidence by her judgment and their affection by her kindness. This throws a softening and gentle influence over their ruder and harsher natures, and compels the parents to say, "She is a second mother to the family."

The servants must not be left out of consideration. They add much, very much, to the comfort or disquiet of families; and they are considerably influenced not only by the conduct of the parents, but by that of the children. Were I addressing young men, I should remind them of the distance without pride, the kindness without familiarity, the purity in thought, word, and deed, which is necessary to be observed in their conduct towards female servants. But I am addressing young women, and therefore remind them that the three things to be practiced are kindness, considerateness, and confidence; and the three to be avoided are haughtiness, oppression, and familiarity.

A young woman displays considerable littleness of mind, as well as forgetfulness of the laws of God, when she treats a servant with scorn and contempt, as a being of an inferior nature. That servant may have not only a finer form and a stronger mind, but a holier heart and a diviner taste, and may be her superior in every respect, except in rank. Nor is this the only kind

of ill treatment that servants are sometimes doomed to bear
from their young mistresses, and, alas, sometimes under the
cognizance of their old mistress. Woman of high rank are
brought up with the notion, and the practice also, that they are
to do nothing for themselves, and they are usually provided
with a waiting-maid to do everything for them, whose place
would be a sinecure, if her young mistress did anything for
herself. But for others in the middle of life to be brought up in
helplessness is a discredit to the mother, and injury to the
daughter, and generally a cruelty to those who are called to
wait on them. Such a system of aping the manners of the
nobility, with scarcely means to command the service necessary
for a tradesman's household, is indeed contemptible.

Mothers, I speak to you. Train your daughters, not to be
fine and helpless ladies, but to be useful wives, mothers, and
mistresses. Be yourselves patterns in these things, and secure
the imitation of your daughters. See to it that they learn to
help themselves in all proper matters, and do not allow them to
press too hard upon the energies of your servants. Much will
depend upon you in this matter. And you, my young female
friends, enter warmly and wisely into this subject yourselves.
Do not play the role of the fine lady, or wish to be only a kind
of dressed dolls, to be carried about and played with by others. I
do not ask you to do anything to degrade yourself below your
rank and station, or anything that would lower you in the eyes
of the servants themselves; but still be ambitious to grow up in
a state of independence, and in preparedness to make your way
through life, even against difficulties and privations, should you
be called to meet with them. Your own happiness, as well as
the comfort of the servants, demands that you should be as
considerate and give as little trouble as possible. It was certainly
a happy invention for mistresses when bell-hanging was in-
vented, but a great misery for some servants, in whose ears the

jingle of the parlor or bedroom bell is ever sounding.

Many a thoughtless young woman will say, "What were servants made for but to wait upon us?" And what were young limbs given you for but to wait upon yourselves? It would do some young persons good if, for one year at least, they were without a servant at all, and had to do everything for themselves.

I now suggest some other matters, partially implied in what I have already advanced, but of sufficient importance to be brought out in full view. Among these must be mentioned amiability; in other words, that sweetness of temper which is ever seeking to please, and to avoid whatever would offend. There is a saying that "Temper is everything." This is going too far, since it is not to be doubted that good temper is sometimes associated with bad principle, while, on the other hand, there are many high-principled and noble-minded individuals who are troubled, equally to their own annoyance and that of their friends, with infirmities of temper. Still, though not everything, good temper is a great thing. Very much depends in this matter upon our physical organization, for we see the same difference in the brute creation that we observe in the human species. But this, though an explanation, is not an apology, because reason and religion may do much, and in myriads of instances have done much, to correct and improve a disposition naturally bad. Begin life, young woman, with a deep impression of the value of good temper, both to your own happiness and to that of the persons with whom you have to do, especially your family circle. Study well your own temper. Know well what it is that you have to contend with in your own case, and set yourself most diligently to subdue it. Be mistress of yourself! Bad temper is a generic phrase; there are several species of the thing, as, for instance, there is a peevishness or petulance about some persons which makes them susceptible of offense, not of either a very deep or passionate kind, but an irritability which disposes them to be hurt at little things, and to complain of the conduct of others rather than to have their resentment excited. Then there is the violent temper, which is excited by some supposed or real offense to sudden outbursts of wrath, sometimes even to a storm, or what we call "being in a passion." There is also the sullen disposition, which, on being contradicted, opposed, or reproved, sinks into a silent, moody, and inwardly resentful state of mind. Persons of this turn will sulk for hours, if not days; retiring into themselves, they will brood over the matter which has occasioned their unhappy state, till they have actually made themselves ill by their bad temper; and yet, if expostulated with, they will assert that they are not ill-tempered, but only "hurt." This is the disposition which, more than anything else, is an interruption of domestic peace. I am no apologist for stormy passions, or for those who indulge them, but those who are soon in a blaze and then as soon are cooled down and the fire extinguished are not so inimical to the peace of a family as those in whose heart the embers of ill will are kept long smoldering under the ashes and not suffered to go out.

Next there is the selfish disposition, which leads its possessor ever to be seeking to concentrate the attentions of the family upon herself, especially if subject to indisposition. All must bend to her, and every hand must be employed by her. Her will must be consulted in everything, and her comfort must be the study of all. She must engross the affection of her parents, the regard of her brothers and sisters, and the time and labor of the servants. This is sometimes fostered by injudicious parents who excite the envy and jealousy of the other branches of the family by this exaction from all for the sake of the one. True, where there is much indisposition, the sufferer should be, and usually is, the center of sympathetic attention; but where the ailments are slight, and especially where the patient is apt to exaggerate them, she should not be petted into an engrossing and exacting selfishness, but should be gently taught to have a little regard to the comfort of others.

In addition to these, there is the jealous and envious disposition, which contends not only for preeminence, but for monopoly and which accounts as a rival everyone who receives the least special notice, and dislikes them on that account. What petty passions of this kind often creep into families and poison all the springs of domestic happiness! Consider how much the tempers of its members have to do with the peace of a household, and how much sunshine one sweet and lovely disposition, constantly in exercise, may throw over a household. On the other hand, consider how much gloom and storm one passionate, sullen, selfish, or envious temper may bring over the little community at home.

Let all, then, begin life with a deep conviction (and it cannot be too deep) of the importance of this subject. A bad temper will torment you through life. With this you will carry your own curse with you everywhere. It will multiply your enemies and alienate your friends; it will cloud your reason and numb your religion; it will embitter your comforts and envenom your trials; it will make you unhappy at home and secure your distress when away from home; it will give you wretchedness at the time, and conscious guilt and painful reflections afterwards; it will deprive your days of peace and your nights of sleep. In short, a bad temper will be to the soul what a chronic and painful disease is to the body, a constant source of uneasiness and distress, with this difference: whereas the former is a visitation from God, the latter is our own doing, and while one brings its own consolation with it to the Christian, the other brings nothing but punishment and shame.

To make home happy you must, of course, conform to its

general rules. This, perhaps, it is less necessary to insist upon in reference to you than it is to your brothers, because you are less in danger than they are of infringing domestic order. Every well-regulated family has its laws and customs, its times and seasons, its government and authority, which must be observed if the little community is to be kept in order and good condition.

I will suppose it is a pious family where God is worshipped, and the morning and evening sacrifice are duly offered upon the domestic altar. At the appointed hour all ought to be present. Nothing can be more unseemly than to see one member after another come dropping in while the Scriptures are being read, as if the Bible were only the prayer bell to call the family together for worship. I have often witnessed this, and heard the remonstrances of the father with his dilatory children whose want of punctuality had been occasioned only by a wretched habit of lying late in bed. It has really, in some cases, given rise to domestic quarrels. Much the same remark will apply to other matters. The father of a family may see reason to object to the late hours of the present day, and may request that all his household shall be home by a certain hour of the evening. It may be thought by his children that he is too precise, too antiquated in his notions, too inconsiderate of their gratification, but still it is his law; he is master of his house, and they are subjects who are to obey him. It is unseemly for the children to be ever maintaining a struggle against paternal rule and maternal counsel. On the contrary, it is the glory and the praise of a good and dutiful child to find what sacrifices of feeling and gratification she can submit to, rather than commit herself to a struggle with parental authority and domestic government. On the other hand, parents should be very careful not to make their yoke oppressive and their burden heavy. The laws of the family should not be too stringent, nor the author-

ity of the father tyrannical, capricious, and unnecessarily precise. But they must be obeyed as long as they last, and the elder
branches of the family, where there are younger ones, should
excel in leading them both by example and precept to habitual
conformity to household law.

If you would make home happy, you must, of course, be
happy at home. No one can diffuse joy who is not joyful. The
passions are infectious, because the heart is sympathetic.
Cheerful persons make others like themselves, and so do
gloomy persons, just as the sun irradiates by its beams, or the
clouds darken by their shadow, the whole landscape. A young
person whose heart finds his or her resting place in the domestic circle; whose sympathies are with household scenes; whose
chosen companions are her parents, and her brothers and sisters; whose pleasures are the sweet interchanges of domestic
offices and affections; whose loved employment it is to make
her daily contribution to the comfort of the little community
within doors; and whose good-humored disposition radiates
from smiling eyes and flows from gently curled lips—such an
inmate is a blessing to the house in which she dwells. The soft
music of her speech, aided by the genial influence of her accommodating and insinuating temper, sheds a benign influence on all the family.

But observe the opposite to all this: the girl who looks upon
her home as a prison rather than a paradise, thinks that to stay
at home is a penance rather than a pleasure; and accordingly is
anxious to escape from it, and is ever seeking opportunities to
effect her purpose. Her gloomy aspect, her sullen disposition,
her discontented air, her repulsive taciturnity, her peevish expressions when she breaks her silence, her unsympathizing
isolation—what a member of a family do they make her! She
has at home no associates, no objects of strong affection,
nothing to engage and interest her heart, but is ever seeking

occasions to slip away, upon any pretense, or for any engagement. She is ever on the watch for opportunities or excuses for absence; ready for any errand; eager for every business that opens the door for her egress. She is not happy but in a continual round of parties, visits, or out-of-door novelties, of which this fertile age is so prolific. Any society rather than that of the family, and any scenes rather than those of home, suit her taste.

Can such a young person make home happy? Yes, if a specter can do it, for such, or little better, is she. Young people, I repeat, be happy at home. Parents, put forth all your ingenuity to make them so, by investing home with its proper attractions. Mothers, this devolves much on you. Be "keepers at home," for a gossiping mother is sure to make gossiping daughters. Let it be seen that you are happy at home in the midst of your families. Put on a cheerful countenance so that your children may love to bask in the sunshine of your smiles. Be the center of attraction to your families, and let the household delight to revolve in sweetest harmony around your maternal chair.

Industrious habits will contribute greatly to the happiness of home, especially on the part of a young female. Slothfulness is a wretched thing, as it regards the subject of it, and as it affects others. A lazy person cannot be a happy one. Indolence is a constant opposition to the law of our being, which is made for activity. That there is a species of indulgence connected with it is true; but it is a very mixed kind of gratification, for as it is against nature, there is sometimes a consciousness of this which awakens the conscience and inflicts remorse. To the remonstrances of conscience are added the reproaches of others. And as it cannot always be indulged, there are to be overcome the repugnance, lassitude, and inertia which make the least exertion more wearisome to the indolent than far greater efforts are to the active.

Slothfulness is a miserable object; the very sight of it inflicts pain upon an industrious person. What a vexation it is to an industrious mother to see the dull, heavy, immovable habits of a daughter whom neither entreaties, persuasions, nor rebukes can quicken into activity nor excite to industry; who, if moved at all, must be moved mainly by force, and needs every minute the same effort to keep it going; a poor, lumpish creature who is enough to wear out the patience of the most forbearing and affectionate mother on earth. Such habits in a daughter must be destructive of domestic happiness. The misery they create may not, like the profligacy of a prodigal son, come upon the family with the noise and destructive force and fury of a hurricane, but it settles down upon its comfort like the silent power of blight or mildew. It is a constant vexation which eats into a mother's heart, when she finds that a daughter who has grown to an age when she ought to be a relief to maternal labor and solicitude is a heavy increase in both. This wretched habit may be overcome, and it must be, or you will be a poor, helpless, useless, and unhappy creature through life. If indolent in your parent's house, what are you likely to be in your own? An idle daughter is likely to make an idle mother; and from my soul I pity the man who is tied for life to a lazy, indolent woman. No personal charms, no mental acquisitions, no brilliance of conversation can make up for the want of domestic industry; and indeed these things are rarely found in the absence of industry, for indolence is usually too lazy to acquire knowledge, the habits of soul and body being in sympathy with each other.

It is essential to your making home happy that there should be much self-denial, a spirit of forbearance, and an occasional surrender, for the sake of peace, of supposed "rights"—a willingness to forego what you could rightfully claim as your own. I am aware that there are limits to this, especially in cases where concession pampers tyranny and encourages oppression. There may be brothers, and even sisters, whose disposition is so encroaching that it should be resisted with parental authority for the protection of the weaker and more yielding members of the household. It is, however, far better in some cases to concede rights, when the sacrifice is not too costly and does not involve a violation of principle, than to contend for them. The contest, even where it is successful, often costs more than it is worth; the victory does not pay for the battle. Be, therefore, content sometimes to lose a little for the sake of retaining more. I cannot give you a piece of advice more conducive to your peace at home, or to your comfort through life, than to be ever ready gracefully and quietly to bear with the infirmities of disposition of those around you, and to yield little things which you deem belong to you, rather than disturb the peace of the family by contending for them.

Never seek an undue share of parental affection. Let there be no ambition to be a favorite, nor any scheming to obtain this distinction. Some young people have made home miserable in this way, being base and guilty enough to attempt to rise in the esteem and affection of their parents, by little arts of detraction in reference to their brothers and sisters, and by their parents being weak enough to encourage the attempt. Partiality was then not only cherished, but manifested. Envy and jealousy ensued, and the peace of the family was destroyed. Abhor this conduct, and be content to share with other branches of the family your parents' justly apportioned regard.

Remember that your power to contribute to the happiness of home does not depend on the performance of great services, opportunities for which occur but seldom, but on attention to little matters which are ever taking place. Our existence, as to time, is made up not only of years, but of moments; our body not only of limbs, but of particles; our history not only of great events, but of little occurrences; and our obligations not only of splendid acts of duty, but of seemingly insignificant ones. Set out in life with a deep sense of the importance of little things, or rather with a conviction that where character, duty, and the happiness not only of ourselves but of others are involved, nothing is little. This applies especially to your conduct in the family.

In that little world, then, keep up a constant attention to what will constitute the felicity of the passing hour. True politeness has been defined to consist in "benevolence in trifles." This is a beautiful definition, and worthy of being remembered by all who would fill the family circle with bliss. By "politeness" here I do not mean the heartless and unmeaning ceremony taught in Lord Chesterfield's pages, nor even the graceful polish of manners which characterizes the intercourse of well-bred people, but a gentle, obliging demeanor and delicacy of behavior towards all around, or that mode of conducting ourselves towards others which is opposed to what is coarse, vulgar, rude, or offensively familiar. The politeness that I mean is not affection's root, but it is its flower, beauty, and fragrance; or, if not the plant itself, it is like the hedge around it which preserves it from being trampled underfoot.

In the family circle, all the little acts that can give pleasure or pain, all words, tones, and looks, should ever be considered and weighed. Woman has perhaps more tact and discernment in reference to the minor affairs of life than men. Her mental eye is more discerning, her touch more delicate, and her taste more refined on all the matters of behavior. Let her therefore keep this up in reference to her conduct at home. Mrs. Copley, in dwelling upon this in her book *Female Excellence*, has the following reference to her own history:

Might I be permitted to say that after the lapse of
twenty-six years, a sensation of pleasure thrills through
my fingers when I recollect the daily task of tying on
my father's neckcloth, and combing back my mother's
silvery locks. . . . But we return to the more ordinary
circumstance of young females, resident under the
parental roof, after having finished the term of their
education, and observe that their conduct should be
marked by a soothing forbearance and tenderness towards the infirmities of their parents. Deafness, lame-
ness, dimsightedness, and other infirmities of age cir-
cumscribe their pleasures, and perhaps a degree of fret-
fulness is sometimes observed. But a dutiful child will
be fertile in expedients to extend their pleasures, to alleviate their privations, and to bear with and soothe
their infirmities. The prompt eye will discern their
needs and anticipate their wishes. The needle will be
threaded before the eye aches with endeavoring, and
before the sigh is excited by inability, to accomplish it;
or, by gentle and playful persuasion, the needle-work
will be exchanged for knitting or netting. The legrest
or the footstool will be presented or exchanged before
complaint of uneasiness is uttered. The large-print
Bible and the spectacles will be placed at hand; the dim
columns of the newspaper will be read aloud; the inquiring eye will be answered by a repetition of the conversation, or of the sacred address, which, uttered by a
stranger's voice, had passed over the dull ear; and in the
most exalted sense, the benevolent pleasure will be enjoyed of being eyes to the blind, feet to the lame, ears to
the deaf, and causing the trembling heart to sing for
joy.

I now return to the idea with which I started, that the
right conduct of a daughter at home is to study to make home
happy. There is a fascination in the very expression, "a happy
home." And so far as what may be called the poetry of home
scenes is concerned, is there a lovelier flower to be found in

that garden of unearthly delights, that paradise of sweets, than a good daughter and affectionate sister, adorning her maiden charms with the virtues that become her sex, her age, and her relationships, and elevating and sanctifying all her other excellences by a saintly piety, which makes her lovely in the eyes of God by all the beauties of holiness? Her father's pride, her mother's comfort, and her brother's companion, she is the ministering angel of them all. How much bliss does this one dear object of their common affection throw over them all! Her absence is mourned as a common loss, and her return to the family circle is hailed as the restoration of a suspended enjoyment. When this lovely one is loved by another not belonging to the family, though about (through her) to be united with it, with what a treasure, at their expense, is he about to enrich his own home! Their hearts, at the thought of parting from her, bleed from wounds which nothing but the hope of her happiness could heal. Her removal leaves a blank, which, as they look upon her vacant seat, calls up recollections, and produces a sense of deprivation, which even the sight of her happiness can scarcely dispel.

But as woman's mission is to make happy her husband's home, suppose her gone forth to fulfill it. Well has she been trained, and well has she trained herself also, at her parental home; for this home of her own, and all the united excellences of the good daughter and the good sister, now develop and blend into the more mature and matronly virtues of the good wife, mother, and mistress. And she who, as the young woman at home, contributed so greatly to the felicity of one family circle has just prepared herself to contribute still more greatly to the felicity of another, and that other is her own. Behold, my young friends, your pattern. May the imitation of it be your study, your prayer, your bliss.

Chapter 7

Life Away from Home

"Behold, I am with thee, and will keep thee in all places whither thou goest." Genesis 28:15

"In all thy ways acknowledge Him, and He shall direct thy paths." Proverbs 3:6

"Thou shalt guide me with Thy counsel, and afterwards receive me to glory." Psalm 73:24

The hour of separation from parental society, home enjoyments, and the scenes of early history is in most cases, and ought to be in all, a season of pensive grief. No affectionate daughter can leave the house of her father, and go from beneath the covering wing of maternal love, without passing over "the bridge of sighs." Even the joys of the bridal morning, when she quits the arms of her hitherto nearest relations for those of one now still nearer, do not prevent her from looking around with something of instinctive regret on the scenes she is leaving, now no longer hers; and amidst the smiles of the happy bride are seen falling the tears of the loving child, like dew-drops sparkling in sunbeams. It would augur ill for the husband if his wife could part from her parents, even for him, without a momentary pang. It is one of nature's loveliest sights to see in that scene and season of delight filial piety blending its luster with conjugal affection, and investing even nuptial charms with new and captivating beauty.

But I now speak of a different kind and purpose of separation from home. I contemplate the young woman not led out by that right hand, the "cunning" of which is to be employed for her support; nor going away, leaning upon that arm which is to be continually stretched over her for protection; but departing solitarily and mournfully on the journey of life, to meet alone its dangers, cares, and toils. It is sad enough to see a young man quitting his father's house, and leaving home to earn his daily bread by the sweat of his brow; how much more to see a young female thus going forth to seek her own support. What is she but a lamb venturing out into the wilderness where wolves abound, or a young dove quitting its nest to fly abroad amidst eagles and vultures? How many in the progress of life, and amidst its changes, some of which are so melancholy, look back to the hour of separation and exclaim, "O my mother, how sad and certain presages of what awaited me were those bitter tears I shed on that morning when I tore myself from your embrace! My heart then sank, and the sun of my life then set never to rise. Every step since then of my dark journey has been one of sorrow, and every change only of one calamity for another."

In some cases separation from home is rendered necessary by a change in domestic circumstances, and she who was brought up tenderly amidst the luxuries, and with the prospects, of opulence is now compelled to quit scenes where she was a stranger to toil and care, to earn her own support. It is a sight to be looked upon with admiration to behold a young woman in such circumstances, instead of hanging upon parents no longer able to support her without additional privations for themselves, nobly resolving to relieve them of the burden, and, instead of sitting down in despairing grief and helpless sorrow, bracing her mind to meet the privations of her altered condition, descending gracefully to a lower level, and going forth with true magnanimity, inspired by religion, to tread life's stormy way alone. No morbid sense of degradation, no feeling of false shame arising from altered circumstances, no haughty sense of humiliation connected with a situation of subordination and dependence benumbs her faculties, paralyzes her energies, or renders the duties of her new situation irksome and oppressive; but, remembering it is the will of Providence, and thankful for her health, her abilities, and her opportunities to take care of herself, she goes to her new sphere without dread, despondency, or reluctance.

Others meet with no such reverse, but are brought up amidst circumstances which have always kept before them the probability that they must go out into the world to support themselves. In these cases, the change does not come upon them by surprise, and, if they are wise, they will endeavor to prepare their hearts and qualify their minds for it. A judicious mother's energies and vigilance will ever be employed not only in helping her daughters, but in teaching them to help themselves. Wherever there is a probability of their leaving home, and even when there is not, her anxiety, considering the vicissitudes of human life, should be directed to the point of qualifying them to become self-supporting. It should be a point of ambition with every young woman whose parents support with difficulty their family not to be a burden to them, but to provide for herself in some honorable and useful occupation. It is a very beautiful scene to witness a young female not only supporting herself, but endeavoring by the produce of her diligence and the savings of her frugality to minister to the comfort of her aged, infirm, or impoverished parents. Many a heroine has left home and endured privations, neither few nor small, for this purpose. All her discomfort and labor were endured with patience, under the idea that by this means she was rendering the home of her beloved parents more happy.

Here, however, a caution is necessary against too great an eagerness to get away from home. A large family, where there is a limited income, brings many cares and some privations not only upon the mother, but upon the elder daughters. In such a case, for a young woman who can be of essential service to her mother, and whom her mother wishes to retain, to determine or even wish to go out into the world, and leave her mother to struggle and almost faint under the load, is a deplorable want of filial piety. It is delightful to hear a daughter say, "Anywhere, or in any circumstances, abroad or at home, in single or in wedded life, my beloved and honored parents, I am ready and eager to serve you."

There is another melancholy occasion which not infrequently causes a young woman to leave home, and that is when home itself is broken up by the death of both parents. How frequently does this happen! Ah, how often are families invaded by the last enemy, and scattered hither and thither by his desolating ravages! The grave covers both father and mother. The dear domestic hearth is forsaken. The family gatherings at prayer, at meals, and at festive seasons are over, and the house of your childhood and youth is deserted. Poor orphans, I pity you; especially, you orphan girls, my heart bleeds for you. Your brothers can provide for themselves better than you can. But even you have no need to despond. Painful I know it is to have no parents, no home, no settled place of abode. Often in your forlorn situation you must and do say, "Alas for me! I am alone in the world. David's expression suits my case. I am like a pelican in the wilderness, or like a sparrow alone upon the housetop. Other young people, though away from home, have a home to think and talk about, and parents to write to, and occasionally to visit. I have none. I have not a house to dwell in except that which I may soon be required to leave; nor have I any friends, except those whom my own good conduct may secure. My heart is often more desolate than my condition; and though I am in the midst of society I feel as if I were alone in this great and busy world."

But I remind you that the orphan's unfailing friend is still left. God lives, and He is the Father of the fatherless. May you say, "When my father and my mother forsake me, the Lord will take me up." Should you be so wise and happy as to become truly pious, you will never be without a Friend, and in the absence of an earthly father, will have an omnipotent one in heaven. You may then set out in life, and go through it, adopting as your motto the reply of Abraham to Isaac, who, when the latter said, "Behold the fire and the wood, but where is the lamb for a burnt offering?" replied, "God will provide." Be that your motto, "God will provide." Fear God, and you may without scruple and with confidence adopt this assurance.

Permit me now to suggest some topics which apply alike to all these different cases, and which it is important that you should dwell upon, either in prospect of leaving home or when you have left it.

Consider that it is in the order of Providence that you should be thus situated. Your lot is fixed in heaven. It is God's will, and not chance. Is there nothing consolatory in this? Consider His wisdom, power, and goodness. He does all things well. He knows what is best for you. He may, in ways which you cannot imagine, be consulting your future and permanent good. You see not the end. When this is revealed, you may be compelled to exclaim, "He leadeth the blind by a way that they know not, and leadeth them in paths that they have not known. He maketh darkness light before them, and crooked things straight." Submit, therefore, without envying others and without murmuring. Would you contravene His purpose? Say, "It is the Lord; let Him do what seemeth good in His sight. I am where He would have me be."

But remember, there are not only privations to be endured away from home, but moral dangers also to be encountered. If these are not so pressing in your case as in that of your brothers, there are some perils even in yours. Happily for you, the guards of female decorum, propriety, and reputation are stronger and stricter than those of the other sex. But they have proven too weak for absolute security in thousands of instances. Multitudes who have stood well at home have unhappily fallen when removed from it. Eve was tempted when alone and away from the protection of her husband. Alas, how many have gone away to sin, and have returned to hide their shame. A mother's watchful eye is no longer upon you; a father's arm is no longer stretched over you; and the shelter of home no longer protects you. Others know this as well as you, and may take advantage of it. And even if there were no danger of vice, is there none of imprudence, folly, or levity? None of bad connections, improper acquaintance, or ill-contracted marriages? None of Sabbath-breaking, of undue love of pleasure, of vanity? Are not the prevailing faults and defects of some women to be found in vanity, love of dress, disposition to court attention and admiration, fickleness, inconsiderateness, love of novelty, want of judgment, and curiosity? And are not all these likely to increase rather than diminish when they are away from the checks which home supplies? Are not these weeds likely to grow faster, and to attain greater strength, when there is no mother's eye to see them, no mother's hand to pluck them up? All this danger is greatly heightened in the case of those who have personal or mental accomplishments. A beautiful young woman, withdrawn from the fostering care and ceaseless vigilance of a judicious mother, and exposed abroad to the rude and licentious gaze of the world, is ever an object of alarm to her friends, and it would be well if she were so to herself. It is perhaps a rare case for such a female to be ig-

norant of her charms; it is rarer still for her to be more afraid
than vain of them, and to be more anxious that they should
not lead her into danger than that they should secure admiration for her. The great source of consolation and protection to a young
woman from home is true religion. It is very easy for anyone to
conceive of the privations and discomfort of many a young
person who leaves the comforts of a happy home to sustain the
character of a governess, a shopwoman, or a servant. The cold,
proud, and perhaps, in some cases, cruel treatment of employers, as contrasted with the affectionate conduct of parents; the
annoying and unfeeling peculiarities of companions in the
house, as contrasted with the sympathizing and loving behavior of their brothers and sisters; the disregard for their comfort,
in all that concerns their food, lodging, and general personal
convenience, as contrasted with all the accommodations and
enjoyments of their father's house; and the general inattention
and neglect of the strangers among whom they dwell, as contrasted with the recognition and kind notice of a wide circle of
friends in their own native place—this, all this, is bitter indeed.
Some hard and unfeeling natures, or gay and frivolous ones,
may be insensible to these things; but oh, that poor girl of
softer mold whose heart was made for home scenes, and whose
bliss was derived from home enjoyments—under all this, her
heart is sometimes ready to burst! What thoughts disturb her
peace, like visions of bliss lighting on her gloomy and sorrowful
path, and then instantly vanishing, only to leave the path still
more gloomy and the darkness still more oppressive! What letters, wet with her tears, she writes to her own sweet home and
to her sympathizing parents!

What is to comfort her? Only the balmy influence of religion, the consciousness that she is in the way of duty, and the
testimony of her conscience that she is discharging her obliga-

tions with scrupulous fidelity. This can and this will do it. She whose heart is renewed by divine grace, who has genuine faith in our Lord Jesus Christ, who walks with God as her divine, unchangeable, omnipotent Friend, and communes with Him as her heavenly Father; whose affections are set on things above, and who considers life as a probation for eternity—she will find, in such a state of mind, a source of consolation, a means of endurance, an element of happiness, which will counterbalance all discomfort, disquietude, and distress. With true dignity she will bow to the will of God, and consider her situation as His appointment. She will find satisfaction in submission. Her religion will impart much patience, and something of cheerfulness; it will control her temper, and throw an air of loveliness over her character, which will give her an interest in the heart of her employer. She will ever find companions in her Bible and other good books; in her closet of devotion and in communion with God, she will find a sweet retreat from the coldness and unkindness of her fellow creatures; and in meditation upon the everlasting rest above, she will find a blessed substitute for the comforts of the home she has left on earth. Faith in God, in Christ, in Providence, in heaven, can comfort, has comforted, and will comfort, in the dreariest situations of life and in the bitterest agonies of death.

I am anxious that all should set out in life with this lofty idea of true piety: that it can sweeten the bitterest cup of human woe, can soften the hardest lot, and can be a substitute for all other pleasures. It must be so, for it made Adam happy in Paradise, and makes saints and angels happy in heaven. It has lighted, as with a lamp kindled in heaven, the confessor's dungeon, has sustained the Christian fugitive in his exile, and has enabled the martyrs to endure even the agonies of the stake.

Adopt religion, then, young women, as your companion, for it will not only comfort you, but also protect you. Yes, it will be a shield for your defense as well as a cup of consolation amidst your sorrows. Expect temptations, for you will certainly have them in one way or another. You cannot imagine in what shape or from what quarter they will come. It may be in a form so fascinating, so plausible, so unsuspected, or so insidious as to contain all the "deceitfulness of unrighteousness." Do not imagine that Satan respects female virtue too much to assail it. Did he thus respect the holiness of Eve in the garden of Eden? Does he reverence any character or any virtue? Did he not tempt our Lord? The more spotless the character, and the more eminent the excellence, the more intense is his hatred, the more malignant his envy, and the more eager his desire to spoil it. Has he not tempted to their ruin multitudes as pure as you are? Against such a foe, whom all but infinite cunning makes skillful, and boundless success makes bold, consider yourself safe only under the protection of Omnipotence; and that protection can be obtained only by faith and prayer. Of these millions of instances of female frailty which the history of your sex has presented, not one would have occurred if they had trusted their virtue to the keeping of true godliness. It is religion that will repel the fiercest assault with the holy and indignant remonstrance: "How shall I do this great wickedness, and sin against God?"

It is not only, however, from such dangers as these, dangers affecting moral character in its most important features, that religion will protect you, but from the lesser ones also, which, if they do not lead to vice, are still injurious. Religion will moderate your love of pleasure by furnishing pleasures of its own. It will check your vanity and folly by producing a devout seriousness and sobriety of mind, without at all destroying your natural and innocent vivacity. It will remove your inconsiderateness and make you thoughtful and reflective, without stiffening you into formality or investing you with gloom. It will induce habits of forethought and frugality, and thus guard you from present imprudence and recklessness, and future improvidence and extravagance. Do not then venture out into the world unprotected by this spirit as your guardian angel.

There are one or two other cautions which it may be important that you should receive and remember. You should never allow yourselves for a moment to imagine that there is anything dishonorable or degrading in your being compelled to leave home and to support yourself, either as a governess, shopwoman, or servant. Those who have been in better circumstances are, of course, most apt to feel this. And no doubt it is a descent, a lower status, according to the conventions of human life; but it is no dishonor. It is from misconduct and not from misfortune, from loss of character and not from loss of rank, that disgrace arises. Nobility of soul is often associated with plebeian descent, while vulgarity of character is sometimes covered with the coronet or the crown. A virtuous, holy, and intelligent young female has, in the heraldry of heaven, a patent of nobility, and is one of God's peers in her own right. Industry is far more honorable than wealthy indolence; and she who willingly, honestly, and cheerfully earns her own support, when Providence has deprived her of her patrimony, is far more to be admired than she would have been had she throughout life rolled in her father's affluence, and been surrounded by every luxury.

Akin to this is another state of mind against which you should most sedulously guard, and that is a conviction that you must be miserable away from home. It is conceded that you cannot be as happy away from home as you would be at home. It is not right that you should be. There can be no perfect substitute for a united and happy family circle. But when called by Providence to surrender it, give it up with submission and fortitude, and yield to the privation with true magnanimity.

Let it be said of you on leaving, as is said by Milton of Eve on her departure from Paradise, "Some natural tears she dropped, but wiped them soon."

Weep you may, and you ought, at giving up the dear delights you have enjoyed from childhood in your father's house; and you cannot help but sometimes feel pensive at recollecting the friends from whom you have been separated. But to allow your love of home to make absence from it intolerable wretchedness; to render you moody and melancholy, discontented and ill-tempered; to make you unfit for business and unpleasant to your employer and companions—this exhibits a weak mind, a feeble heart, and a sickly character. Rise above this. If Providence calls you away from home, bear it with composure. Go out expecting to meet with privations, and make up your mind to endure them with fortitude. Make the best of your situation. Do not doom yourself to misery on this account. You may be happy anywhere with religion, good temper, submission to your lot, and usefulness. If you determine to find out such pleasures as your present situation affords, instead of always looking back upon that which you have left; if you resolve, by God's grace, to please and be pleased; if you give up your mind to piety, industry, and usefulness—you will find that felicity is a flower that blooms, and a fruit that grows away from home as well as at home. A cheerful spirit, like a lamp lighting any darkness into which it may be carried, lessens the discomfort of any situation, recommends you to your employer, and promotes your interest as well as your happiness.

Perhaps it may not be amiss to say a few things on the choice of a situation, and they appertain to your parents, where they are living, as well as to yourselves. Let the subject be made the matter of earnest and believing prayer to God. "In all thy ways acknowledge Him, and He will direct thy paths."

"Commit thy way to Him, and He shall bring it to pass." These are precious declarations, and they are sustained by promises no less precious. "The meek will He guide in judgment, and the meek will He teach His way." "I will instruct thee, and teach thee in the way which thou shalt go. I will guide thee with Mine eye." With such exhortations and assurances, what should be your resolution? "Thou shalt guide me with Thy counsel." There is Providence in everything. Even your mean affairs are under divine direction. Your times are in His hand. Do not doubt it. Hold fast the truth that God hears your prayer, casts your lot, and fixes the bounds of your habitation. Pray, pray earnestly, believingly, and expectingly. All situations and all hearts are at His disposal.

In selecting, accepting, and retaining a situation, consult its religious advantages. In these are included such means of pulpit religious instruction as are likely to build up a young disciple in her holy faith, and to quicken into activity the principles of godliness planted in her soul by the Spirit of God. It is not ordinarily desirable, where a selection can be made, to choose a situation where even the minor matters of the sacraments and church government differ from those to which you have been accustomed. This exposes you, if not to a change of sentiment, yet to antagonism and perplexity, which are unfavorable to the quiet enjoyment of your own personal religion, and may do you injury by producing a spirit of controversy. Where the differences of opinion are of a more serious kind, affecting even the fundamental doctrines of the gospel, no pious young person should expose herself to any hazard of this kind.

I will now address a few special counsels and cautions to two or three classes of those who are in the circumstances contemplated by this discourse.

Many are occupied in the very important and responsible duties of a resident governess. This is a situation of delicacy,

difficulty, and momentous consequence, and requires much
wisdom, prudence, and conscientiousness. There are many
parties concerned, all of whose interests and comfort should
and must be consulted. You who are in this situation owe
something to yourself. Those who have engaged you will be
most likely to pay you the respect due to you when they see you
respecting yourself. If they so far confide in you as to entrust
you with the education of their children, they ought to treat
you in such a manner as to teach them also to confide in you
and esteem you. But this will depend much upon your own
conduct and bearing. Let them be duly aware that you expect
all that is your due in the way of kind and respectful conduct,
but that you expect no more. Any apprehension on their part
that your demands in this respect are too high, or are presented
in an obtrusive and exacting spirit, will be sure to set them on
their guard against you as a person of encroaching disposition,
and will dispose them to yield you less than you are entitled to.
A kind, attentive, respectful, and dignified bearing towards
them, as far from servility on the one hand as it is from familiarity on the other, as well as a right behavior towards their
children, will in most cases accomplish all you wish.

If you have taken your present situation after coming down
in life, let there be no such sense of degradation and mortified
pride, no such hauteur or loftiness, as will make you gloomy,
dissatisfied, unhappy, and repulsive. Even should it appear that
you have exchanged places with your employers, and that they
once were in the situation of inferiority which you now occupy, give no evidence that you are aware of it, and take no
notice of little outbursts of vulgarity, or even purse-proud insolence, not uncommon to those who have risen in life. If
sometimes you cannot be insensible to this, and you feel your
spirit rising within you, and your cheek growing flushed and
warm, so that your mortification cannot be concealed, call in

religion to your aid; comfort yourself in God, and exemplify a Christian spirit of meek forbearance. In such circumstances, many a tearful look will be thrown back by memory of that home from which you have been driven by misfortune (or rather by Providence), and you will need to retire to calm your perturbation and repress your indignation. In such cases, go and by prayer invite the hand of your heavenly Father to wipe your weeping eyes, and compose your ruffled spirit and agitated heart.

Then there are the children entrusted to your care for their education. Enter upon your task with a deep and solemn sense of responsibility to them, to their parents, and to God. Abhor the meanness, injustice, and cruelty of being satisfied with any manner of discharging your duty just as long as you get your board and salary and respectful treatment. The future character and comfort, for both worlds, of those girls depend much upon you. They have been placed in your hands, and look up to you as their instructress and oracle. As you would desire to give your account at last to God with joy and not with grief, do your very uttermost; tax your energies to do them and their parents justice in instructing their minds, forming their characters, and fitting them for the station they are to occupy in life. Prepare yourself for your task by constant reading and study. Do not be satisfied with your present qualifications. The education of a rational and immortal creature, for this world and the next, is a great work. Improve your own mind so as to be better fitted to improve theirs. Win their confidence by your ability, their affection by your kindness, their reverence by your dignity, and their application by your own diligence. Let your aim be not only to communicate knowledge, but wisdom; not only to fill the memory, but to strengthen the judgment, to fortify the will, and to make the conscience tender; to teach them not only to think correctly, but to act with propriety, discretion, and promptness in any situation in which they may be placed.

As regards religion, that, of course, must depend much upon the views of the parents. If they are similar to your own, and you have unrestricted liberty on this point, labor to the uttermost to form the religious character of your youthful charge. Ever consider the education of an immortal being incomplete without instruction in that which alone can fit her for immortality. But never act the part of a covert zealot by inculcating principles opposed to those of the parents. I would encourage a religious young woman to go into no situation where you are not allowed to teach what you consider to be the truth as it is in Jesus. Do not conceal your sentiments, and then teach them secretly and stealthily. You would abhor such conduct in a Romanist; do not be guilty of it yourself. Of course you should not and cannot conscientiously teach what you believe to be error; therefore do not go where you would be required to do so.

Then come the parents to be considered by you. Of course you will do everything you can to uphold their authority, even as they ought to do their uttermost to uphold yours. You should also most assiduously labor to secure the affections of their children for them rather than for yourself. It would be treachery of the basest kind to steal away the hearts of their children. Your aim should be to secure the love of the children toward you for their parents' sake as well as your own, and then their love for their parents for your own sake as well as theirs.

There is another thing to be observed, and one which I shall touch upon with the delicacy it demands; that is the fact that a wife has sometimes been made uncomfortable by the presence of a governess. Jealousy, it is true, is sometimes suspicious without reason. But are there no cases in which such uneasiness is not entirely the result of an over-sensitive and morbid imagination? Respect your own character and dignity, the wife's peace, and the husband's honor too much ever to seek or accept attentions which, coming from him, even though playful and innocent, may excite uneasiness in that one bosom the tranquility of which is so easily disturbed by any act of his. Conduct yourself so as to be not only without blame, but without suspicion.

Apart from this, do nothing, by becoming the depository of secrets, hearing tales, or uttering insinuations, to loosen the bonds or violate the affection of the husband and wife, or to disturb the peace of the family. If, unhappily, a difference should exist, keep yourself as much as possible out of the way of witnessing it, or let your wisest and kindest offices be exerted to heal the breach. Win for yourselves the blessing which will come upon the peacemaker, and cause the family to bless the hour which made you a member of their household. Remember that you are bound in honor never to make the transactions or condition of the family a matter of conversation with others. Without being actually sworn or even pledged to secrecy, you are solemnly bound to observe it; you are a traitor to the family which has received you as an inmate if you make their affairs known to others. Keep to your own sphere, and diligently discharge your own duties. You will find sufficient scope there for all your time, your energies, and your anxiety.

To maintain a course of conduct, seek by prayer the grace and wisdom which come from on high, and under all the trials of your situation, whether the waywardness of the children or the ingratitude, pride, or petulance of the parents, seek the comfort which comes from the Father of mercies and the God of all consolation.

Governesses in a school are a class of young females who, though acting under the direction and supervision of another, and therefore with less responsibility than those who reside in a family, have to discharge very important duties, for which high qualifications, both intellectual and moral, are essential.

I next consider the case of those young persons who are employed in retail shops, and they form a very large class. Their situation is often one of far greater discomfort and moral danger than that of the class just mentioned. In addition to the oppressive and exhausting labor which modern competition imposes upon them, in common with all who are engaged in trade, they have to bear in some cases the unkindness of their employers, who are not infrequently deplorably wanting in regard to the comfort of those whom they have received into their service, as to their food, lodging, and general treatment. A surly master and his unfeeling wife, intent only upon what they can get out of the flesh, bone, and muscle of their servants, and caring little for their welfare; never satisfied with even the most exemplary diligence and competent ability, and therefore ever urging to greater labor, and ever uttering the language of complaint; always suspicious, even where there is no ground for it, of the honesty of their servants—such are the trials which some of these hapless young people have to bear. In such a case, you who have to endure it need comfort. The recollections of home, where all was kindness, happiness, and confidence, embitter, by the power of contrast, the ills you have to sustain. Bear all with as much patience as you can command. Seek consolation in true piety. Carry your sorrows to God by prayer. When the bitter contrast between your position at home and your present situation away from home forces itself upon your thoughts, and sends a tear to your eye and a pang to your heart, go to Him whose gracious presence is ever with you, and whose infinite love is ever ready for you.

But it is not thus with all shopkeepers. I am not describing the class, but only some of its members, the exceptions rather than the rule. I know heads of retail establishments, employing a large number of young people, who cherish for them something of the feelings of parents, and regard them almost as children; nor is it their temporal comfort exclusively, but also their spiritual welfare, which is the object of their solicitude. And this is obviously the incumbent duty of employers.

Whether your employers are generous and kind or neglectful and oppressive, do your duty, and seek to possess all the qualifications which will commend you to their esteem. Diligence is indispensable. It is the first excellence of one in your situation. Be anxious to please, and as earnest to serve your employer as if the business were your own. No one will or can employ an indolent servant. Be an early riser. Comply with all the rules of the shop. Aim at excellence. Seek to be clever. Cultivate an attractive, winning, and even polite address. Be in the best sense of the term a clever shopwoman. Especially let your honesty be above suspicion. Deem it no insult or reproach that I caution you on this subject; you are exposed to temptation. Money in small sums is continually passing through your hands; your salary is low, and through the deceitfulness of the heart you may dwell on the injustice of your small stipend until you imagine it lawful to pay yourself, and make up what you should in justice receive. Resist every temptation of this kind. Rather starve and die than appropriate to your own use an article of clothing or decoration, or a farthing of money, belonging to your employer. As a guard upon your integrity, and a check to temptation, avoid expense in dress and ornament. Vanity is insatiable, and has led more persons into dishonesty than any other passion. A taste for finery fostered and indulged, with a salary too small to yield the means of its gratification, has in innumerable instances led to acts of pilfering to supply the deficiency.

In some establishments, young persons of both sexes are employed. Where this is the case it brings new perils, and requires additional caution. Your honor, your respectability, and your safety require that you should be most anxiously upon your guard. How earnestly as well as sincerely should you present those beautiful petitions of our Lord's prayer, "Lead me not into temptation, but deliver me from evil." Avoid all undue familiarity, all flippant and trifling conduct, all jocularity, with the young men employed in the same establishment. Maintain a proper self-respect, a becoming reserve, and a dignified bearing; they will be a fence around your character, and prevent even the approach of anything that would insult your purity or offend the most fastidious modesty.

You have need to be upon your guard against the influence of companions even of your own sex. In large and even in moderate establishments, many young women are associated together without, in some cases, any matronly superintendent being placed over them, and with almost unrestricted opportunities for free conversation and general intercourse. It is no severe reflection on the sex to suppose that in such a number of young persons there may be some who have no personal religion, whose sense of female decorum and propriety is not the most delicate, and who, without being vicious, are still so given to levity, vanity, and romance as to exert an unfavorable influence over the rest. Be upon your guard against influence of this kind. Gain all the good you can from those who are your associates, but avoid all the evil. Be good-tempered, accommodating, amiable, and conciliatory; but set yourself against all that is improper. Be an example of all that is good, and then you may be a reprover of all that is evil. Let there be no affected superiority, nothing like "Stand back, I am holier than you," but all the consistency, gentleness and sweetness of unaffected goodness, of true piety and good conduct; then you may be a blessing to those around you. Be especially careful in the selection of a particular friend from the rest of your companions. Be not led away by specious appearances, nor induced to commit yourself by professions of friendship on the part of another, or by the first feelings of partiality on your own; but take time to ascertain the correctness of her principles, the consistency of her conduct, and the respectability of her family—otherwise you may be led into snares and dangers which you very little anticipate.

For your conduct towards your employers, if you have a master, I refer you to what I have said to the governess. Instances have occurred within my knowledge to prove that cautions on this heading are not altogether unnecessary. An evil eye has sometimes lighted on an unsuspecting female, and men bound by every tie of honor, and by their solemn vow to a wife, have been base enough to assail and, in some instances, to destroy the purity, the honor, and the peace of those whom they were bound in duty to protect. Spurn, then, with disdain and indignation any such attempts; receive no special attentions, and quit the service of the wretch whom you suspect of a design against that which ought to be dearer to you a thousand times over than even life itself.

I shall now conclude this chapter by some few general remarks, which will apply alike to all classes of those who are away from home.

Again and again, I say, commit yourselves by true faith in Christ into the hands of God for protection and consolation. How many beautiful passages and examples of holy Scripture, in addition to those already quoted, could be adduced which apply with peculiar force to your case. Look at poor Hagar, who was much to be pitied as well as much to be blamed, alone in the wilderness, "when the angel of the Lord found her by the fountain of water, and she called the name of the Lord that spoke unto her, 'Thou, God, seest me.' " If, when God found her there, notwithstanding some past misconduct and self-reproach, she comforted herself in that desolate place with the consideration that she was compassed about with the presence of the Lord, with how much greater confidence and peace may you cheer your heart with the thought of an ever-present God, you who have not been driven out as she was by misconduct from your home, but have been led out from it by Providence! Yes, God is in every place. He is with you. He compasses your path, knows your sitting down and rising up, and is acquainted with all your ways.

You have left your earthly father, but your heavenly one is with you. You are far from your earthly home, but, if you are a Christian, you are as near as ever to your heavenly one. The eyes that lately beamed affection upon you do not see you now, and you do not see not; but lifting your voice to God, you can say, "Thou, God, seest me." His eye is upon you. His heart yearns over you. His arms are underneath you. Then, what promises are on record for you! Do you fear the want of adequate provision? "Trust in the Lord, and do good; so shalt thou dwell in the land, and verily thou shalt be fed." Do you lack protection? "He that dwelleth in the secret place of the Most High shall abide under the shadow of the Almighty. He shall cover thee with His feathers, and under His wings shalt thou trust; His truth shall be thy shield and buckler." Do you need direction? "Thine ears shall hear a voice behind thee, saying, 'This is the way, walk ye in it.'" Do you dread the forlorn circumstances that await you away from home? "None that trust in Him shall be desolate." Are you trembling with apprehension at the absence of all who were dear to you, and the unknown difficulties of your new situation on earth? "Fear thou not, for I am with thee; be not dismayed, for I am thy God; I will strengthen thee; yea, I will help thee; yea, I will uphold thee with the right hand of My righteousness." "My presence shall go with you and give you rest." Do you ever dread the idea of being forgotten by the friends you are leaving? "Can a woman forget her sucking child, that she should not have compassion on the son of her womb? Yea, she may forget, yet will I not forget thee." "I will never leave thee, nor forsake thee."

Can anything be more consolatory than such assurances? Need you be afraid to leave home and go out into the world with such promises? What, when omnipotence, omnipresence, omniscience, all-sufficiency, and boundless love go with you? Why, with such assurances you may quit not only your father's home to dwell in any other part of this land of railways and easy and speedy methods of conveyance, but may embark on board an emigrant ship, quit your native country for the antipodes, and exultingly exclaim, "If I take the wings of the morning and dwell in the uttermost parts of the sea, even there shall Thy hand lead me, and Thy right hand shall hold me."

But then to apply the truth and feel the comfort of these precious assurances, you must have that genuine faith which alone gives you a title to them. Personal religion will, in all probability, procure you earthly friends wherever you go, for it is the soil in which all those virtues grow that conciliate affection, ensure respect, and invite confidence. God will go before you to prepare the way for you, for when a man's ways please the Lord, He "maketh even his enemies to be at peace with him." Remember how He gave Joseph favor in the eyes of the governor of the prison, and how He turned the heart of Esau, brooding over purposes of revenge, into brotherly endearment. The best way to get the friendship of man is first to secure the friendship of God.

Connected with this, acquire in an eminent degree the general good qualities which I have already alluded to. Add to piety amiability of disposition, kindliness of temper, and gentle, artless, and attractive manners. Let there be a substratum of the solid gold of excellence, bearing at the same time the polish of the amenities of life. Those who have to make their way in the world must be attentive to external and to what some may call "little things." It is not enough to be holy and virtuous, or even to be conscious that you are such; you must also be attractive. You must aim to please. Real excellence may sometimes be repulsive on account of eccentricities, acerbities, and blunt coarseness with which it is associated. It is like grapes amidst nettles or thorns, which few will attempt to gather for fear of the sting or the prickle.

There is a word of very difficult definition, but which, without being defined, is perfectly understood and very impressive: "She is an *interesting* young woman." This is a very common expression. Perhaps the best explanation of it is the power of giving pleasure and engaging affection. This includes, I am aware, more of nature than of art, and something of personal attraction. A manifest intention to secure the favor of an individual is almost sure to defeat its own end and to inspire disgust. But the general good opinion of those among whom we live can, in most cases, be secured by attention to their wishes and consideration for their feelings. And surely it cannot be improper to ask, "How can I interest others in my behalf?" And those who depend upon the interest they create for themselves in the hearts of others should study how to ensure it.

Combine a due and tender recollection of home with a noble fortitude in surrendering its comforts. You are not required to forget your father's house and your mother's endearing society. You would be unnatural if you could. Indeed, you are in little danger of this. "Forget you, my honored father? Forget you, my much loved mother? Forget you, my brothers and sisters? Forget you, sweet home of my childhood? Oh, no! Memory must perish before I can be guilty of such oblivion. I muse on you all in my solitary walks. I give up many an hour's sleep to think of home. I wet my pillow with my tears as I think of the years and joys that are gone, never to return. I dream often that I am in the midst of you all, and wake to the sad reality that I am away from home." But these are not the only thoughts you are to cherish as to your home. Nor is the frequent and affectionate letter, so welcome and so precious to those who love and think of you, the only way to send comfort to your parents. Let there be the never-varying excellence of character and conduct, the uniform good behavior, the growing usefulness, which when they know of it shall comfort their hearts. Avoid that fickleness which would make you soon tired of a situation; let no unsuitable connection of a tender nature, which they would not approve, be formed; let no conduct which, if they knew it, would distress them be carried on by you. They have lost the comfort of your society; add not to the affliction by causing them to lose the comfort of your character.

Let your situation in a social point of view remind you of your circumstances in a religious one. If you are a true Christian, what are you here upon earth but a child away from home? Yes, heaven, and not earth, is the home of the believer. How simply and sublimely beautiful is the language of our Lord: "In My Father's house are many mansions; if it were not so, I would have told you. I go to prepare a place for you. And if I go and prepare a place for you, I will come again, and receive you unto Myself, that where I am, there ye may be also." Delightful idea! Heaven is the home of the Christian, which the Savior has fitted up and made ready for him. There is God the Judge of all, the Father of whom the whole family is named. There is Jesus the Mediator of the new covenant, who calls Himself "the Firstborn, the Elder Brother." There are the spirits of the just made perfect, the brothers and sisters. There is the innumerable company of the angels, the ministering spirits now sent forth to minister unto the heirs of salvation. What a glorious household assembled in the third heaven, the eternal home of the redeeming God, the great Redeemer, and the redeemed family! There you are going, if you are a true believer. All the dispensations of Providence and all the means of grace are preparing you for that state. All things, and among them your present situation, with all its disquiet and discomfort, are working together for your good. You are away from home here that you may be at home there. Let this cheer and comfort you. When distressed by looking back upon the home you have left, comfort yourself by looking on to that to which you are going. Heaven, glory, and eternity are before you. You are educating yourself for your Father's house, preparing to go in and dwell forever in His presence. Half a century hence at most, and in perhaps a much shorter time than that, it will be of no consequence to you whether you passed through life agreeably or not. The only thing about which you should be supremely anxious is not to be shut out from the heavenly home, not to be excluded by sin, impenitence, and unbelief from the mansions which Christ has gone to prepare. In the blessed hope of reaching that state, you might endure, not only with fortitude but with comfort, all the trials of a young woman away from home, though they were ten times greater than they are.

Chapter 8

The Character of Rebekah

"And before I had done speaking in mine heart, behold, Rebekah came forth with her pitcher on her shoulder; and she went down into the well, and drew water. And I said unto her, 'Let me drink, I pray thee.' And she made haste, and let down her pitcher from her shoulder, and said, 'Drink, and I will give thy camels drink also.' So I drank, and she made the camels drink also." Genesis 24:45–46

Everyone must be struck, I should think, with the narratives in the book of Genesis, and their correspondence to the state of society to which they relate. Their verisimilitude guarantees their truthfulness, and explains their peculiarity. We find all that charming simplicity which is in keeping with the primeval life of the persons referred to; together with all the defects in their conduct, which their partial instruction might be expected to bring with it. Another kind of narrative, more in conformity with the advanced and artificial refinement of modern society, would excite suspicion of the truthfulness of the story.

Where shall we find in all the range of fiction anything so exquisite as the history of Joseph, or even as the beautiful story which furnishes the example to be contemplated in this chapter? I invite those accustomed to criticism and endowed with taste to the investigation of this portion of Holy Writ. True, it relates rather to the history of a family than of a nation. And it is worthy of remark that the Spirit of God preserved in the inspired chronicles this little gem of historic narrative rather than the record of anything going on at that time among the great kingdoms of antiquity, not excepting Egypt, the birth-place and cradle of science. The secular historian delights to emblazon his page with the conflicts of empires, the exploits of heroes, and the prowess of armies; but what is the influence of such records upon the moral habits, social happiness, and individual character of mankind compared with that of the story of the holy courtship of Isaac and Rebekah?

Sarah, the beloved and faithful wife of Abraham, had died, and had been laid in the cave of Machpelah. Sadness and desolation were reigning in the patriarch's household. His tent was empty; the grief of Isaac, who loved his mother most tenderly, was unsoothed; and upon him the heart of the venerable widower was now turned with more concentrated affection. Isaac, the miraculous child of promise, though forty years of age, was unmarried. The holy patriarch, amidst much domestic disquiet, the consequence of polygamy, had known the happiness of possessing a faithful and devoted wife; and he now became naturally anxious to see his beloved son in possession of a companion in life before he himself should go the way of all flesh. His solicitude, however, was not merely that Isaac should be married, but well married, which in his view meant not wealthily, but religiously. He was a worshipper of Jehovah, and abhorred idolatry, by the votaries of which he was on every hand surrounded; and it pierced his heart with anguish to think of the child of his love contracting a marriage with one of them. He knew that his character as well as his happiness depended upon his choice.

Moreover, it was not only a private matter of personal and family arrangement, involving Isaac's happiness and the comfort of his father, but also a public concern, intimately affecting the covenant which the Almighty had entered into with him, and the countless millions who were to be blessed in his seed. Isaac sustained a sacred character; he was the child of promise, and inherited (and was to transmit) the promises concerning the Messiah. As Abraham had relatives in the land of Mesopotamia who worshipped the living God, he determined to send his confidential servant to engage a wife for Isaac from their family. We must suppose, of course, that all this was with the knowledge of Isaac and met with his cordial consent, though parental authority was then more extensive, and filial submission to it more exemplary, than they now are. Parents, in those times, chose wives for their sons, and husbands for their daughters, and often were regulated in their choice more by regard to wealth and rank than by the adaptation and affection of the parties to be united. I do not wish this custom to be revived; it is unnatural, and reduces marriage to a matter of bargain and sale. But I do wish parental counsel, consent, and approbation to be always sought in a matter of so much importance to all parties concerned, whether directly or remotely.

The trusty servant selected by Abraham proceeded on his mission, so delicate, difficult, and momentous to both the father and son—not, however, till religious solemnities had been observed, and the patriarch had commended Eliezer to God by prayer. If we wanted the character of a faithful servant delineated in life, where could we find a picture so perfect as this man? I shall not follow him through his long and wearisome journey of nearly five hundred miles, nor will I dwell upon the anxious ruminations of his mind during the weeks it occupied. Yet I cannot but imagine how constantly that mind was lifted up to God for protection, direction, and success.

At length he arrived at the city of his destination. It was a summer evening, and spying a well outside the walls he stopped to give his camels drink before he passed through the gates. Aware that it was the custom for the young women to come and draw water for household purposes, he first placed his camels by the well, and then set himself to prayer for divine direction. "And he said, 'O Lord, God of my master Abraham, I pray Thee send me good speed this day, and show kindness unto my master Abraham. Behold, I stand here by the well of water, and the daughters of the men of the city come out to draw water; and let it come to pass that the damsel to whom I say, "Let down thy pitcher, I pray thee, that I may drink"; and she shall say, "Drink, and I will give thy camels drink also"—let the same be she that Thou hast appointed for Thy servant Isaac; and thereby shall I know that Thou hast shewed kindness unto my master.' " It is noticeable that he did not fix upon the one who would first offer her services, but upon the one who would first willingly grant the service asked of her. In this he proceeded wisely, conceiving, it would seem, that a maid who tendered unasked, to a stranger, even so slight a service as a drink of water at a public well showed no maidenly spirit; he considered perhaps, that such attention might be an excuse for curiosity, and an evidence rather of officious forwardness than of an obliging disposition. Eliezer's conduct in all this is worthy of notice, as furnishing a beautiful comment upon Solomon's advice, "In all thy ways acknowledge Him, and He shall direct thy paths."

Let us thus begin, carry on, and end all our works in God. What is begun in prayer usually, as in this case, ends in praise. So thought Eliezer when he knelt down by the side of the well of Nahor, and poured out this simple and beautiful prayer. In his case it, no doubt, was well, but ordinarily it does not become us to ask (much less to prescribe) special tokens by which God shall indicate His will.

Having presented his prayer, he waited for the answer, and waited in strong faith that he should receive it. He did not wait long. There came a damsel with a pitcher upon her shoulder towards the well. By her appearance, perhaps by an impression from God, he was possessed with the idea that she was the person sought, and that the Lord had answered his prayer. He therefore addresssed her in the language which he had resolved to employ, and received the very answer which was to be the sign of her being the object of his mission. Her gentleness, cheerfulness, assiduity, and courtesy, manifested towards a stranger of whom she could have had no knowledge, were truly admirable, unmixed and uncorrupted as they were by any unbecoming forwardness or levity. She was frank without being obtrusive, kind without being familiar. She neither ran away frightened from his presence, for her innocence gave her courage, nor did she step beyond the decorum of her sex, nor allow her courtesy to infringe upon her modesty. It was well for Rebekah that she did not answer with a proud and haughty contempt, and a surly refusal. Yes, and it was well for another woman, who long after met another stranger, wearied with His journey, at another well, when she met His request, "Give Me to drink," with the surly question, "How is it that Thou, being a Jew, askest drink of me who am a Samaritan?"—it was well, I say, for her that she had a different person from Abraham's servant to deal with.

The words in which Rebekah's answer and conduct are described paint the scene. " 'Drink, my Lord'; and she hastened and let down her pitcher upon her hand. And when she had given him drink, she said, 'I will draw for thy camels also, until they have done drinking.' And she hastened and emptied her pitcher into the trough, and ran again unto the well to draw, and drew for all the camels." Conduct so amiable overwhelmed Eliezer; and so slow of heart are we often to believe in the answer of our prayers that he, "wondering at her, held his peace, to wit whether the Lord had made his journey prosperous or not."

There are cases in which the mind, like the eye, is lit up by a sudden light. It was so here. Finding at length that she was indeed the object of his journey, he could not repress the feelings of his full heart, but expressed them in two ways. The first has, in all ages and in all countries, been considered as one inlet to the female heart—that heart which has, at any rate, been ever thought accessible to finery, presents, and praise. "For it came to pass, as the camels had done drinking, that the man took a golden earring of half a shekel in weight, and two bracelets for her hands of ten shekels' weight of gold." But this was not the only expression of his joy and gratitude, for, unrestrained by the presence of Rebekah, "he bowed down his head and worshipped, saying, 'Blessed be Jehovah, God of my master Abraham, who hath not left destitute my master of His mercy and His truth. I being in the way, Jehovah led me to the house of my master's brethren." Did the heart of Rebekah, true to instinctive perception in all such matters, begin to divine what this present and this praise to God meant? Did a thought glance across her mind of the nature of this man's visit to Nahor? Or was the scene beheld by her in awe and wonder at the character and errand of the mysterious stranger? She must have known of her august relation, Abraham, whose name she now heard in prayer from the lips of Eliezer.

But let us for a moment forget Rebekah to look upon this holy, faithful, loving servant. Never did piety and fidelity more truly blend the sanctity of the one with the devotedness of the other. Happy master, to have such a servant! Happy servant, to be blessed with such a master!

It is not necessary for me to enter very minutely into the incidents of the scenes which followed: how Rebekah hastened with the intelligence to her father's house, and how Laban, her brother, went forth to greet the stranger and conduct him to their home. We mark, as if we saw them, the courtesy of the opening interview, the frank interchange of kindly greetings and good offices, the admirable delicacy of the servant's introduction of himself to the family of Bethuel, the servant's impatience to discharge his trust, the simple recital of what the Lord had done for him, and the full development of the object of his visit. Upon hearing them, Laban, as the surviving representative of his father, replied, "The thing proceedeth from the Lord; we cannot speak unto thee bad or good. Behold, Rebekah is before thee; take her, and go, and let her be thy master's son's wife, as the Lord hath spoken." This was dependent, as the later part of the narrative shows, upon the damsel's consent.

To help to gain this, a second splendid present was prepared for her, comprised of jewels of silver, jewels of gold, and raiment. This was, and is still, the oriental custom of contracting all bargains and entering into all covenants relating to marriage, trade, or politics. Very natural was the remonstrance which the brother, and especially the mother of the bride, addressed to the impatient servant of Abraham, when in the morning he said, " 'Send me away to my master.' And her brother and her mother said, 'Let the damsel abide with us a few days, at the least ten; after that she shall go.' " Whether it is a respite of ten days, or, as some say, of ten months, or even years, that the mother joined with her son in soliciting before the daughter should bid her a last adieu, this is a touch of genuine tenderness which we would not willingly lose from the narrative. For it is a narrative which proves its own truth by its being so thoroughly, all throughout, true to nature.

Rebekah was now called in and the question put to her, "Wilt thou go with this man?" Was she deficient in virgin modesty, in prudence, in thoughtfulness? Did she display an unseemly haste to become a wife? Did she venture too carelessly to commit herself and her happiness for life to one of whom she knew nothing but by report? Did she not take the decisive step in the dark when she consented to risk in such haste the comfort of her life, upon the truth of the lone ambassador who had come to her? In ordinary circumstances I would unquestionably reply to these questions in the affirmative; and I would earnestly recommend to all young females, and to all who have the care of them, whether parents or guardians, more delay, inquiry, and caution than were observed in this case. Hasty offers of marriage should be met either by immediate refusal or lengthened consideration. It is too momentous an affair to be decided without much investigation and reflection.

But there was a peculiarity here. Something, perhaps, may be justly imputed to the times, but far more to the religious state of Rebekah's mind; a sense of duty overwhelmed a feeling of reluctance, together with every inferior consideration. She was doubtless in the habit of daily intercourse with God, and in fervent prayer had sought divine direction. She saw an overruling providence. God was in the affair. His finger, visible to the eye of faith, pointed the way in which she should go, and with unhesitating obedience she confessed her readiness to part from all the felicities of home and seek a distant alliance, at the voice of the almighty Being to whom she had committed her destiny. Flattering as the scene before her must have appeared to a worldly eye, the sacrifices she made at this moment of compliance were certainly considerable. What could have led to such an answer—when standing between the tears of parental and fraternal affection and the urgency of a mere stranger, the servant too of her future home—but a faith which overcame the world and dictated her holy resolution? Heaven appointed her journey, and nature pleaded in vain.

That religion had something to do with it, I have no

doubt; that the promptings of the female heart had also some influence, I have as little doubt. "What woman," says Monod, "under a sense of her dependence, has not wished once in her life for the arm of a man to support her, and his name to shelter her? But at the same time, what woman, under the feeling of reserve, has not kept her secret closely shut up within her own bosom, waiting silently till she is sought for, even though she should wait till the hour of her death, hastened, perhaps, in some cases by that internal fire by which she would be consumed within rather than suffer it to be blazed abroad? The invariable order of marriage which cedes the initiative to man, and does not accord even the appearance of it to woman, is not a refinement of civilization; it is not even a nicety of the gospel; it is a law imposed on woman in every age, not excepting the most barbarous, and among all people, not excepting the most savage."

Rebekah partook of this feeling, but she worshipped the true God, and lived amidst those who worshipped idols, where perhaps few opportunities for a holy union presented themselves; and now one was offered, in which was combined all that piety could desire, and even vanity crave. She therefore required little or no time to deliberate upon it, and at once consented to accompany the servant of Abraham. Rebekah took leave of her friends, and proceeded on her eventful journey under the care of Eliezer, and accompanied, both for her comfort and her protection, by Deborah, an old and faithful servant who had nursed her since she was a child.

For a moment we leave her, proceeding on her journey, to speak of her future husband, of whom good Bishop [Joseph] Hall says, "Of all the patriarchs, none made so little noise in the world as Isaac; none lived either so privately or so innocently; neither know I whether he proved himself a better son or husband. As the one he gave himself over to the knife of his father when about to be offered up in sacrifice, and mourned three years for his mother; to be the other he reserved himself in chaste forbearance twenty years and prayed." He appears to have been a quiet, retiring, domestic, and devotional character; good, rather than great, and altogether blameless, with the exception that he was a little too much addicted to the gratification of his palate.

Dr. Candlish, in his commentary on Genesis, writes, "It is a calm and peaceful summer evening. The oxen have been lodged in their stalls, and the implements of husbandry are at rest in the furrows of the field. Not a breath of wind rustles in the noiseless leaves. Not a stray sheep wanders in the dark shadow of the hills. It is a time of profound repose. One solitary figure is seen slowly pacing the sweet-scented meadow path. Unconscious of nature's charms, although his soul is melted into sweet harmony with the peace that reigns all around, he is wrapt in holy fellowship with the God of his salvation. It is Isaac, who had gone out into the fields to meditate."

This is no improper description of the good man, who, surrounded by the glories of creation, looks through nature up to nature's God. In such an exercise and such a frame of mind, Isaac was well prepared to receive the best possible earthly blessing, a good wife. Perhaps he was then meditating upon Eliezer's mission, and beseeching heaven for its success. Behold the answer to his prayers! A cavalcade is seen in the distance approaching. It draws nearer and nearer. Can it be the return of Eliezer, the faithful servant? And are there not two females in the retinue, one young and the other far advanced in life? The vision of his future wife now flashed through his imagination as the procession drew nearer, and his eyes with fixed attention rested upon the beauteous form of Rebekah. "And who," says Rebekah, whose eyes are as busy in looking towards

Canaan as Isaac's are in the direction of Mesopotamia, "is that meditative man approaching us?" The secret is disclosed by the faithful, joyful Eliezer: "My master, Isaac."

As she approached her destined lord, see how female delicacy, and maiden diffidence and reserve, resume their empire. "She alighted off the camel, and took a veil and covered herself." This act had more meanings than one; it expressed her subjection, as his already espoused wife, to him as her future husband. It would also prevent that confusion which the suddenness of the interview and the important consequences that were to follow it would naturally produce. "And Isaac brought her into his mother Sarah's tent, and took Rebekah, and she became his wife, and he loved her. And Isaac was comforted after his mother's death." In this tender manner does this admirable story close.

Peace be to that dwelling, the residence of a dutiful son and a tender husband, and of a kind, generous, open-hearted, pious wife. Dutiful sons promise to be affectionate husbands; and were I a woman, and received an offer of marriage, one of the first inquiries I would make concerning the man who solicited my hand and heart would be, "How did he behave to his mother?" For conjugal affection could scarcely be expected to dwell in that heart from which filial regard had been excluded. He who is insensible to a mother's tender affection, believe me, my young friends, is not to be entrusted with the care of a woman's heart and happiness.

We may here pause and remark that all the circumstances continue to make this portion of the sacred record peculiarly attractive. In reading it we feel at home amid these patriarchal incidents and descriptions, recognizing them as if they were familiar. The stately pomp and ceremony, reserve and coldness and suspicion of a more artificial social state, all pass away. The freshness of nature's early truth and tenderness returns, artless,

guileless, and fearless. We breathe a purer and freer air. We are
touched with a deeper sense at once of a special providence in
heaven, and of a real and true sympathy on earth. We feel that
there can be such a thing as the exercise of a frank and generous trust, relying both upon God and upon man, and that it is
possible to act upon the belief both in God's superintendence
and in man's sincerity.

Before we consider what is to be learned from the conduct
of Rebekah as a wife and a mother, let us for a few moments
contemplate her in reference to the act which made her such,
her marriage. The circumstances connected with this were peculiar to the times, and partook of a simplicity, as I have already
remarked, to which your history is not likely to supply a paral-
lel. One thing, however, may be noticed: it was with the
awareness and consent of her friends. I cannot account for the
fact of Bethuel, Rebekah's father, being passed over in silence,
and Laban, her brother, being mentioned as conducting the
transaction, except upon the supposition that Bethuel was
dead. It is true that the name occurs once in the history, but
this probably was a brother. But Laban was consulted. There
was nothing clandestine in the affair. And, moreover, it was a
marriage in which the claims of religion were considered. On
this delicate subject I cannot enlarge. If Rebekah had shown
too great an eagerness for quitting the single state, and somewhat too hasty a decision, I would not recommend this to you.
From this, however, we have exculpated her. It may be natural
enough to prefer the married to the unmarried state, when an
opportunity offers for entering into it. But let not your minds
be unduly restless and anxious in realizing the object of your
wishes. Avoid all romantic and poetic imaginativeness on this
momentous affair. Do not allow yourselves ever to treat it with
levity, or to sustain or adopt a line of conduct which would
look as if you were more anxious to be a wife than to be quali-

fied for such a state. Never come to the conclusion that you
cannot be happy if you are not married, and cannot but be
happy if you are. Let the multitude of happy maidens and the
equal number of unhappy wives correct such mistakes, and dispel all the illusions with which the idea of marriage disturbs
the propriety of some young women's conduct. Treat the
whole subject not as a matter of poetry and romance, but as
one of the gravest realities of life. It is an affair of love, but it is
also an affair of prudence. It is a matter of taste, and even of
poetic delight, but it is also a matter of judgment and of conscience. It is not a thing to be laughed and joked about, but to
be pondered in the deepest recesses of the soul, and prayed over
in the most solemn seasons of devotion. It is momentous to
both parties, but more so to the woman.

Jeremy Taylor wrote in his *Marriage Ring*, "Life or death,
felicity or a lasting sorrow, these are in the power of marriage.
A woman indeed ventures most, for she has no sanctuary to
retire to from an evil husband. She must dwell upon her sorrow, and hatch the eggs which her folly or her infelicity has
produced; and she is more under it, because her tormentor has
a warrant of prerogative; the woman may complain to God, as
subjects do of tyrant princes, but otherwise she has no appeal
in the causes of unkindness. And even of the man we may say
that, though he can run from many hours of his sadness, yet
he must return to it again, and when he sits among his neighbors he remembers the objection that lies in his bosom, and he
sighs deeply."

It is not necessary for me here to lay down many rules for
your guidance in this affair. When, however, it comes your
way, consult not only your heart, your imagination, and your
young companions, but your judgment, your God by prayer,
and your parents for advice. Enter into no acquaintance without the cognizance of those natural guides and guardians of

your youth. It is at the beginning of connections of this kind that parental counsel should be sought. Never commit yourselves by a word till the domestic oracle has been consulted, nor allow your affections to be entangled till a father's and a mother's judgment have been pronounced. Be determined that similarity of taste, especially in the most important of all matters, religion, shall form the basis of any union you may form.

Should it be that God has not destined you to wedded bliss, forget not, as Mrs. Sendford writes, "that there are advantages peculiar to single life, that it affords an immunity from many cares, an opportunity for intellectual pursuits, and a power to do good extensively, which married women may not enjoy. And if these privileges are improved, if cheerfulness and benevolence characterize the temper, there will be no want of occupation, happiness, or sympathy. The kind sister or aunt will be always welcomed; she will be hailed as the agreeable companion or the tender nurse, as the participator in joy or the sympathizer in sorrow, as the helper in business or the companion in affliction. She will be the ready assistant in every good work; the children will run to greet her arrival; the poor will rise up and call her blessed. And if in truth, as we see in some bright examples in our own day, her energy grows with her desire of doing good, and in the assiduous and painstaking efforts of Christian charity she seems to forget the weakness of her sex, she realizes in one of its most pleasing forms primitive devotedness. She is in pious exercises more spiritual, in self-denial more mortified, in faith more pure than any of the cloistered nuns of the strictest habit; while at the same time her religion is without superstition and her sobriety without gloom. She is one of a holy sisterhood, whose order is truly 'catholic,' whose vows are scriptural, and whose voluntary service is the labor of love."

We now turn to another chapter in the history of

Rebekah, in which she appears to far less advantage than she does in the one we have just reviewed, where the artless simplicity of the virgin is lost in the crooked policy of the designing wife and the too-partial mother. Perhaps it will be thought by some that, as I am addressing young women, I might have cut short the story with her marriage and her virtues, and drawn a veil over her future failings. But bear in mind what I said in a former chapter, that the matron should be held up to the maiden so that from the outset she may learn what to copy and what to avoid. And here is a striking example to serve this purpose, an affecting instance to prove what a transformation a change of circumstances may produce in the same character. Isaac and Rebekah, like Abraham and Sarah, had their faith tried in waiting long for the son who was to be the heir of promise. Twenty years elapsed and Rebekah bore no child. In answer to the earnest prayers of her husband, God gave her the prospect of becoming a mother. Before this happy event took place she received a communication from the Lord that she would give birth to twins, who would be the heads of two separate nations, and that, contrary to the order of nature and the custom of nations, the elder brother would serve the younger.

Esau and Jacob were born, grew up, and exhibited great difference of taste and character. Into this family of Isaac and Rebekah there entered that which has rent myriads and myriads of households, setting the husband against the wife, the mother against the father, and one child against another; disturbing the harmony of domestic peace; poisoning the springs of domestic happiness; and preventing the progress of domestic improvement. I mean parental partiality. In the case of Isaac and Rebekah, the parents had each their favorite child, and, what was worse, manifested their fondness. It may in some cases be almost impossible not to have a preference for one child above another, but what anxious carefulness should there be to conceal it! Policy and justice both demand from parents an equal distribution of their affection, their countenance, and their goods; for if there is one folly which more certainly punishes itself than another, it is this ill-judged and wicked distinction between equals. Parental partiality injures both the one who is preferred and the one who is slighted; it inflates the one with pride, insolence, and vanity, and corrupts the other by jealousy, envy, and revenge. Isaac loved Esau, and for a reason not very honorable to his character: "because he did eat of his venison." Rebekah loved Jacob, for what reason we are not told; it is probably on account both of his superior excellence and of the revelation which God had given her concerning his future history. She was undoubtedly a woman of sincere faith, and even her most censurable conduct arose from misdirected piety. She, like another female in later times, pondered in her heart all the things which had been spoken of God concerning her child of promise. It was not long before the effects of parental partiality appeared in the family. A competition for precedence, and for the right of primogeniture, engaged the attention of the brothers, and whetted their spirits against each other from their earliest years; the result was alienation, separation, and hostility on the part of the children, and sorrow and distress on the part of the parents. Jacob's conduct was ungenerous, and Esau's profane. The younger son knew that he was destined to precedence, and, instead of leaving God to fulfill His own purpose, sought to accomplish it in a manner unworthy both of himself and of the blessing.

Time, which moves on with ceaseless tread, had brought Isaac to old age; and he now thought of his approaching end and the propriety of settling his domestic affairs. His great concern was to direct the descent of the patriarchal blessing, which in this case implied more than that ordinary benediction which every good man would pronounce on all his children without distinction; it comprehended the great things contained in the covenant with Abraham, according to which his posterity was to be selected and distinguished as the peculiar people of God, and to give birth to the Messiah. Isaac ought to have remembered the communication made to Rebekah, and by her doubtless told to him, that this blessing was to be bestowed upon Jacob. Natural attachment for a while overcame his faith, and he prepared to divert the blessing from the channel marked out for it by the purpose and providence of God. To kindle his affection for Esau by the remembrance of past gratifications, he wished to have some savory meat, certainly a carnal introduction to so divine an act, partaking more of the flesh than of the Spirit, and betraying more of that parental partiality under which he had acted than of the faith of a son of Abraham. See how important it is to avoid contracting bad habits early, as time, indulgence, and habit interweave them with our very constitution till they become a second nature, and as age confirms instead of eradicating them. We find the two great infirmities of Isaac's character predominant to the last: a disposition to gratify his palate with a particular kind of food, and partiality to his son Esau.

Rebekah, whose affection was ever wakeful, active, and jealous for her favorite, overheard the charge given by her husband to Esau, and instantly set about a scheme to divert the blessing into another, and, as she knew, into its right channel. What should she have done? She should have expostulated with Isaac on the impropriety of acting in direct opposition to the revealed purpose of God. Such an appeal to a mind as devout and contemplative as his evidently was, notwithstanding its weaknesses, would in all probability have succeeded. Instead of this, she manifested what has ever been considered to be one of woman's infirmities: a disposition to have recourse to finesse, stratagem, and maneuver, a wish to achieve her object by a tortuous and circuitous way rather than by an open and straightforward course.

It is unnecessary for me to enter into the details of her plan, its prompt execution, and its success. It is a sad story. There was nothing but shameless trickery and imposition, a disguised person, a stolen name, sham venison, and a false answer. Everything was bad except the motive, and that could not alter the character of the action, and transmute evil into good. It was a disgrace to Rebekah, a cruel fraud practiced upon Isaac, and a most grievous injury inflicted on the moral character of her son. We must not load Jacob with more of the infamy of this transaction than what really belongs to him. He was not first in the transgression. His feelings revolted from it when it was proposed to him. He remonstrated against it. His remonstrance, however, was founded more upon the consequences of the evil than the evil itself. And there is a striking difference between his reasoning and that of his son, Joseph. Jacob said, "I shall bring a curse upon me, and not a blessing." Joseph's pious and noble reply was, "How can I do this great wickedness, and sin against God?" The resoluteness of Rebekah is astounding and effective, confirming the general opinion that woman, in a bad purpose, is often more bold and determined than man. "Upon me be thy curse, my son; only obey my voice." An appalling spectacle, to see a mother, a religious mother, so far forgetting what is due to her sex, her relationship, and her piety as not only to lead, but to goad and drag on her son to perpetrate falsehood, and to practice deception upon his half-blind father! O mothers, read this account and tremble!

The plan moves forward, but the whole plot was in danger of exploding. The conference between Isaac and his son Jacob is deeply affecting. The half-awakened suspicion and artless simplicity of the father invests, by the power of contrast, with deeper shades of infamy and guilt the shameless, undaunted effrontery of the son. Such is the way of transgressors: one sin prepares for and leads on to another, till the sinner is forced by a kind of necessity to add another and another lie to sustain the former one. Isaac's ears were truer than his eyes, and his faculties were not so blunted by age as not to be capable of reasoning upon some improbabilities; for there is something about falsehood which, though it may silence, yet will not ordinarily satisfy. Craft, however, in this case was too deep for honesty, and Isaac, kind and incredulous to evil thoughts, soon had his suspicions lulled, ate the venison, and bestowed the blessing. It is no part of my design to paint, or rather to copy, the scene which followed when the return of Esau revealed the plot and proclaimed the deception. The shock to poor old Isaac was almost overwhelming. As an aged and an afflicted man, the imposition which had been practiced upon him would excite his indignation. Yet a moment's reflection would convince him of his mistake in intending to convey to Esau that blessing which God designed for Jacob. Such considerations, rushing upon his mind at once, sufficiently account for all his feelings; it was to him like a place where two seas meet, or as the union of subterranean fires and waters which causes the earth to tremble. Esau is to be pitied, and would be more so if his distress arose from any other feelings than disappointed ambition. He who profanely despised his birthright cared for the loss of the blessing only as it deprived him of some earthly distinctions and temporal possessions.

Rebekah's policy had succeeded. But she soon began to reap its bitter fruits in perceiving the feud which she had occasioned between the two brothers. The same tent could no longer contain them. And intelligence having reached her that

Esau was contemplating revenge, even the murder of his fraudulent brother, she hurried away Jacob to the land of Paddan-Aram to seek protection and a home among her own relatives.

With the sequel of this interesting story you are acquainted, and we return to Rebekah. The best explanation that can be given of her conduct, and it has been advanced by her apologists as her defense, is that she acted from religious motives. Perhaps it is in part true, but I think not wholly so. There is much of the mother mixed up with the believer, and no small share of regard for the interests of a favorite child blended with regard for the purposes of God. But if it is true that religion had the principal hand in this odious deception, then we see how early pious frauds were practiced for the furtherance of the faith, and Rebekah, so far as this part of her conduct is concerned, is presented to us as anticipating the principles of the Jesuits; for even if we concede to her a religious end, we must admit that she adopted the most sinful means to obtain it. She was unquestionably right in her belief that God designed the blessing for Jacob, and in this one respect, I mean her faith, she was stronger and more unswerving than her husband. Yet this faith was mixed with some unbelief after all; for what else was it but a partial distrust that led her to adopt such sinful means to secure the accomplishment of the divine purpose? Does God's truth require man's falsehood to fulfill it? Cannot we leave God to find means to perform His own word without supposing that He requires our sins to help Him out of a dilemma? The urgency of the temptation was, no doubt, very great. In her view, an hour or two would decide the matter, and the blessing intended for Jacob would be transferred to Esau; and how then would the declaration be fulfilled? She should have left it to God.

Let us now leave the history, and learn the lessons with

which it is fraught. The Scripture narratives are intended to exhibit holiness and sin embodied in living characters—the one for our imitation and the other for our warning. And not infrequently we find both sin and holiness blended in the same character, requiring a careful analysis and an accurate discrimination. This discrimination is required in looking at the character now before us.

As you see Rebekah with her pitcher on the shoulder coming to draw water, you cannot fail to notice her domestic and industrious habits. Yes, it was when she was thus occupied, and not indolently reclining upon the couch of ease, nor sauntering with a company of associates as idle and gossiping as herself, nor wasting her time in useless occupations of frivolity and amusement, that Eliezer saw her. Though she was high-born, wealthy, and beautiful, bearing the pitcher upon her shoulder to the well to draw the evening's supply of water for the family. I admit that the artificial habits of society had not then introduced those distinctions in household occupations which the advance of civilization has now brought into our habitations. At that time, and long after, the women of wealthy families were engaged in services which are now with propriety consigned to servants. There was nothing unseemly then in the daughters of men of rank being found with their pitchers upon their shoulders at the public well. Anything like this would with us be altogether out of character. I have, however, not only heard of, but have known at least one who, though high-born, yet, under the influence of mistaken views of the obligations of religion, performed those menial services which belong to and are usually discharged by domestics. Surely such "voluntary humility," as the apostle calls it, this unprescribed, fictitious lowliness, neither honors its subject nor does any good for Christianity; for when mistresses thus do the works of servants, they, by a natural ambition and exchange, will seek to take the place of mistresses. I ask no woman to step out of her place, or to descend from her rank, but only to be industrious in the domestic duties which belong to it. Every young woman should aim to be useful at home, and she is not a wise or good mother who does not train her daughters for such occupations. But as I have already dwelt on this, it is not necessary to enlarge upon it here any further than to say that the humble yet useful employments of domestic life are a virtuous woman's most honorable station. Whether in single life, wedlock, or widowhood, God and nature have destined you, my female friends, to occupation, not perhaps highly honorable in the eyes of unfeeling wealth or giddy dissipation, but highly important to the happiness of others, and therefore essential to your own.

We cannot fail to notice in Rebekah's early deportment an artless, unaffected simplicity, noticealy in contrast with her subsequent artifice and duplicity. This it is which invests her character, and most of the excellent ones in Scripture, with such an irresistible charm. Wherever we look we find that simplicity is beauty. This is true of nature as the great model. Amidst all its grandeur and complexity, its processes appear easy and spontaneous, being all originated and directed by a wisdom and a power which operate not only without visible effort, but in perfect repose. Simplicity is no less beautiful in art than in nature, and the very perfection of art is to hide itself in copying the simplicity of nature.

All this holds true of manners; there especially, affectation is hateful and repulsive. Studied display of any kind, whether of intellect or virtue, of conversation or even of pronunciation, or of singularity, whether in dress or habits, is always odious. It cannot secure respect, but must excite ridicule. Perhaps this is one of the principal follies against which women, and especially young women of education, have to guard. An artificial

character has a deeper meaning, involving immorality, as signi-
fying a tendency toward artifice, equivocation, and the simula-
tion of virtue not really possessed. This in its fixed and consoli-
dated form is hypocrisy, the most odious vice on earth. But I
now refer to artificial manners, to the affectation or parade of
superiority in any particular, to a studied mannerism for the
purpose of display. This generally springs from that vanity
which has been considered by many female writers as one of
the foibles of their sex, and the prevalence of which really
spoils many otherwise useful and amiable characters. It is in
woman what ambition is in man, and though it may be a less
dangerous, it is a meaner fault; it is a form of self-love equally
jealous and insatiable. Nothing can be more opposite to the
spirit of the gospel, and the only security against it is genuine
humility. Be clothed, young women, with this; it is your most
becoming and beautiful garment, and where will you obtain it
but from the wardrobe of Christianity?

Observe the courteous affability of this interesting young
woman. Here was a stranger, a servant, though evidently a servant of no mean master; and yet how respectful, how gentle,
how affable was her address. Josephus, fond of adding in his
paraphrastic manner to the terseness and simplicity of the
Scripture narrative, relates that there were other young females
with Rebekah who were asked for water, but refused, and that
she reproved them for their churlishness. Courtesy is a becoming grace in both sexes, but especially so in the female, while
rudeness, which is a blemish upon other characters, is a blot
upon hers. A female churl is a monstrosity, from which we
turn away with insufferable disgust. Courtesy is one of the
cheapest exercises of virtue; it costs even less than rudeness—
for the latter, except in hearts that are petrified into stone,
must put the subject of it to some expense of feeling. Even a
rough voice issuing from female lips is disagreeable; much more

rough manners exhibited by a female form.

There are various things which prevent the exercise of courtesy. In some cases, it is to be traced to pride, a vice which befits a demon, but not a woman. In others it is the result of absolute ill-nature, a morose, sour, and ill-conditioned mind, which knows no genial seasons and experiences no soft emotions. Some are petulant and irascible, and when putting on a mood of civility are easily driven from it by the slightest touch of their irritability. Be courteous, then; this is, if not of the solid substance of holiness, at least its polish. It is a Christian grace, for an apostle has said, "Be pitiful; be courteous."

Akin to this was Rebekah's kindness. There was not only an external affability of manner, but a real benevolence of disposition. Here was a stranger, tired and faint from a day's journey in a hot country, asking her kind offices to procure a supply of water for himself and his weary beasts. To grant his request for himself would have cost her no great labor; but it must have been a considerable effort to draw water enough for a number of thirsty camels! And this is more apparent when you know the construction of eastern wells, which are not like ours, but are a kind of sunken cistern to which you descend by a flight of steps. How many tiresome descents must this young creature have made before she satisfied the thirst of Eliezer's camels! And there is another little circumstance which marks her kindness. Eliezer asked only for a "sip" of water, for so the original word signifies, and she said, "Drink, and thy camels." It was a solitary act, I admit; but it was so promptly, so generously done as to indicate a habit. It is said, with as much beauty as simplicity, "Love is kind"; and with, if possible, still greater beauty, it is given as one of the traits of the virtuous woman that "In her tongue is the law of kindness," the tongue here, as in all cases, commanding the hand.

Insensibility in a man is bad enough, but worse in a

woman. An unfeeling woman is a contradiction in terms, for the female heart has ever been found to be the dwelling-place of kindness where misery, when all other hopes have failed, is sure to find an asylum. In what age, or in what country in the world, has woman forfeited her character as the ministering angel of humanity? When and where has the female bosom disowned the claims of misery and repudiated the virtue of benevolence? Arctic snows have not frozen up the springs of mercy in the female heart, nor tropical suns dried them up. Tyranny has not crushed it out, nor barbarism extinguished it. Look at Mungo Park, when alone in the midst of Africa, and lying down to die in want and despair, found by the black women of that wild land, carried to their tent, fed, clad, and cherished amidst the tender strains of the impromptu song with which they cheered the feelings of his heart and expressed the benevolence of their own. Young women, cherish in your bosoms the purest philanthropy. Abhor selfishness; you are made for kindness. Oppose not the design of your Creator. Do no violence to your own nature. A stony heart does not become you. A tearless woman is a revolting scene in our sorrowful world. She may be pure and beautiful as the marble statue, but if, withal, she is as hard and cold, who can admire her?

I cannot yet pass from the contemplation of this sweet and amiable young creature to behold her in her future character till I have referred again to the veil of modesty under which all this affability and kindness were concealed. In listening to her language, in witnessing her conduct, will the most fastidious, prudish, or censorious of her sex find aught to condemn in anything that she said or did? Did she in the smallest measure violate decorum? She did not stand to gaze upon the stranger and his camels, or do anything to attract his attention, but was intent upon the object for which she came, and was diverted from it only by an opportunity to do good, thrown in her way, without her seeking for it. She did not anxiously or confidently enter into discourse with the man, but waited till she was addressed, and then answered him modestly. Modesty is the most attractive of all female graces. What is intelligence without it but bolder impudence, or beauty but a more seductive snare?

There is, I know, a reserve that degenerates into repulsive pride, as on the other hand there is a frankness that corrupts into forwardness. Woman is intended neither to avoid man by a bashful timidity nor to court him by an obtrusive advance. A genuine modesty guards against each extreme. It is that semi-transparent veil which, by revealing half her excellence, makes more lovely that which it reveals, and excites desire to know the rest. It is her shield as well as her veil, repelling all the darts with which, either by acts, words, or looks, anyone would dare to assail her purity.

It is also her ornament, investing all her other excellences with additional charms, the blush of purity upon the cheek of beauty. It is her power, by which she subdues every heart that is worth the conquest. Yea, what is not modesty to woman? Lay not aside your veil. Cast not away your shield. Divest not yourselves of your brightest ornament. Enfeeble not your power to influence others. Avoid everything in which the absence of this virtue can show itself. See how the want of it is reproved by the prophet Isaiah in his third chapter, and how the practice of it is enjoined by the Apostle Paul: "That women adorn themselves in modest apparel, with shame-facedness and sobriety, not with braided hair, or gold, or pearls, or costly array, but, which becometh women professing godliness, with good works." Neither in dress, nor in conversation, nor in action, nor in the toleration in your presence of improper discourse, should you violate this law. Chastity is the robe which every woman should wear, and modesty is the golden clasp that keeps it upon her, and the fringe that adorns it. When the clasp is lost, the garment is likely to fall off; and when the fringe is torn away, or carelessly allowed to be trampled upon, the disfigurement of the robe has commenced, till at length it is cast away as not worth being retained.

I do not wish you to mistake a silly and affected bashfulness for modesty. You do not live amidst Asiatic ignorance, tyranny, sensuality, and female degradation, where woman is used mainly to pander to the appetite of her lord, and where, by a cruel jealousy, she is excluded from intercourse with all but her fellow slaves and their common tyrant. You are the women of an enlightened age and country, and you are admitted on equal terms to all the enjoyments of social intercourse. Assert in this respect your rights; maintain your standing, and, while you throw off all boldness, cast away with it all unworthy prudishness. In one of my previous chapters, I remarked that the over-prudish mind, which can never speak to one of the opposite sex but with a blush, is not always the purest one in reality.

There are, my young friends, one or two momentous lessons for you to learn from Rebekah's conduct in later life, lessons which you must carry with you through all your future existence on earth. The first is general: a change of circumstances often produces a considerable change of character and conduct. How unlike the maid of Nahor was the wife in Canaan! And is it an uncommon thing now for a change far more extensive and more powerful than this one to be effected by the new condition into which marriage brings the female character? Learn also this special lesson, that we should never seek a good end by bad means; in other words, never do evil that good may come. Abhor the great principle and favorite maxim of Jesuitism, that the end sanctifies the means; and especially abhor the application and operation of this most detestable principle in reference to religion, a principle which is more or less interwoven with the whole history of Popery. What crimes have been perpetrated by the zealots of Rome, in the abused name of religion, for the good of their church! The pages of history which record the progress of that dreadful apostasy are not only stained with blood, but steeped in it. And even by other professing Christians, holding a purer creed and animated by a milder spirit, how much has been done, ostensibly for religion but really for sectarianism, in contradiction of every principle of the law of God and love for our neighbor! Religion refuses to be served by any principles of action but its own, and disdains to accept any offering which is contrary to truth, love, holiness, and honor. And just as the stronger our zeal is for an object, the more we are in danger of resorting, in times of difficulty or in prospect of defeat, to unworthy means, so the more fervent we are to promote any religious cause, the more watchful should we be against being seduced into the use of unholy means to obtain success. The wife of Isaac was right in her object, but wrong in her means, to obtain the blessing for Jacob.

But we must take leave of Rebekah. It is somewhat remarkable that the sacred narrative takes no notice of her death. One might have hoped that she, who came upon our notice at first like a bright and lovely vision, would have been seen to depart with as much gracefulness, simplicity, and beauty as she exhibited when we first saw her with such delighted attention. Is it that this act of her history so disrobed her character of its pristine beauty that censure is pronounced upon her by this most impressive silence? But is hers the only instance of painful contrast between the maid and the matron? The only instance that has disappointed the hopes raised by youthful excellences? The only instance in which the full-blown flower has not answered to the bud? Happy would it have been for thousands if it were.

Let it then be your first solicitude to exhibit, in your early life and single state, all those general and moral beauties which form the character of virgin excellence. Be holy, industrious, modest, benevolent, and useful; inspire hope in every beholder, and awaken expectation. But, then, be ever anxious, studious, and prayerful, so that in the transition from the single to the wedded state, in the development of the girl into the woman, all that was lovely, artless, and simple in youthful charms shall, with unbroken and unvarying consistency, ripen into all that is holy, estimable, and venerable in the wife, the mother, and the matron.

Chapter 9

The Ornaments of a Profession of Religion

"That they may adorn the doctrine of God
our Savior in all things." Titus 2:10

"Whose adorning, let it not be that outward adorning of
plaiting the hair, and of wearing of gold, or of putting
on of apparel; but let it be the hidden man of the heart,
in that which is not corruptible, even the ornament
of a meek and quiet spirit, which is in the sight
of God of great price." 1 Peter 3:3–4

There is in human nature an instinctive propensity to decoration. To whatever principle the taste may be traced, whether to innate perception of the beautiful or to a desire to excite admiration, the fact is indubitable. It is seen equally in savage and civilized nations, and is manifested by them alike in attention to their persons and their dwellings, and indeed in all their social customs and usages. The string of shells, fishes' teeth, or bits of bone around the neck of the Polynesian, and the blaze of diamonds or rubies upon the brow or breast of the British queen, indicate the same instinctive propensity. This taste, however in many cases it may be altogether corrupted in its object, wrong in its principle, or excessive in its degree, is in its own nature an imitation of the workmanship of God who, by His Spirit, has garnished the heavens and covered the earth with beauty. Who can look over one of creation's lovely scenes and behold the display of elegance of form, and beauty of color in the flowers of the field and garden, in the plumage of the birds, in the meandering rivers and the gentle undulations of the ground, exhibiting wood and copse, hill and dale, all gilded with the beams of the glorious sun—I say, who can witness all this without being convinced that God Himself delights in decoration! He has made a world which He has ornamented so profusely that He has scattered beauties where there are no eyes but His own to behold them:

> Full many a gem of purest ray serene
> The dark unfathomed waves of ocean bear;
> Full many a flower is born to blush unseen,
> And waste its fragrance on the desert air.

To reject all ideas and efforts to add the fair to the good, the beautiful to the useful, would be to oppose and not to imitate, to condemn and not to approve, the works of the great Creator. And, indeed, no sect has ever arisen among Christians which has even pretended to disclaim all attention to what is ornamental. Even those who conscientiously repudiate the pearl, diamond, and ruby, the feather and the flower, erect their buildings, select their furniture, plant their gardens, and choose their garments according to their ideas of taste, and with some regard to the laws of beauty. Hence, I think that both of the apostles who touch on the subject of personal decoration for Christian women are to be understood not as condemning all ornament, but only regulating it. The propensity to personal decoration is, without all doubt, peculiarly strong in the female heart. That a maid should forget her ornaments or a bride her attire is spoken of by the prophet in a proverb as being unlikely. There is nothing wrong in the instinct itself. It serves important purposes. Its total absence is felt as a serious interruption of the pleasure of social intercourse. A slovenly woman is disagreeable, a slattern intolerable. Christianity makes no war on any of man's natural propensities, but only on their abuse. Its object is not to eradicate our instincts, but to prune and train them, and make them bear good fruit.

Now it is well known that some, in what the apostles say on this subject, find an absolute prohibition of all ornaments of dress, and an injunction to wear only the most plain and unadorned apparel. I think Christian women may fall into much more dangerous misinterpretations of Scripture than this; yet I have no doubt that it is a misinterpretation. The prohibition seems to be comparative rather than absolute, and contains an injunction to be far more attentive to the ornaments of the soul than to those of the body. "I will have mercy, and not sacrifice" means, "I prefer mercy to sacrifice." At the same time, there can be no doubt that in the words of the text it is taken for granted that women at all times are, and that the women of those times were, far too much addicted to ornamental dress; that they violated both modesty and economy by their habits; and therefore that in these verses the apostle laid down some very important hints as to the principles on which Christian women should regulate their attire. They inculcate modesty in opposition to what is immodest, economy in opposition to extravagance.

"Excessive costliness," says Robert Leighton on this passage, "argues and feeds the pride of the heart, and defrauds, if not others of their dues, yet the poor of their charity, which in God's sight is a due debt too; and far more comfort shalt thou have on thy deathbed, to remember that 'at such a time, instead of putting lace on my own back, I helped a naked back to clothing; I abated something of my former superfluities to supply the poor with necessities'; far sweeter will this be than to remember that 'I could needlessly cast out many pounds to serve my pride, while I grudged a penny to relieve the poor.' "

Albert Barnes has given, I think, the true meaning of the apostle: "It is not to be supposed that all use of gold or pearls as articles of dress is here forbidden; but the idea is that the Christian female is not to seek these as the adorning which she desires, or is not to imitate the world in these personal decorations. It may be a difficult question to settle how much ornament is allowable, and when the true line is passed. But though this cannot be settled by any exact rule, since much must depend on age, one's relative rank in life, and the means which one may possess, yet there is one general rule which is applicable to all, and which might regulate all. It is that the true line is passed when more is thought of this external adorning than of the ornament of the heart. Any external decoration which occupies the mind, and which engrosses the time and attention more than the virtues of the heart, we may be certain is wrong. The apparel should be such as not to attract attention, such as befits our situation, such as will not be particularly singular, and such as will not leave the impression that the heart is fixed on it. It is a poor ambition to decorate a dying body with gold and pearls. It should not be forgotten that it will soon need other ornaments, and will occupy a position where gold and pearls would be a mockery. When the heart is right, when there is a true and supreme love for religion, it is usually not difficult to regulate the subject of dress."

It is somewhat remarkable that Plato, the loftiest of all the Grecian sages, has a passage which strikingly resembles that of the apostle: "Behavior and not gold is the ornament of a woman. To courtesans, these things—jewels and ornaments— are advantageous to catching more admirers; but for a woman who wishes to enjoy the favor of one man, good behavior is the proper ornament, and not dresses. And you should have the blush upon your countenance, which is the sign of modesty, instead of paint, and worth and sobriety instead of gold and emeralds." It is impossible not to notice this similarity between the apostle and the philosopher, and equally impossible, one should think, not to mark the superiority over the one's reason of the other's inspiration. The philosopher is of the earth, earthly; the apostle brings the authority of God and the power of the unseen world distinctly into view. While Plato leads wives to seek exclusively the honor that comes from men, Peter teaches them to seek the honor which comes down from God, the true Judge of excellence, the great Fountain of honor.

Before I pass from this subject of personal decoration, I will just notice the very beautiful reference which the apostle makes to that part of our nature which it is to be your chief concern to beautify. "Let it be," he says, "the hidden man of the heart, in that which is not corruptible, even the ornament of a meek and quiet spirit, which in the sight of God is of great price." How exquisitely is this put! How impressive the ideas which are conveyed! It is the decoration of the soul rather than of the body about which Christian women should be chiefly solicitous, and about the ornaments that are suitable to its own nature. The soul is indestructible and immortal; so should its ornaments be. What can jewels of silver or jewels of gold do for this? Can the diamond sparkle upon the intellect? Or the ruby blaze upon the heart? Or the pearl be set in the conscience? Or the gorgeous robe clothe the character? Or the feather or the flower wave over the renewed and holy nature? No! The appropriate ornaments of the soul are truth, holiness, knowledge, faith, hope, love, joy, humility, and all the other gifts and graces of the Spirit. Wisdom, prudence, fortitude and gentleness—these are the jewels with which the inner man should be adorned.

The outer man is corruptible. Dust it is, and unto dust it

shall return. That beautiful woman, glittering in all the profusion of diamonds, the admiration and envy of the court or the ballroom, must ere long be a mass of putrefaction too ghastly to be looked upon, and then a hideous skeleton, a collection of bones, a heap of dust; and where will be the immortal spirit? Will it wear the cast-off jewels of the body? Oh, no, these remain, rescued from the grasp of the king of terrors, but only to ornament other bodies and not to prepare souls for immortal glory. But turn now to that other female, the woman who, regardless of the decoration of the body, was all intent upon the beauty of the soul. Look at her, I say, who was clothed with the robe of righteousness and the garment of salvation, and decorated with the ornaments of a meek and quiet spirit. She too dies, and whatever of her beauty there was in her person dies for a season with her; but the indestructible and immortal spirit over which death has no dominion goes not unadorned into the presence of the Eternal, for the jewels with which it decorated itself on earth are as indestructible as its own nature, and go with it to shine in the presence of God.

"Men," says Leighton, "think it poor and mean to be meek. Nothing is more exposed to contempt than the spirit of meekness; it is mere folly with men; but that is no matter. This spirit outweighs all disesteem; it is with God of great price. And these are indeed as He values them, and no otherwise. Though it is not the country's fashion, yet it is the fashion at court; yea, it is the King's own fashion; 'Learn of me,' says He, 'for I am meek and lowly in heart.' Some who are court-bred will send for the prevailing fashions there, though they live not at court; and though the peasants think them strange dresses, yet they regard not that, but use them as finest and best. So care you not what the world says; you are not to stay long with them. Desire to have both your stuffs and your fashion from heaven. The robe of humility and the garment of meekness

will be sent to you. Wear them for His sake who sends them
to you. He will be pleased to see you in them, and is not this
enough? It is never right in anything with us till we attain to
this: to tread on the opinion of men, and eye nothing but
God's approbation." (See also Dr. John Brown's masterly ex-
position of this passage of Peter.)

But I now pass from the ornaments of the Christian
woman's person to those of her profession; and these indeed
are the chief subject of this chapter. There is something impressive in the exhortation, "Adorn the doctrine of God our
Savior." The great truth of our divine Savior, the Lord Jesus
Christ, is thus represented as susceptible of decoration on the
part of those who profess it. The sentiment conveyed is that
the holy life of a consistent Christian is an adornment of the
profession of this sublime doctrine. This, more than all splendor of tasteful architecture, gorgeous forms, imposing ceremonies, or anything else which can appeal to the senses, is the
decoration of Christian doctrine. It is this, as it shines forth in
the beauties of holiness, that truly decorates religion:

> Beyond the pomp that charms the eyes,
> Or rites adorned with gold.

A very large proportion of the members of all Christian
churches are females, and young females too. This, on many
accounts, is a very delightful fact. It has, however, been sometimes complained that, like others, they are not so anxious to
sustain their profession well as to make it. And it is for their
sake, and to lead them to consider what would set off their
profession to the best advantage, that this chapter is designed.
What is truly ornamental attracts attention and excites admiration, and these are advantages which the friends of religion
should secure by their conduct. I shall divide what I have to

advance on this subject into four particulars.

1. I will first consider the personal qualities which will have the effect here desired. As incongruity of conduct in reference to any profession whatsoever is a blemish and not a beauty, a deformity and not a decoration, remember that inconsistency would be so in you in reference to religion. Study your profession, and thoroughly understand what it implies and enjoins. Consider well what sanctity of conduct, what spirituality of mind, what separation from the world in spirit and taste, what devotional feelings, what faith, hope, love, and humility, what amiableness of disposition and amenity of temper are included in the declaration (and that declaration you have actually made), "I am a Christian." You should not have made such a profession if you did not understand it, or mean to sustain it. I must remind you, it is a solemn thing to profess to be a disciple of Christ. It supposes that you are a new creature; that old things are passed away and that all things have become new with you; that you have new principles, new motives, new ends of life, new tastes and new pleasures. Now, your profession is to be maintained with a due regard to this. Your conduct must comport with it. You must be dissimilar in these things, very much so, to those who make no such profession. They must see the difference as well as hear of it. You must commend yourselves to them as consistent with yourselves. You must compel them to say, "Well, we do not like her religion, but it is quite in harmony with her profession." But what is this consistency? The following remarks will perhaps explain it.

There must be earnestness without enthusiasm, fanaticism, or bigotry. Lukewarmness with regard to any duty is odious. Earnestness, on the other hand, excites attention, and sometimes admiration, even where its object is far from commendable; how much more where that object is holy, benevolent, and useful. It is a noble and a lofty spectacle to see amidst a race of frivolous mortals a soul which, being immortal, is intent upon its immortality and, though surrounded by the frivolities of this visible world, is intent upon the realities of the unseen state. Nothing can be more dull and repulsive than a lukewarm and heartless profession of religion—a pale, sickly, and shriveled form, which has all the decay of tuberculosis without its hectic flush or lustrous eye.

On the other hand, how impressive a spectacle is it to behold a young woman amidst the wonderment of some of her companions, and the laughter of others, rising upon the wings of faith and habitual devotion above the region of their levities into that of devotion; to see her eye, as it is upturned to heaven, sparkling with the beam of eternity that has fallen upon it; and to follow her in her ardent career, pursuing her seraphic course, undeterred by contrary examples or opposing influence. But there must be no enthusiasm leading her to violate the law of sobriety; no fanaticism leading her to tie down others to all the rules she has imposed upon herself, and to cherish a hostile, much less a malignant feeling towards them, because they seem to differ from her in some things which she deems important. There must be the most profound humility blended with all this intense earnestness, and the mildest forbearance towards others combined with the utmost conscientiousness as regards the laws which she imposes on herself. Earnestness implies a resolute determination never to allow others to interfere with our convictions; a courage that dares to be singular; a fortitude which braves opposition, though it should be united with gentleness even under persecution. Earnestness must be shown by an intelligent and well-regulated zeal to bring others under that influence which is the spring of its own energies. Mild in persuasion, gentle in entreaty, and with a loving, insinuating manner, the female religious professor must aim at the conversion of others. Usefulness, in the sense of holy activity for the temporal and eternal happiness of mankind, must be a conspicuous trait of her character. Selfishness, indolence, and inertness are disfigurements of character, while benevolent activity is one of its richest ornaments.

There must be seriousness without gloom. On the one hand, she who is bent upon eternity and anxious for salvation cannot sink down into the levity of those who are all taken up with fashion, amusement, and folly. On the other, true religion includes such an intelligent joy as makes its possessor satisfied with her own sources of enjoyment, without running to the amusements of the world for pleasure and excitement. The young female professor must let it be seen and felt that her religion is her bliss and not her penance, that it is her song and her solace. She must appear as irradiated with sunbeams, and not invested with shades. Her countenance must be the index of a heart at peace, of a bosom serene and happy.

And in addition to all this, there must be a most anxious desire to cultivate that prime virtue in the composition of womanly and Christian excellence, meekness. See how this is commended in the passage which I have already quoted from the writings of the Apostle Peter: "The ornament of a meek and quiet spirit, which in the sight of God is of great price." God values it above all gifts of intellect, delights in it above the most splendid genius, and honors it above all that men delight to honor. It is woman's ornament above all others; it is her defense, for who can oppress the gentleness that never provokes, and can scarcely resist or complain? Who can wantonly tread on that lowly, lovely floweret which, as it lifts its unpretending head, silently says, "Can you crush one that hurts nothing?" Nothing is more unsightly than the reverse of this: an irritable, discontented, peevish, domineering woman.

Hence the declaration of the inspired Israelite sage, "It is better to dwell in the corner of the housetop alone than in a wide house with a brawling woman. It is better to dwell in the wilderness than with a contentious and angry woman. Whoso hideth her, hideth the wind." Mr. [William] Jay has drawn a beautiful picture of this virtue in his character of a Christian wife. He says that she is one "who can feel neglects and unkindnesses, and yet retain her composure; who can calmly remonstrate, and meekly reprove; who can yield and accommodate; who is not 'easily provoked,' and is 'easily entreated'; who would endure rather than complain, and would rather suffer in secret than disturb others with her grief." Such is meekness, the highest form of the peculiarly Christian life, and such is the ornament of female Christian profession.

2. I now touch upon another branch of the subject, and that is the importance of social excellence to the adornment of religion.

Great injustice has been done to religion, and a great hindrance thrown in the way of its diffusion, by those descriptions of it which represent it as an abstract thing, almost exclusively pertaining to the Sabbath as to time and to the church as to place; a mere matter of devotion, a transaction between God and the soul about salvation and heaven, but having nothing or little to do with secular affairs, social relations, and the interactions of human life—in short, as a thing which looks entirely heavenward, but which casts no glance upon earth. This is superstition, and we find enough of it in Popery, which overlays with cumbersome ceremony the moral duties of the law, as well as the free grace of the gospel; cuts in many instances the ties of social life, and isolates men and women from their fellows; and, by the devotions of the cloister, the convent, and the church, supersedes the duties of the house, the shop, and the exchange, thus setting forth religion as fitting men for the next world, but having very little to do with their abode in the present one.

On the contrary, true religion, the religion of the Bible, is seen under two aspects: one looking up to heaven, the other looking down to earth. It gathers all the interests of man under its protection and fostering care. Like the sun which, though fixed in the heavens, pours the flood of its light and glory and cherishing influence upon earth; or like the atmosphere which, though above the earth, enters into every place upon it, and sustains the insects that creep as well as the birds that soar—so religion irradiates with its light, guides by its revelations, animates with its stimulus, sanctifies by its power, and blesses with its influence, in all their relations and all their interests, all those who yield themselves up to its authority and government. It goes to palaces and teaches kings, to the legislature and teaches senators, to the exchange and teaches merchants, and to the cottages and teaches peasants and workmen, instructing all in the various duties which they owe to God and to their fellow men.

Religion is also a household thing, a family law. It lifts the latch of the house and goes in and takes its seat at the parental board, and joins the circle around the hearth as well as around the altar; it swells the joys of the domestic fellowship as well as responding to the morning prayer or chanting the evening hymn; it founds the duties of the second table of the law upon those of the first, employs the loftiest theology to enforce the commonest morality, and enjoins the most ordinary obligations of social existence by motives drawn from the cross of Christ. Hence the necessity for professors to pay the greatest attention to the various duties of social and domestic life. We are commanded to "let our light shine before men, that they, seeing our good works, may glorify God."

So in the beautiful passage quoted from the Apostle Peter,

where he gives directions to Christian wives, he says, "Be in subjection to your own husbands, that if they obey not the Word, they also may without the Word be won by the conversation of the wives, while they behold your chaste conversation coupled with fear." Here again the fact is set out that religion is intended to regulate the intercourse, and form the character, of domestic and social life, and that where its influence so exerted is seen it must be beneficial to the observers of it. I wish to press this point most earnestly upon your attention: the faith of the gospel is intended and calculated to carry social excellence to the very highest perfection. It is the soil in which all the seeds of domestic happiness will best flourish.

It should not be forgotten that social excellence is often seen apart from religion. Very exemplary instances of the home duties of life are sometimes found in those who make no profession of religion. Good husbands and wives, parents and children, brothers and sisters are found outside the circle of vital piety—a fact which ought to make those who are within it still more anxious to be exemplary in the discharge of their obligations. A real Christian should excel unconverted persons not only in religion, but in morality. She should not only be more holy, but more socially excellent. She should excel the world in those things which the latter makes her boast, and rise above the level which the world has prescribed as its highest elevation in moral and social virtue. Select, therefore, the most dutiful and affectionate daughter, the most kind and attentive sister you can of this class, and say to yourself, "She makes no profession of religion, and yet she excels, in a manner worthy of attention and admiration, in all the duties of domestic life. Now, as I do profess religion, I must, if possible, be still more exemplary than she is in all social obligations; for surely nothing could possibly bring religion into greater disrepute than for my parents, or my brothers and sisters, or even the servants, to make a comparison to my disadvantage between my conduct and hers."

You probably have heard of that Roman daughter who, when an aged father was in his condemned cell and left to starve, all having been prohibited from carrying him food, nourished him from the same breast which sustained her infant. The authorities were so struck with the report that the old man was pardoned, the daughter raised to public esteem, and the prison demolished to make way for a temple dedicated to filial virtue. If paganism furnished such an example of devoted affection, and if pagans could so admire it, what ought Christianity to do?—not, of course, in the same mode of action, but in every other way in which genuine and strong affection can show itself. If you would adorn your profession it must be in this way of domestic excellence. There may be the most seraphic piety, so far as the raptures of devotion go; there may be a most punctilious performance of all the rites and ceremonies of religion; there may be a most eager and regular attendance upon all the public services of religion; there may be an ardent zeal for the spread of the religious peculiarities of your denomination; but if, at the same time, there is a deficiency of duty, honor, and obedience to your parents, or of kind interest and affection for your brothers and sisters, or of humane consideration for your servants, all this religious profession will only excite disgust, and raise a suspicion of your sincerity and a prejudice against religion itself.

No one can possibly be attracted to or conciliated by a religion which is to any great degree destitute of social and domestic excellence. It is a terrible taunt to be thrown at anyone: "Yes, she is, if her own profession and supposition is consulted, a very good Christian. But it is a pity she is not a better daughter, a kinder sister, and a more accommodating neighbor." The most flaming profession must be at once

thrown into eclipse by such a sarcasm. If you were to study
how most effectually to discredit not only your own profession,
but religion itself, you could not be more successful than by
associating with it such a line of conduct as this. I therefore
most solemnly and anxiously entreat you to once again enter
very deeply into the subject of the chapter entitled "The
Parental Home" (chapter 6).

3. There are intellectual ornaments of your profession
which you should seek both on their own account and on that
of religion. True it is that genuine and consistent religion is its
own recommendation, and depends upon nothing extraneous
for its real value. Still, since there are those who have imbibed
prejudices against it, and have taken up mistaken views of its
nature, as if it were at war with the gifts of the intellect and
the graces of the character, it would be well to disabuse their
minds and, by your attainments, accomplishments, and elegance, convince them that piety is not, as they may suppose,
another name for ignorance, stupidity, and vulgarity. For their
sakes, then, as well as for your own pleasure, cultivate your
minds by study. Acquire an eager thirst for knowledge. Be
fond of reading, and of the best kind of reading. Disprove the
slander that girls are only fond of tales and novels, of stories of
love, female adventures or heroism. Prize knowledge; desire to
arrive at truth; be anxious to investigate the wonders of nature;
and seek to enrich your minds with the treasures dug up and
distributed in such abundance in this wonderful age. Fill your
minds with this wealth.

But let other faculties be brought into exercise besides your
memory. Cultivate your judgment; be inquisitive, reflective,
and discriminating. There are many young persons whose
memory is a storehouse crowded with facts, names, and dates,
but who are nevertheless lamentably deficient in judgment.
They may speak French, quote history, and display other ac-

complishments, but their intellect is too feeble to form, hold, or defend an opinion of their own. I do not, of course, expect all women to be profound logicians or subtle metaphysicians, but most tolerably well-educated females may, by vigorous and well-sustained efforts, arrive at some maturity of sound judgment. Let it then be seen that the highest kind of wisdom and knowledge does not lead you to despise the lower kinds, lest those who are adept only in them should, by what they see in you, despise that which is the highest. Make it clear that they who are the children of God are most solicitous to become acquainted with all the works of their heavenly Father, not excepting the wonders and glories of creation. Convince the worshippers of the God of nature (or rather of the *false* god, Nature) that while you are chiefly anxious to pass on and worship Him who sits enthroned between the cherubim, upon the mercy seat in the Holy of Holies, you can bow and adore with them in the vestibule of His temple, and ascend with them to the highest altitude of earthly subjects and general knowledge. Show them that when, like birds of weaker pinions and dimmer vision, they droop the wing and stop their flight, you, like the eagle soaring still upward to the sun, can still pursue your heaven-bound course, and rise into the regions of celestial splendor.

Nearly allied to this faculty of judgment is taste, or a perception and love of the beautiful and sublime in nature, in literature, in accomplishments, in conduct, yes, and in holy Scripture. The Bible is full of instances of this. With a correct literary taste you will relish even more this bread of life that came down from heaven, the Word of God. Inspiration has garnished its page with beauties that are hidden from eyes whose vision has not been strengthened by education. The Scripture is a paradise of flowers to be admired, as well as of fruits to be eaten.

Taste displayed even in what are called "accomplishments" is ornamental to piety, when not carried to excess. As I observed in a former chapter, these matters of elegance are not to be despised. True, it is a sin for a Christian woman to spend hours and hours of each precious day in the fashionable modes of killing time—by embroidery, crotcheting, painting, languages, and music—to the neglect of religion, useful reading, and all benevolent effort. It is truly saddening to see a rational, immortal, and accountable creature dwelling in this world of ignorance, sin, and misery, which she could do something to enlighten, reform and bless (and also advance herself on her way to eternity and the bar of God), consuming the best and preparatory period of her whole existence in this world and, for the next in painting figures upon canvas, or drawing them upon paper; in playing and singing; or in acquiring German, French, or Italian.

Let me not, however, be misunderstood. I am not such a rigid utilitarian as to be the advocate of the merely useful in human character, for I really love and admire the ornamental. I am not all for Doric strength, but contend also for Ionic grace and Corinthian elegance. I am not for young women laying down the needle and the pencil, for their leaving the piano silent and untouched or foreign languages unlearned. No such thing! Religion forbids not these matters. Nature, and the Bible too, are full of the sweetest embroidery and enameling, full of music and painting, and of all the varieties of a language not our own. Instead of forbidding what can add embellishment to the female character, I enjoin it. Woman, formed to please, yea, made in Paradise, where beauty was in perfection, and where the first lessons in taste were taught by the great Master of all created beauty, go on to sprinkle your character and to interweave your conduct with every flower of elegance; and especially Christian woman, let it be seen by your sex that you have not so learned Christ as to throw off all delight in the tasteful, the decorative, and the picturesque, with which, pointing to the lily, the vine, the birds, and the flocks, He was pleased to enliven and adorn His own discourses. To me it is always a beautiful sight to behold the robe of righteousness and the garment of salvation in which genuine piety is ever attired and adorned (not encumbered) with the jewels of elegant accomplishments and tasteful decoration.

All this is important to you as young unmarried women; and the importance of it is augmented by your looking forward and contemplating yourselves in future life as wives and mothers! Without intelligence and taste, are you fitted to be the companion of a wise and sensible man, or to preside with advantage over the education of children? Remember the character of the age in which you live. But even in these days of knowledge and taste we know very well that the aptness and ability of a good housewife are always invaluable; for it is a poor commendation to say of a woman, "She is exceedingly well informed in all the literature of the day, quite learned, but she knows very little of household affairs." I believe her husband often thinks, if he does not say it, "I would dispense with a great deal of her bookishness and her knowledge if I could have the house kept in a better condition, and enjoy a little more comfort at home." Still, a wife and a mother, to all the household prerequisites, should and may add intelligence and taste. It is indeed the perfection of womanly character at once to "look well to the ways of her household," and also to "open her mouth with wisdom." How impressive and attractive a scene is it to see a pious, well-informed, accomplished woman, respected as well as beloved by her husband, as his intelligent companion, esteemed by his guests, and looked up to with confidence, reverence, and affection by her children, over whose general education she presides with dignity and ability.

4. There are some things which do not fall under any of the other headings, and which may therefore be called general excellences of a decorative nature. These have been already dwelt upon in former discourses, and therefore need only to be briefly mentioned here. We find them set forth in the early character and conduct of Rebekah, in which we beheld modesty without silliness, frankness without forwardness, courtesy without affectation, and complaisance without servility—in short, all that maidenly reserve which would restrain whatever is obtrusive, rude, impudent, and bold, and which yet would allow an artless, ingenuous, and unembarrassed mode of intercourse with the other sex. I have sometimes seen good women so bold, obtrusive, and imposing as to repel and disgust. I could not doubt that they had really some religious principle within this indecorous outside, but it could scarcely be seen. In some cases it has happened that even the very profession of religion, which should have led women to draw closer the veil of modest reserve, has led them to throw it off altogether; and they seemed to act as if the Christian name, which ought to be a guarantee for all that is meek and gentle, was a sanction for unseemly forwardness. On the contrary, there are others whose profession of religion has so disfigured them with the airs of assumed sanctity, so stiffened them into prudish reserve, and so distorted the simplicity of nature with the formalism of gloomy superstition that they are repulsive as specters and lead many to exclaim, "If this is religion, it may be pure, but it is surely unlovely, and, one should imagine, as unfit for heaven, where all is joyous, as it is for earth, where, if happiness is wanting, this certainly cannot supply it."

Good temper, or amiability, is essential to the adornment of a Christian profession. This has been alluded to already in more places than one, but its importance justifies the repetition. I have already admitted that there is a great difference in this respect among natural constitutions. Hence it costs some immensely greater pains to acquire a small degree of this excellence than it does others to manifest ten times the amount. And really there may be more of principle and virtue in the modicum of the one than in the abundance of the other. Some indulgence should therefore be shown to those who are born with a crabbed disposition, and they should not be judged too harshly. We see the fault, but not the contrition with which it is followed; nor do we witness the deep self-abasement which the outburst of the moment inflicts for hours, if not days. But still we would enjoin on those who are conscious of this infirmity a most anxious, earnest, and prayerful attention to the subject. Let every woman who is troubled with an over-wrought sensibility, a morbid susceptibility of offense, or an unusual liability to passion put her heart under discipline, or her constitutional tendency will be a prolific source of misery to herself, and to others around her.

It is not, however, as a source of disquietude that I now allude to it, but as a cause of scandal. A bad temper not only troubles the heart, but it disfigures the profession. Observers can see nothing to love and admire in religion when found in company with so much ill temper. There are some persons whose bad temper is unassociated with piety, or indeed with moral worth of any kind, and they are wasps, hornets, scorpions, all venom and no honey, according to the degree of malignity they possess. There are others who have real godliness and some sterling excellence of other kinds, and they resemble bees who, though they have honey, yet are somewhat irritable, and have also a sting for those who offend them. Cultivate, then, a lovely and amiable temper as one of the brightest ornaments of religion. It is to religion what the burnish is to the gold, the polish to the steel, the fragrance to the rose, and the sunshine to the prospect.

There is one thing which, in addition to all that has been mentioned, is required to give the finishing stroke of ornament to the character of the young female professors of religion, and that is the virtue that is sometimes designated "good sense," at other times "prudence," and at others "thoughtfulness." I know such dispositions are thought by some minds to partake too much of the grave to be ornamental in youth. They may hang like rich, ripe clusters around the character of the matron, but such persons think the beauty of youth consists in the picturesque and the romantic, with a tinge of the wild, the visionary, and the enthusiastic. There is no poetry they imagine in prudence, no imagination in good sense, no fancy in thoughtfulness. I will concede so much as to allow that a precocious gravity, an anticipation of the sobriety of threescore years and ten, is not what I enjoin or wish to see in youthful maidens. Even religion with all its solemn proprieties, all its heavenly sanctities, does not extinguish the vivacity, the sprightliness, or the buoyancy of a girl in her teens. I love to see her sparkling eye, her sunlit countenance, her elastic step, and to hear the merry note of her laughter, and the music of her cheerful voice. These are ornamental; they belong to her age and the natural flow of her spirits, and it is only superstition that would turn that young and joyous creature into the stiff and silent statue, the nun-like figure, or the unsmiling devotee. But then, is it any detriment to all this innocent hilarity to have meditative thoughtfulness, an instinctive sense of propriety, cautious reserve, and accurate discrimination? Is it a blemish rather than a beauty to be able to consider what in all circumstances is best to be done, and to be able to do it well? To act from principle rather than from impulse, and be guided by reason rather than by feeling? To weigh words before they are spoken, and estimate actions before they are performed? Is not propriety beauty? Are freaks and caprices, whims and eccentricities, imprudence and follies, ornaments? Yes, in the estimation of that silly girl (but in hers alone), who would rather be smiled at for her wildness and her weakness than commended for her more solid excellence. What kind of a mother is this romantic and wayward creature likely to make? Let the Christian young woman be very jealous then of this romanticism, and consider it to be not in keeping with the dignity and sanctity of religion. The matrons are admonished by the apostles to teach the young women to be sober, a word that refers there not to wine, but to a prudent thoughtfulness.

Such, then, are the ornaments of early female religious profession. It has been supposed throughout this chapter that there may be real piety without some of these accompaniments—a rough unpolished godliness, true but unadorned religion. One young female may be sincere in her profession of religion, and yet have an uncorrected infirmity of temper; another may be very illiterate or very weak-minded; another may be guilty of various little inconsistencies which tarnish the beauty of her profession; another may be rash, restless, and imprudent; another may be spiritually proud, and something like affectedly sanctimonious; another may be wanting in agreeable and accommodating manners or habits at home. In all these ways, and in various others, religion may be disparaged, shorn of some of its beauty, rendered less attractive, and made even repulsive to those who observe it. "Let not your good," says the apostle, "be evil spoken of." Religion is itself so transcendently excellent (being the highest glory of man, the image of God, and the temper of heaven) that it should be exhibited to the greatest possible advantage. Who, if he wore the portrait of some dear friend, or suspended a picture of the queen in his house, would not wish to have it so framed as to be worthy of the subject? Who would not deprecate the idea of his keeping it covered either with dust or defilement?

Religion is the only thing that can make people happy in this world, or guide them to eternal felicity in the world to come. How solemnly, tremblingly anxious should all who profess it be to exhibit it in the most advantageous light, and with the greatest and most powerful attractions! How deeply solicitous should we be, lest by anything others see in us they should form a prejudice against it, and we should thus cast stumbling blocks in their way! How desirous should we feel, and how studious should we be, to invest our profession with whatsoever things are lovely, so that others, beholding our good works, our peace of mind, our meekness, gentleness, and kindness, our usefulness and humility, should be won to Christ—so that if they will not love religion in the first instance for its own sake, they may be conciliated to it by the ornaments with which, in our case, it is decorated!

Before this chapter is concluded, I may with great propriety suppose that some will read it who have not made a profession of religion, who are not in visible connection with a Christian church, and who are living in the habitual neglect of the Lord's Supper. Making no profession of religion! How is this? Have you none to profess? Melancholy idea! No religion! Better, I admit, not to profess at all than to profess what you do not possess, and thus add hypocrisy to your other sins. But is it not painful and fearful to think of a rational, immortal, sinful being living without penitence, prayer, faith, and love? How can you live another hour in such a state? What are all the intellectual ornaments spoken of above without personal piety, but a garland of beautiful flowers around the brow of a corpse, or but as diamonds sparkling on the breast of death? Oh, for your soul's sake, live no longer without remembering your Creator in the days of your youth!

Others, perhaps, will read this discourse who, though partakers of true faith in Christ and love to God, are not yet professors of the religion they possess. I again say, How is this? Have you pondered that language of the apostle, "With the heart man believeth unto righteousness, and with the mouth confession is made unto salvation," or that solemn injunction of Christ, when He instituted the sacred supper, "Do this in remembrance of Me"? Is this the command you select from the law of the New Testament as the only one you feel at liberty to disobey? This one, so tender, so pathetic, so loving! This, delivered in sight of the cross, only a few hours before our Lord endured those agonies by which you are saved! What, neglect the command of dying love, a command so positive, an invitation so gracious, an injunction obedience to which is at once so honorable, so happy, and so useful! What is your reason for this neglect? Do you tremble to make a profession because it is so awful? Does not this arise from superstitious rather than religious dread? Is it awful to profess the faith you exercise, and to commemorate the death of Christ? Have you not mistaken the design of the Lord's Supper? It is simply a commemorative ordinance, and are you not deluded and terrified by the mystery in which priestcraft has sought to envelop it?

But, you may say, "I tremble to make a profession lest I should dishonor it, as so many have done." They have indeed, and the painful fact should lead to caution, self-examination, and earnest prayer for grace, that another stumbling block should not be furnished by you. But the very fear will, if sincere, be your preservation from the object of your dread. The path of duty is the way of safety. Besides, are you less likely to sin outside the pale of communion than within it? I invite you, therefore, if you are partakers of true faith, to profess, or, to use a scriptural synonym, to "confess" it. The communion of saints and the participation in the Lord's Supper will, by God's grace, strengthen the principle and call forth the exercise of the divine life, and will be at once your honor and your joy.

And as to you who are already to be found in the fellow-ship of the faithful, I congratulate you on the choice you have made, and on the decision to which you have come. To your pastors it was a source of unspeakable pleasure to receive you among the number of the followers of the Lamb. You, in a special manner, are their hope, joy, and crown of rejoicing, inasmuch as they look to you, and those who may descend from you, to fill up the places of more aged disciples when they, according to the course of nature, shall be removed to the church triumphant. Acknowledge practically and gratefully the grace you have received from the Lord by using your influence with labor and judgment, to engage other young persons, your relatives and companions, to come and share with you the privileges, and enjoy the blessings, of Christian communion. And to give effect to your persuasions, exhibit all the beauty of consistent example. Let religion be seen in you, combining with all its sanctities and spiritualities, the amenity of life, ami-ability of temper, general intelligence, correct taste, and general social excellence, which shall prepossess them in favor of gen-uine piety. Make it evident to them that true godliness is as happy a thing as it is a holy one. Convince them by what they see in you, as well as by what they hear from you, that you have found the secret, and that your soul has touched the center of bliss. Let the richest excellences that can adorn the female character, all the most rare and delicate beauties that are ad-mired in it, be strung together upon the golden thread of emi-nent piety, and be hung like a necklace of heavenly pearls round your profession. Thus adorn the doctrine of God your Savior in all things.

Chapter 10

The Character of Martha and Mary of Bethany

"Now it came to pass, as they went, that He entered into a certain village; and a certain woman named Martha received Him into her house. And she had a sister called Mary, which also sat at Jesus' feet, and heard His word. But Martha was cumbered about much serving, and came to Him, and said, 'Lord, dost not Thou care that my sister hath left me to serve alone? Bid her therefore that she help me.' And Jesus answered and said unto her, 'Martha, Martha, thou art careful and troubled about many things; but one thing is needful. And Mary hath chosen that good part, which shall not be taken away from her.'" Luke 10:38-42

This beautiful little gem of sacred history is replete with instruction in reference to every one of the individuals which it brings before us. It is a group of characters, each possessing its own peculiar excellence and interest. It says much for the condescension, kindness, and fidelity of the chief personage of the scene, and no less for the feelings and the excellences of the other two. In the person and conduct of Jesus Christ are always combined, without being confounded, all the uncreated glories of the Godhead, and all the milder beauties of the perfect man. And if, in the admiration of His humanity, we are not to lose sight of His divinity, so neither in the contemplation of His divinity are we to forget His humanity. Human nature had its consummation in Him. He is its representative in its best estate, the pattern man. His greatness did not raise

Him above any kind of goodness or the manifestation of it. Is friendship one of the virtues of our nature, one of the bonds of society, one of the blessings of life, a sweet and lovely flower that unfolds its beauty and exhales its fragrance in the garden of our social existence? Behold in Jesus Christ this virtue in perfection! He had His attachments, not indeed capricious ones; they were all founded on the characters of their objects, but He had them. His nature was susceptible of special regards. He felt more complacency in some of those He loved than in others. Hence the groundlessness of the cavil against Christianity that it nowhere positively enjoins the practice of friendship; for it does more: it exhibits it in the character and conduct of its divine Founder. For "Jesus loved Martha, and her sister, and Lazarus." And this was so well known that, when Lazarus was ill, "his sisters sent unto Christ, saying, 'Lord, behold, he whom Thou lovest is sick.' " And where shall we find a more beautiful manifestation of friendship than in the gospel narrative of Christ's conduct when Lazarus was dead?

In entering upon this interesting history, I observe that it is one of the peculiarities of our Savior's discourses that He often takes occasion to graft general truths on special incidents, and makes comparatively small occurrences the vehicle of momentous instructions, in a few words bringing everlasting truth, in some important view of it, home to all times and circumstances. Standing on the spiritual center point, He, without violence, entwined the minutest and least important circumstances of the present with the loftiest eternal verities. Thus, in the conduct of the two sisters before us, He places together the nothingness of all love and care for the body in comparison with care for the soul and solicitude about that which is everlasting.

Bethany was a little village about two miles from Jerusalem, inhabited as a suburban retreat by many wealthy and respectable Jews. There dwelt Martha, who appears to have been the elder sister and mistress of the house, her sister Mary, and a brother named Lazarus. Whether the sisters were maidens or widows, we are not informed. All we know of the family is (and it is the best and most worthy thing to be known of them) that they were all united not only by the ties of nature, but of grace; they were all one in Christ, partakers of "the common salvation," by a "like precious faith."

In the bosom of this little quiet and holy family, it is probable that Jesus occasionally found repose after His bodily fatigues and mental sufferings in the unbelieving city; for His humanity was susceptible on the one hand of both of these, as indeed of all the sinless infirmities of our nature, and (on the other) of the relief afforded by rest and pious conversation. "Oh, happy house," says pious Bishop Hall, "into which the Son of God vouchsafed to set His foot! Oh, blessed women, who had grace to be the hostesses to the Lord of heaven and earth! How should I envy your felicity herein, if I did not see the same favor, though in a different way, if I be not wanting to myself, lying open to me!" There are two ways of receiving Christ even in the present day: in Himself, by opening to Him our hearts in faith, and in His members, by opening our hands in charity and our doors in hospitality. And Christ will esteem Himself better served in these ways than He would, were He again upon earth, by being entertained in our houses.

On one occasion when the divine visitant made His appearance by an unexpected visit, Martha—as the head of the household, the presiding spirit of the domestic economy, with an anxiety prompted by a loving and generous heart towards her illustrious guest, not altogether, perhaps, unmixed with a desire to display her skill in good housewifery—set about providing the best and fullest entertainment the larder could afford. We can see her in the fullness of her cares and the activ-

ity of her temper, cheerfully and busily engaged in getting
ready the supper, eyeing everything with minute inspection
and provident forethought so that nothing might be wanting
that was worthy either of her Lord or of herself. Generous but
mistaken woman, do you know so little of your Lord as to
imagine He needs, or can be gratified with, all this care and
provision for His sake? Had you never heard that He once said
to His disciples, when pressed to take food, "My meat and My
drink are to do the will of My Father in heaven"? Yet it was
love, though mistaken love. I can fancy her saying to herself,
"Can I ever do enough for Him who deserves infinitely more
than all I can do? Cheerfully will I give Him the best I have,
and the most I am able to perform. To give to Jesus and labor
for Him are my delight. He has my heart, and He shall have
my hand, my feet, my house, my all."

And where was Mary all this while? Eagerly availing herself of the precious opportunity afforded by the presence of the
Great Teacher, sitting at His feet to receive instruction. Such a
season might never return, and she was determined to make
the best of it by listening to every word the Savior said. Yet we
are not to suppose that Martha had not been at the Master's
feet at all, listening to any part of Christ's instructions; for it is
said of Mary that "she also sat at Jesus' feet and heard His
word," evidently implying that some other had been there also
(which no doubt was Martha) who, just then, like some of her
sex, thinking of the house and its duties while in the sanctuary
and service of God, recollected the provision which she supposed necessary, and somewhat abruptly rose up and retired
from the presence of Christ to the scene of her domestic solicitude, leaving Mary to be feasted by Christ while she went to
make a feast for Him. "I know not," says the good bishop already quoted, "how to censure the holy woman for an excess of
care to welcome her Savior."

How apt are we to measure other people's sense of propriety and rightness of conduct by our own, and to blame them for not exercising their religion and expressing their love and obedience to Christ in our mode! Mary perhaps wondered that Martha could on any ground whatsoever cease to listen to the instruction of Christ, while Martha wondered no less that Mary could sit still and be a learner when she ought to have been active as a provider. Martha would be ready to blame Mary for her want of love in keeping Christ talking when she ought to have been caring for His refreshment, while Mary would be apt to blame Martha for the lukewarmness of her regard in not eagerly catching every word that fell from His lips. Let us learn that those may equally love Christ who do not take exactly the same mode of showing it. Goodness is very ingenious, and, while it is uniform in essentials, is multiform in circumstantials.

After waiting some time, and expecting Mary to come out and assist her, and often, perhaps, casting a silent but reproachful look at Mary, as the door stood ajar and she remained still sitting at the feet of Jesus, Martha's patience could endure it no longer and, in unseemly haste, ruffled temper, and irreverent manner, she entered the room and thus addressed herself to Christ: "Lord, carest Thou not that my sister hath left me to serve alone? Bid her that she come and help me." It was a sad speech, which in her cooler moments she must have condemned. It was irreverent to Christ, for it accused Him in an angry tone of neglect of her comfort. It was unkind to her sister, for it implied that she was wanting in love both for Christ and for herself. It was well she had one to deal with who knows our frame, and remembers that we are but dust.

Why did she appeal first to Christ, and arraign her sister before Him? Might she not have beckoned Mary away, or whispered in her ear? Or why, when she saw her so devoutly engaged, did she not leave her to her rapt enjoyment, and say, "Happy sister, to be thus enjoying thy Lord's presence and instructions. Would that I could feel at liberty from these cares, and be at your side; but somebody must provide for the comfort of the Master, and this belongs to me." Those are not always in the right who are most forward in their appeals to God. Many are more anxious to get God on their side than to be on the side of God. We must take heed lest we expect Christ to espouse our unjust and groundless quarrels. I am afraid there was in Martha's mind at this time a little of that envy and ill will which is not infrequently felt by one person at witnessing the superior piety of another. The more eminent religion of one professor is often felt to be a reproach to those who are lukewarm and worldly, and is therefore really in some cases the cause of ill will and dislike.

We do not find that Mary uttered a syllable in reply to this vehement accusation. I can fancy her lifting up her meek and invoking eye to the Savior, with a look which seemed to say, "O my Lord, I leave the vindication of my love for Thee and for my sister in Thine hands." Gentle spirit! May we learn from this example, when we are complained against for welldoing, to seal up our lips in silence, and to wait till the manifestation of our innocence comes from above. And how surely will Jesus undertake our cause, and bring forth our righteousness as the light and our judgment as the noonday. When Christ might have retorted with keen and cutting severity, He replied only with a kind but faithful answer, in which He first rebuked her, and then justified and commended her sister. The very repetition of her name is instructive, showing how serious Christ was in this act of reproof: "Martha, Martha." It is as if He had said, "O woman, thou art very wrong." Though the wrongdoing was out of love for Him, He reproved it; for as many as He loves He rebukes and chastens. No faults, mistakes, or sins are more dangerous than those which originate in misdirected love; and none should be more faithfully yet tenderly pointed out to those who commit them, as there are none which the deceitfulness of the human heart will be so backward to see and confess, none which it will be more ready to excuse and defend. The ill-directed love of friends is sometimes more mischievous than the open hostility of foes. Now observe the rebuke of Jesus: "Thou art careful and troubled about many things, but one thing is needful; thy mind is full of unnecessary anxiety about those domestic matters and disturbed by restless agitation. And what thou discoverest on the present occasion is too much thy wont on others. There is one thing far more important and far more needful than all these matters, which, by losing the opportunity I now afford thee of receiving instruction, thou art sadly neglecting the care and salvation of thy immortal soul."

It has been contended by some that, by "the one thing needful," our Lord intended to suggest to Martha that instead of the abundance she was preparing, the many varieties of food she was about to place upon the table, one *dish* only was necessary. I will not deny that this might seem to harmonize with the occasion; much less will I deny that it would furnish on the part of our Lord a perpetual and merited rebuke to unnecessary and sinful care, trouble, and expense on the part of professing Christians to provide costly entertainments for their friends. Good John Newton has some admirable remarks on the subject of entertainments given to ministers: "Some of us would be better pleased, whatever kindness our friends design to show us, to be treated less sumptuously, and in a way more conformable to the simplicity of our Christian profession. We would not wish to be considered as avowed epicures, who cannot dine well without a variety of delicacies; and if we could suppose that such cost and variety were designed to remind us how much better we fare abroad than at home, we might think it rather an insult than a compliment." The interpretation, however, which would make our Lord refer to such things is obviously a false one; for as Mary's conduct is opposed to Martha's, that which she chose, the good part, must be the same as the one thing needful; and if the one thing needful means one dish, Mary's good part must also be one dish, which she chose or provided, rather than the many which her sister was intent upon. But the suggestion of such a meaning is trifling with Scripture rather than explaining it.

Having rebuked Martha, our Lord next vindicates her sister, whom she had so severely and unmeritedly reproached. "Mary hath chosen that good part which cannot be taken from her." By the "good part" we are to understand her sitting at Christ's feet to hear His words rather than bustling about domestic affairs. That was the good part for the moment, but I believe our Lord meant to extend His meaning in what He said to each of the sisters, to their habitual character and conduct; and as He intended, when He said to Martha that she was too careful and too much troubled about many things, to describe her usual temperament, so, when He said that Mary had chosen the good part, He designed to describe her uniform attention to the high and sacred concern of religion, and to represent her as one who had given herself to the pursuit of eternal salvation. This was a matter of choice, and neither of compulsion nor of unintelligent and heartless formality. She voluntarily took up a life of piety; and in doing this she secured an inheritance "incorruptible, undefiled, and that fadeth not away." I reserve for the conclusion of the chapter some remarks on this description of true piety.

How difficult it is to inflict reproof and not excite anger, and to bestow deserved praise without doing mischief by inflating vanity! No such injury was done in this case. The ef-

fect, both of the censure and of the praise, appears to have
been beneficial; for in a subsequent chapter of this scriptural
history, to which we shall presently have occasion to refer, we
find the two sisters as united in affection as ever, and Martha
considerably improved.

I shall now attempt an analysis and discriminating delineation of the character of the two sisters. I have already remarked that they were in one feature, and that the most important, alike: they were both pious women; they both loved
Christ. And what is religion without love for the Savior? In
making the inquiry after true piety, fix your attention, concentrate your thoughts, terminate your researches, and settle your
conclusions on this simple but comprehensive idea: it is a
scriptural, supreme, practical, and grateful love for Christ. This
Martha, as we have already asserted, undoubtedly possessed as
well as Mary. She, too, notwithstanding her failings, could
have returned the same answer as did Peter, "Lord, Thou
knowest all things; Thou knowest that I love Thee."

Underneath the superficial earthliness of that careful and
troubled mind, there burned a sacred fire of strong attachment
to the Savior. With this sameness of general character, there
were circumstantial differences—just as we have seen two
flowers springing from the same root, possessing the same
general characteristics, yet one bending towards the earth
while the other stands erect and opens its petals more expan-
sively to the sun. Martha and Mary are the exemplars of the
peculiarities of two distinct varieties of character and religious
tendencies. One was the type of a naturally energetic, the
other of a quiescent mind. One exhibited excellence in action,
the other in repose. One was busily devoted to externals, the
other careful only for her own religious instruction as the one
thing needful. In the one we see the contemplative Christian
musing and feeding in silence upon holy thoughts, and look-

ing up in rapt meditation into heaven; in the other we see the
practical Christian, now lavishing her indefatigable cares upon
a brother whom she loves, and now ministering in ordinary
life to a Savior whom she adores; invoking Him in the bitterness of grief, and blessing Him in the joy of deliverance. In
one we see too much of the busy, careful, anxious housewife;
in the other, perhaps too much of the contemplative, quiescent
devotee. You cannot mistake all this; it is patently obvious to
every reader.

There was much that was good and useful in Martha's
character. She possessed great quickness, alertness, and energy,
with practical ability and good sense, which qualified her both
for taking a lead herself and for giving an impulse to others, so
that she was well fitted for going through with any work to be
done, and was always awake to the common calls and the
common cares of the ordinary domestic routine of life. And
more than this, she was well prepared to work her own way,
and to help others, in those emergencies of trouble and of difficulty which frequently occur in the changing scene of human existence. It is a blessed temperament, my young friends,
to have that noble hardihood, untiring energy, and undaunted
boldness of character which can grapple with difficulty, sur-
mount obstacles, and, instead of being crushed by misfortune,
rise triumphantly above it. But such a temperament has its
dangers, and Martha fell into them. She was impetuous, irritable, intolerant, and somewhat rude. She was angry that
others were not as energetic as herself, a common fault with
persons of such a turn of mind. She could not make allowance
for differences of disposition. She was, however, an excellent
woman after all.

Mary was characterized by more depth of thought, more
reflection, and more sensibility. She was more easily engrossed
by an affecting scene or any spiritual subject; more alive at any

time to one single profound impression, and apt to be abstracted from other concerns.

We see the characteristics of these two sisters brought out in an affecting scene in their later history, to which I will now advert, and for the particulars of which I refer you to the eleventh and twelfth chapters of the gospel of John. Sickness in an alarming form entered this little family at Bethany, and arrested Lazarus. Jesus was at that time in Bethabara, about thirty miles from Bethany. In the agony of their grief the sisters despatched a messenger to Him, under the supposition that He would come and restore their brother to health. Lazarus, it would seem, expired soon after the messenger left. On receiving the information, Christ, who knew all about the matter, and also what He would do, lingered where He was for two whole days in order that the miracle which He was about to work might, from the circumstance of the longer continuance of death, be the more signal and convincing.

At length He set out for Bethany. Observe in this act His usual mercy, to travel thirty miles on foot to restore a dead man. How delightful is it thus to trace the Savior in His journeys, justifying the description which is given of Him as one "who ever went about doing good." Martha was the first to receive information of His approach on this occasion to Bethany, either because, as the mistress of the house, the intelligence was first conveyed to her, or because, from her bustling and active disposition, she was most likely to hear of it. And now, acting according to her character, she lost not a moment, but immediately hastened forth to meet her Lord, to render Him the offices of courtesy and respect, to inform Him of the calamity that had befallen them, to pour out to Him the sorrows of her heart, and to receive the expressions of His sympathy. She was thus, as ever, ready to be up and doing.

But Mary, either not being informed of the coming of

Jesus or absorbed in a deeper grief, sat still in the house and waited for the entrance of the Comforter. This intensity of sorrow did not escape the notice of the Jews. Hence, when at length she arose at the call of her sister to go forth and meet her Lord, they said, "She goeth unto the grave to weep there." They said this from a knowledge of her character, for they made no such remark about Martha when she went forth. She might be bent on other errands. Mary could go only to weep.

It is well observed by Dr. Candlish, in his discourse on this subject: "In different circumstances the same natural temperament may be either an advantage or a snare. Martha was never so much occupied in the emotion of one subject or scene as not to be on the alert and ready for the call to another. This was a disadvantage to her when she was so hurried that she could not withdraw herself to wait upon the Word of Life. It is an advantage to her now that she can, with comparative ease, shake off her depression, and hasten of her own accord to meet her Lord. The same profound feeling, again, which made Mary the most attentive listener before, makes her the most helpless sufferer now, and disposes her almost to nurse her grief, until Jesus, her best Comforter, sends specially and emphatically to rouse her. Nor is it an insignificant circumstance that it is the ever-active Martha who carries to her more downcast sister the awakening message; so ought sisters in Christ to minister to one another, and so may the very difference of their characters make them mutually the more helpful. She went her way, and called Mary her sister secretly, saying, 'The Master is come and calleth for thee.' "

The two sisters, both deeply affected with a sense of their loss, meet their Lord, and exhibit in this interview the same difference of character as pervades their whole history. Martha's grief is not so overwhelming as to prevent her utterance; she is calm, cool, and sufficiently collected to enter into

argument. She can talk of her sorrow, refer to her loss, express
her faith, and even modestly suggest to Christ, in a delicate
and covert manner, the possibility of His restoring her brother.
It was different with Mary. In piety she is, of course, equal
to her sister; but in composure and serenity she is inferior. Her
gentle spirit is paralyzed with grief. All she can do is to cast
herself prostrate at the feet of Christ; all she can say is to sob
out, "Lord, if Thou hadst been here my brother would not
have died."

We cannot pass over one more characteristic, exquisitely
delicate and true to nature. Jesus, having asked where Lazarus
had been laid, is conducted to the grave, which was a cave with
a stone upon it, and He gives orders to take away the stone. It
was not Mary who offered the objection founded on the
commencement of decay; she is silent still in the unutterable
agony of her grief, and the deep reverence of her soul before
the Lord. But Martha's marked officiousness makes her forward when it might have been more becoming to be silent and
to stand in awe. Dr. Candlish, with nice and just discrimination, points out the wise and considerate manner (which will
be observed by every judicious, critical reader of the narrative) in
which Christ adapts His behavior towards the two sisters.
Martha's distress was of such a nature that it admitted discussion and discourse. Jesus accordingly spoke to her and led her
to speak to Him, and made to her, as suited her circumstances,
some of His sublimest communications touching the resurrection of the body and the life of the soul. But to Mary, who is
wrapped in such deep grief, He shows His sympathy in a different way. He is much more profoundly moved. He does not
reply to her in words, for her words are few. Sorrow has
choked her utterance and overpowered her soul. But the sight
of one so dear to Him, lying in such helpless grief at His feet,
is an appeal to Him far stronger than any supplication. And

His own responsive sigh is an answer more comforting than any promise. "When Jesus therefore saw her weeping, and the Jews also weeping who came with her, He groaned in spirit and was troubled." And when He had asked the bystanders where they had laid him, and received the reply, "Come and see," like Joseph, "He could no longer refrain Himself." And this is where we are told that "Jesus wept."

O most blessed mourner, with whose tears your Savior mingles His own! Oh, sympathy most unparalleled! To each of the two stricken and afflicted ones, our Lord addressed the very consolation that was most congenial. With Martha, Jesus discoursed and reasoned; with Mary, Jesus wept. It is thus that He who knows our frame adapts the communications of His grace, as our temperament and circumstances most need them.

Before we quit this scene of domestic grief and pass to another incident in the history of Martha and Mary, shall we not turn aside to see this great sight exhibited in the conduct of Jesus? I know I am giving the history of Martha and Mary, but was not Christ so blended with it as to form a part of it, and to constitute the glory of it? Shall I take you to the grave of Lazarus, point you to the mourning sisters, and omit to notice the weeping Savior? Shall I pass over that short but wondrous verse, which tells us with such sublime simplicity that Jesus wept? Every view of Christ is glorious, whether reigning upon His throne in the glory He had with the Father before the world was; agonizing in the garden when He sweated, as it were, great drops of blood; hanging upon the cross, the great sacrifice for sin; rising from the grave with the keys of death and of Hades at His girdle; or ascending to His glory amidst the retinue and acclamations of angels. Now all these manifestations produce feelings of awe and wonder. But, oh, His weeping at the grave of Lazarus! The Son of God in tears, not as on the Mount of Olivet, when He signed the death warrant of Jerusalem, and looked onward from the destruction of the guilty city to the torments of eternity, of which its fires and plagues were a dark type. No! His tears on this occasion were those of human tenderness, the exquisite sympathy of His noble and perfect manhood with the afflictions of those whom He loved. How many lessons are taught us by those tears. Have they not vindicated and defended humanity from the insults and injuries of Stoicism, and made chastened sorrow one of its genuine workings? Have they not consecrated sympathy as one of the virtues of humanity? Have they not made tenderness the adornment of greatness? Have they not raised friendship to the rank of a Christian excellence? Have they not proved that he has not the mind of Christ who knows not how to weep for the woes of our nature? Jesus wept. There were critics in ancient times who with ruthless fingers canceled this verse, thinking it beneath the dignity of Jesus to weep. Barbarian critics! Stoical scholars! You would rob the Scriptures of one of their brightest gems, and spoiled the character of the Savior of one of its richest beauties.

But now after this not, I hope, ungraceful episode, let us pass on to one more scene in the history of this happy, holy family. About four months after the resurrection of Lazarus, a supper was given to our Lord and His disciples (most likely on account of the resurrection of Lazarus, who, with his sisters, were perhaps relations of the host) by a man named Simon who had been a leper, and who had, in all probability, been healed by Christ. At this supper Lazarus and Martha and Mary were present. Here also we find the contrast between the characters of the two sisters maintained with unbroken continuity and unvarying uniformity. Martha, ever active, ever generously attentive to the comforts of others, ever to be found where energy is required, served. She had assisted in the preparation, and now busied herself in waiting upon the guests, and especially upon the most distinguished of them all, her Lord and Master whom she loved. Not so with Mary; in that assembly all were forgotten by her but one, on whom she gazed long with the silent rapture of love and devotion, waiting and watching for her opportunity to give Him a meditated, practical, and personal expression of her adoring gratitude and affection. While, according to the custom of the times, He was reclining at table on His couch (not sitting upright as we do on chairs), she stole behind Him, and, unrestrained by the presence of the guests, brought an alabaster box of spikenard, and with it anointed the feet of Jesus and then wiped His feet with her hair. She gave him the most costly article of her toiletries, and employed for Him the most ornamental part of her person. For what persons who love Christ will not give Him the richest and best of their possessions? Was not this Mary all over? Sensibility, gratitude, affection—does it not harmonize with the listener and mourner whom we have already witnessed?

From one of the company, I mean the traitor who sold his Master for thirty pieces of silver, this act of pious affection and liberality drew forth a censure, and, under a hypocritical profession of concern for the poor, he expressed his regret that the precious ointment had not been sold and given to the fund for charity. Ah, how often has a plea of charity served as a cloak for covetousness! True it is, as a general principle, that great expense in external magnificence, even when designed to honor Christ, would most commonly be better employed in feeding and clothing His members; but there are some extraordinary occasions when some sort of profusion is not to be blamed. And everything which is given to Christ is acceptable to Him when, as in this case, it is love that gives it. Happy is the person who knows, like Mary, to make that an offering and expression of love to the Savior which, in her days of worldliness and folly, she has offered at the shrine of vanity. Jesus became her vindicator against the cavils of Judas, and pronounced an eulogium which the loftiest monarch on earth might covet to receive: "She hath done what she could." Of how few can this be said; and yet what lower rule of conduct ought any of us to prescribe for himself than this? Is less than what we can do for Christ enough to do for Him? Have you ever weighed in seriousness of mind this noble testimony, "She hath done what she could"? What can you do for Christ? What have you done? What ought you to do? What will you do? Let Mary's memorial be yours.

And to what renown did it raise her? "Wherever this gospel shall be preached throughout the whole world, this also that she hath done shall be spoken of for a memorial of her." How literally has this been fulfilled. Wherever the Bible has gone, in one hundred and fifty languages, this has been published to the world. And all nations will know of Mary's alabaster box of ointment consecrated to Jesus, and will venerate her memory for this act of pious zeal. The world is a poor judge in matters relating to God; and God takes delight in honoring those actions which the world blames through a spirit different from His. Happy are those who are content with the approbation of Him who sees the heart. The contradictions and groundless censures of men pass away like the clouds that occasionally veil the sun; but the good actions which are the subject of their envy or their calumny will remain forever, splendid as the great luminary itself. Good works embalm the memory with an odor more precious and lasting than the perfume of Mary's spikenard.

Reference has been made to this incident, and especially to the praise bestowed by our Lord upon Mary, to prove that the contemplative life is more acceptable in the sight of God than the active. It is this mistaken notion which led to the establishment of convents, a system which is no less opposed to the dictates of revelation than it is to the impulses of nature and the welfare of society; which does violence to humanity in order to do honor to Christianity; which stifles all the instinctive yearnings of the heart under the pretext of giving better opportunity for the exercises of devotion; and which, as a natural and necessary consequence, has deposited a muddy soil of immorality upon the surface of Christendom, where the fruits of righteousness cannot grow, though the weeds of superstition may flourish with a rank luxuriance. The supposition that superior sanctity attaches to celibacy, on the one hand, is one of the supports on which the whole Papal system rests, and on the other has been the cause of more abomination in the world than any other single opinion claiming to have a religious sanction. That the history before us will furnish no support to this system is evident. Mary was neither (at the time spoken of) a nun, nor did she ever become such. Hers was a piety that blended with and sanctified the duties of social life. Whatever was her devotional taste and disposition, it did not drive her from her home, nor cut the ties of her relationships. The design of our Lord's language is not so much to form a comparison between two courses of life, so separate and distinct as not to allow of the mixture of one with the other, as to administer a rebuke to a person who, pursuing one course, had too much neglected the other. It was not to prevent Mary from attending at all to temporal matters, but to engage Martha to less anxiety about them, and to a stricter regard to things unseen and eternal.

And now, my young friends, what in the review of this beautiful little narrative do I recommend? Which of the two characters do I enjoin you to imitate? I answer, all that was excellent in both, without the imperfections of either. Martha's household diligence without her excessive anxiety, united with Mary's fervent devotion without her somewhat superabundant sensibility. So far as it could be said of Martha, "She looked well to the ways of her household," let my female friends imitate her due attention to home duties, her cleverness, her diligence, her dispatch, and her generous attention to the comfort of her guests, especially those who represent their Lord. Let them be skilled in all the important functions of good housewifery. Let them, if wives, know how to make home comfortable for their husbands; if mothers, for their children; and, if widely connected, for their friends. Hospitality is a virtue which should never be wanting in a female heart. She who will not seek to please her husband's friends, but receives them with a frown, will soon learn to leave off pleasing him, and make their home unhappy for all parties. But then, let all this be without carefulness, and with that graceful and pleasant ease which will be ensured by order, method, punctuality, and dispatch.

There are various kinds of slavery in the world, and many classes of victims of this cruel bondage. There is, among others, the domestic slave, whose tyrant is her husband, and the scene of whose bondage is her home. His parsimony is so niggardly that he will not allow her enough servants to do the work of the house, and therefore she must herself unite the character of a servant with that of a wife, a mistress, and a mother; his selfishness is so engrossing and exacting that his demands for his own personal ease and indulgence are incessant, and leave her no time for the consideration of her own comfort. And, withal, his temper is so bad that all her assiduities to please are unavailing to give him satisfaction, and to avert the sallies of his irritability, discontentedness, and complaint. When such a man declaims against the slavery of blacks, let him begin the work of emancipation at home, by raising the oppressed woman he holds in bondage there from the condition of a drudge into the station of a wife. How can she help being careful and troubled about many things?

But then there are cases, not a few, in which the slavery is self-imposed. The bondage comes from the wife herself, from which the husband would gladly release her, but she will not let him. Some are slaves to neatness, and make their fidgety anxiety about this matter a misery to themselves and all around them; others to fashion, and are always careful and troubled about elegance and refinement; others to domestic display, parties and amusements, and are always full of anxiety about making an appearance; others to frugality, and are ever vexing themselves to economize. In these ways women will torment themselves and fill their minds with unnecessary cares and self-imposed troubles. To all such we say, "Martha, Martha, thou art careful and troubled about many things."

With Martha's better qualities, her domestic cleverness and diligence, unite then the fervent piety of Mary. Will you be satisfied with that excellence which fits you only to fill up your place in a habitation from which you may be called away at any hour? Be as diligent, I entreat you, in business, as Martha was; but be also as fervent in spirit, serving the Lord, as Mary was. Seek to unite all the holy virtues of the eminent saint with all the household excellences of the good wife, mother, and mistress. Be all you should be in your own house, and all you ought to be in the house of God. What your husbands, when you have them, will desire and expect is to see you at your post of duty in the family; meet their desires and fulfill these expectations. You ought; you must! What Christ desires and expects is to see you sitting at His feet and hearing His words. Meet these desires and expectations also. You ought; you must! Study the following portrait of a good wife, a cultivated mind, and a sincere Christian, drawn by the pen of Jane Taylor:

And she whose nobler course is seen to shine
At once with human knowledge and divine;
Who mental culture, and domestic rites,
In close and graceful amity unites.
Striving to keep them in their proper place,
Not interfering with her heavenly race;
Whose constant aim it is, and fervent prayer,
On earthly ground to breathe celestial air.

Oh! you too-anxious-and-careful housewives, lessen your solicitude. "Be careful for nothing, but in everything by prayer and supplication let your requests be made known unto God." The spirit and influence of vital piety will soften the cares of domestic life, alleviate its sorrows where they exist, and inspire an alacrity which will make you go cheerfully about the business of the family, while well-regulated attention to domestic duties, so far from making you unfit for the exercise of devotion, will furnish the subjects of your prayers, and prompt the approaches of your soul to God.

And now, in conclusion, let me exhibit to you the description of true religion as set forth in the language of Christ to Martha. It is indispensable: "One thing is needful." Yes, the care of the soul is indeed needful. Mark the restriction and emphasis, "one thing"; and it deserves this emphasis. It is a matter of universal concern, necessary for all alike: for the rich and the poor, for the young and the old, for male and female. Some things are necessary for one person, but not for another; this is necessary for all alike. It is in itself a matter of the highest importance, of infinite moment, compared with which all the most valuable objects of time and sense are but as the small dust of the balance. It will promote every other lawful and valuable interest on earth. It has been pronounced indispensable by those who are most capable of giving an opinion. God has declared it to be needful by giving His only-begotten Son to die for it upon the cross. Jesus Christ has declared it to be needful by enduring the agonies of the cross to obtain it. Angels have pronounced it needful by their solicitude for the salvation of men. Apostles, martyrs, reformers, missionaries, and ministers have given their emphatic testimony to its necessity by their labors, prayers, tears, and blood. Your own judgment, in the cooler moments of reflection, declares its necessity; so does your conscience when you are listening to sermons or suffering affliction. So does your heart, when the world stands revealed before you in its vanity, emptiness, and deceit.

It is needful now in youth to be your guide; it will be no less so as your comforter amidst the vicissitudes of life, your prop under the infirmities of age, your living hope amidst the agonies of dying hours, your defense in the awful day of judgment, and your preparation for the felicities of heaven. Must not that which alone can do this be indispensable, and be, in fact, the one thing needful? Dwell, I beseech you, upon this representation. If religion were as miserable and as melancholy as your mistaken notions of it represent, yet it is needful. It is not something you may do well without, a superfluity rather than a necessary item. No, it is needful. Nothing else can be substituted for it or, in the smallest degree, compensate for the want of it. In the absence of this, you lack the most necessary thing in the universe; you must be poor amidst abounding wealth.

And it is the only thing that is indispensable. There are many other things which are desirable, valuable, pleasurable, and may be lawfully pursued; but they are not indispensable. This is absolutely so to secure solid happiness here and eternal felicity hereafter. O young people, call in your vagrant thoughts, your discursive inquiries, your divided and scattered activities, and concentrate them upon this one thing. Settle it with yourselves that, whatever else you may not have, you must have this. It is well at the outset of life to be informed, by an authority which is infallible, what is most necessary for the pilgrim upon earth. Let me entreat you to remember your own interest in it; it is necessary for you, whose eye shall read this page. Do therefore inquire, solemnly and seriously inquire, into your own conduct in reference to it. Say to yourselves, "Have I thought seriously about it? Have I seen the importance of it? Has it lain with a due and an abiding weight upon my mind? Has it brought me in penitence, prayer, and faith to Christ as my Savior? Am I acting in life as if I considered religion the one thing needful? Am I striving or willing to make everything subordinate to it, my interests, tastes, pleasures, and passions?"

And then how transcendently excellent is true religion. It is the good part which shall never be taken from us. Excellent it is in every view we can take of it, for it is the reception of the first truth and the enjoyment of the chief good. It makes us good, for it makes us like God; it brings good to us, for it leads us to enjoy God. It was the bliss of Adam in Paradise, and is the happiness of the spirits made perfect in heaven. It is the beginning of heaven upon earth, and will be the consummation of heaven when we have left earth. It is far better than knowledge, wealth, fame, or pleasure, for it will stand by us when all these things leave us.

Yes, it is the good part, which can never be taken from us. Neither force nor fraud can deprive us of this. It is above the vicissitudes of life, and unaffected by the changes of fortune. Oh, it is glorious to think of our possessing something that bids defiance to all the assaults of men or demons! Go where you will; it will go with you. It will be as inseparable from you (till you yourself shall abandon it) as your soul is from your body. How much then is included in that precious declaration,

"The good part which cannot be taken from you," which shall remain with you, in you, for you, when friends have left you, health has left you, fortune has left you—a portion all-sufficient, inalienable, and eternal.

Religion is a voluntary thing. "Mary hath *chosen* that good part which cannot be taken from her." It is not the external compulsion of authority, nor the internal compulsion of fear, but the free choice of love. It is not mere blind, unintelligent custom, or an unmeaning, heartless round of ceremonies, performed without motive or design. No, it is the freewill offering of the soul to God, who says, "Give Me thine heart," and to whom the soul replies, "I give myself to Thee." Where there is no choice, there is no religion. Hence the language of Moses to the children of Israel, "I call heaven and earth to record this day against you, that I have set before you life and death, blessing and cursing; therefore choose life, that both thou and thy seed may live."

So it is with you at this moment. There, on the one hand, is religion with all its duties and its privileges, its present enjoyments and its future eternal happiness; this is life, the life of the soul now, and eternal life hereafter. There on the other hand is ungodliness, with all its sins and sorrows here, and its unutterable and eternal miseries hereafter. There are you, so fearfully and wonderfully placed between the two. And I am (oh, solemn and momentous position!) urging you, by every motive that can appeal to your reason, your heart, your conscience, and even your self-love, to choose life. You must make your choice. You cannot evade it. One or the other must be yours. Were you to attempt neutrality, it would be impossible. Those who do not, by true religion, choose life are considered by God as choosing death.

By what witnesses are you surrounded in this crisis of your being! What spectators are looking upon this eventful scene of your history! Parents are waiting, watching, and praying for your decision on the side of eternal life. With silent, breathless earnestness they are agonizing for your soul and her destiny. Ministers are fixing their minds intently upon your situation, and in yearning anxiety for your welfare are saying, "Oh, that they may choose the good part which can never be taken from them!" Angels, with benevolence, hover over you, ready to commence their benevolent activities, and become as ministering spirits to your salvation. Devils, with malignity, are collecting to rejoice (with such delight as demons can experience) in your choice of death. Father, Son, and Holy Spirit are waiting, witnessing, and ready to assist your election. Yes, such value is attached to one human soul; with such importance is its decision for the choice or refusal of religion invested that heaven, earth, and hell are in some measure moved by the scene of its being called to choose between life and death, and thus three worlds are interested in the outcome. Make then your choice. Pause, ponder, and pray; it is a choice which eternity will confirm to your unutterable torment or to your ineffable felicity. Almighty God, direct their choice!

Chapter 11

To Young Mothers

"I call to remembrance the unfeigned faith that is in thee,
which dwelt first in thy grandmother Lois, and thy mother
Eunice." 2 Timothy 1:5

"The aged women likewise, that they may teach the young
women to be sober, to love their husbands, to love their
children, to be discreet, chaste, keepers at home, good, obedi-
ent to their own husbands, that the Word of
God be not blasphemed." Titus 2:3–5

What associations with all that is lovely are connected with
that blissful word, "mother"! To that sound the tenderest emotions of the human heart, whether in the bosom of the savage
or the sage, wake up. The beauty of that term is seen, and its
power felt, alike by the prince and the peasant, the rustic and
the philosopher. It is one of the words which infant lips are
first taught to lisp, and the charm of which the infant heart
first feels. It is a note to the music of which it is difficult to say
whose soul most responsively vibrates, that of the parent or the
child. Humanity, however semi-brutalized by oppression, ignorance, or even vice, has rarely been sunk so low as to have
the last spark of maternal love extinguished, or the last sensibility of this kind crushed out of it. This strength of woman's
love for her child must be turned to good account, and be directed in its exercises to the best and most useful purposes.

There is this difference (and it is a momentous one) between the maternal care of the lower tribes and that of woman: in brutes it goes no farther than provision and protection; training forms no part of it. The same power which endowed the parent bird or beast with the habits which belong to its nature endows also its offspring. The latter, without any pains bestowed on its education, or any solicitude cherished for its welfare, will learn the lessons of its existence by the intuitions of nature, and be capable of rising to its specific perfection, unaided by either parent or teacher. Not so the young of the human species; they also require provision and protection, but more than this they need instruction. And who must be their instructor? First of all, and chief of all, their mother.

But before we reason and descant upon the subject of a mother's duties, let us look at facts. It is universally admitted that scarcely any great man has appeared in our world who did not owe much, if not most, of the formation of his character to his mother's influence. In a very useful little volume by Dr. Jabez Burns, entitled *The Mothers of the Wise and Good,* there is a series of biographical memorials of eminent sons of pious and judicious mothers, amounting to about fifty, among whom are included Alfred the Great, Lord Bacon, Sir Isaac Newton, Dr. Samuel Johnson, Sir William Jones, and General Washington (among the illustrious of this world), with St. Augustine, President [Jonathan] Edwards, Dr. [Phillip] Doddridge, Dr. [Timothy] Dwight, Mr. [John] Newton, Mr. [Richard] Cecil, Leigh Richmond, and many others among the good—all of them blessed with pious or eminently judicious mothers to whom they owed their eminence in the church or in the world. From among these I select the following:

Richard Cecil, of London, when but a young man, had pursued a bold and determined career till sunk in sin, hardening himself in infidelity, and instilling the same principles into others; there seemed no prospect of any change in him. His excellent mother, however, had performed her part, and still remembered that it was good not only to pray always, but not to faint or desist upon any account. At last, one night he lay contemplating the case of his mother. "I see," said he to himself, "two unquestionable facts: first, my mother is greatly afflicted in circumstances, body, and mind, and yet I see that she cheerfully bears up under all by the support she derives from constantly repairing to her closet and her Bible; second, that I, who give unbounded permission to my appetites, and seek pleasure by every means, seldom or never find it. If there is such a secret in religion, why may I not find it as well as my mother?" He instantly rose and began to pray, but was soon dampened by recollecting that much of his mother's comfort seemed to arise from her faith in Christ. "Now," thought he, "this Christ I have ridiculed. He stands much in my way, and can form no part of my prayers." In utter confusion he lay down again; but over time, conviction of sin continuing, his difficulties were gradually removed and his objections answered. He now listened to those admonitions of his mother, which he had before affected to receive with pride and scorn (though they had fixed themselves in his heart like a barbed arrow), and tears would fall from his eyes, as he passed along the street, from the impression she had made on his mind, though the effects were concealed from her observation. He would, however, discourse with her, and hear her without outrage, which revived her hopes, especially as he also attended the public worship of God. Thus he made some progress, but felt no small difficulty in separating from his favorite connections. Light, however, broke into his mind, till at last he discovered that Jesus Christ, so far from "standing in the way," as he once thought, was indeed "the way, the truth, and the life," to all who come unto God by Him.

At a pastoral conference, held not long ago, at which about one hundred and twenty American clergymen, united in the bonds of a common faith, were assembled, each was invited to state the human instrumentality to which, under the divine blessing, he attributed a change of heart. How many of these, do you think, gave the honor of it to their mother? Of one hundred and twenty, over one hundred! Here, then, are facts, which are only selected from myriads of others, to prove a mother's power, and to demonstrate at the same time her responsibility. But how shall we account for this? What gives her this influence? What is the secret of her power? Several things:

First, there is, no doubt, the ordinance of God. He who created us, who formed the ties of social life, and who gave all the sweet influences and tender susceptibilities of our various relationships, appointed that a mother's power over the soul of her child should be this mighty. It is God's ordinance, and the woman who forgets or neglects this is disobedient to a divine institution. God has made the child to be peculiarly susceptible to this power over his nature.

Then comes a mother's love, which is stronger, at any rate more tender, than a father's. There is more of instinct, if not of reason, in her affection. She has had more to do with the physical being of her child, having borne him in her womb, fed him from her breast, and watched him in his cradle. All this naturally and necessarily generates a feeling which nothing else can produce. Now love is the great motivating power in and for human conduct. "I drew them," said God, "with cords of a man, with bands of love." Here is the true philosophy of both man's natural constitution and evangelical religion. Human nature is made to be moved and governed by love, to be drawn with the cords of affection rather than to be dragged with the chains of severity. Woman's heart is made to

love; and love is exerted more gently, sweetly, and constrain-
ingly upon her child by her than by the other sex. It makes her
more patient, more ingenious, and, therefore, more influential.
Her words are more soft, her smile more winning, and her
frown more commanding, because they are less terrific and repulsive. The little floweret she has to nurture opens its petals
more readily to the mild beams of her countenance. Hence, to
repeat an expression of Monod already quoted, "The greatest
moral power in the world is that which a mother exercises over
her young child." Nor is there much exaggeration in that other
expression, "She who rocks the cradle rules the world." The
truth of this expression will appear to be founded on the next
particular.

The mother has most to do with the child's character
while yet in the flexible state in which it receives its shape. The
earliest exercises of thought, emotion, will, and conscience are
all carried on under her eye. She has to do not only with the
body in its infancy, but with the soul in its childhood. Both
mind and heart are in her hands at that period when they take
their first start for good or for evil. The children learn to lisp
their first words and to form their first ideas under her teaching. They are almost always in her company, and are, insensibly to themselves and imperceptibly to her, receiving a right or
wrong bias from her. She is the first model of character they
witness; the first exhibitions of right and wrong in practice are
what they see in her. They are the constant observers of the
passions, graces, virtues, and faults which are shown in her
words, temper, and actions. She is therefore, unconsciously to
herself, educating them not only by designed teaching, but by
all she does or says in their presence.

Children are imitative creatures. During the minority of
reason, imitation is the regent of the soul, and they who are
least swayed by the former are most governed by the latter.

Speech is the effect of imitation, not intuition; and as children so early and so insensibly learn to repeat sounds, so may they also learn to copy actions and habits. This applies to the mother in a fuller sense than it does to the father, of course, just because she is more constantly with the children in the early stages of their existence. It is therefore of immense importance that everyone who sustains this relation should have a high idea of her own power. She should be deeply and duly impressed with the potency of her influence. This has peculiar force in reference to the mothers of the middle (and still more to those of the working) classes. In the upper circles of society, the task of educating the infant is usually devolved upon servants. The nursery is not much, it is to be feared, the resort of many titled or wealthy mothers. Aristocratic habits, in some cases, can scarcely be made to square with maternal ones. Happy are the women who are not lifted by rank or wealth out of the circle of those tender and constant assiduities which an infant family requires, and out of whose hand fashionable etiquette or luxurious indolence has not taken what the poet so pleasingly characterizes as the

> Delightful task to rear the tender thought,
> And teach the young idea how to shoot.

Mothers, then, should be thoroughly acquainted with the work that is allotted to them. I speak not of the physical training of the children (that is not my department), nor primarily of their intellectual culture, but of their social, moral, and religious education. A mother's object and duty is the formation of character. She has not merely to communicate knowledge, but habits. Her special department is to cultivate the heart and regulate the life. Her aim must be not only what her children are to know, but what they are to be and do. She is to look at them as the future members of society, and heads of families of their own, but above all as probationers for eternity. This, I repeat, must be taken up as the primary idea, the formation of character for both worlds. Governesses, tutors, masters, will most probably be employed in the future intellectual training, but a mother's part is from infancy to form habits.

Many have no other idea of education than the communication of knowledge. Much has been said in recent years on the distinction between instruction and education. They are by no means synonymous. The etymology of the two words is worth considering. To "instruct" is derived from a Latin word which signifies "to put on or in." To instruct is therefore simply to put knowledge into the mind. The word "educate" comes also from a Latin word, which signifies "to lead or draw forth." To educate, therefore, means to draw out the faculties of the soul, to call into exercise and invigorate its intellectual and moral powers. Both together constitute the duty of those who have to form the character. Ideas must be poured in, and the recipient must be taught what to do with them.

We hear much said about accomplishments, which may be well enough in their place and in their measure, but they are only subordinate to something higher and better. They are not the whole of education, nor even the best part of it. They are only the polish of the surface; there should be solid gold for the substance. The intellectual part of our nature may be considered as merely the casket, the moral part as the jewel. Yet many leave the diamond uncut and unpolished while they are careful to load its case with tinsel. A mother should look upon her offspring with this idea: "That child has to live in two worlds, and to act a part in both; and it is my duty to begin his education for both, and to lay in infancy the foundation of his character and happiness for time and eternity too. What ought to be my qualifications, and my diligence, for such a task?"

Ah, what? Deep thoughtfulness certainly on the momentous nature of your charge. It is an awful thing to be a parent, especially a mother, and to be responsible for the training of men and women, both for time and for eternity. A distinguished philosopher has said that "all the world is but the pupil and disciple of female influence." Every mother, therefore, has, so far as her individual influence goes, the world for her scholar. O woman! your child's welfare for all time, and all eternity too, depends much upon your conduct towards him during the period when he is under your influence, in the first years of his being. To you is committed the care of the infant's body, the healthfulness, vigor, and comfort of which for all his future existence upon earth depend much upon you. What would be your feelings of poignant remorse if, by any neglect of yours, whether by a fall or an accident, the result of your carelessness, the poor babe was injured in his spine or distorted in his limbs! Oh! to see that young cripple injured for life in bodily comfort, ever presenting to you the sad reminder of your guilty neglect! Yet what is this to the sadder spectacle of a deformed and crippled soul, a character distorted into crooked and frightful shapes, and to have the tormenting reflection that this was the result of your neglect! The poor child in the former case may have his compensation in all the sweet influences of religious submission and consolation; and the distressed mother may assuage the anguish of remorse by the thought that her neglect may have been among the "all things" that worked together for good to her son. But where in the latter case is consolation to be obtained, or who can wonder that such a Rachel mourning over her lost child, lost through her neglect, refuses to be comforted?

Qualify yourself for maternal duties above all things by sincere and eminent piety. A mother should never forget that those little engaging creatures which sport about the room so gaily and so innocently, with all the unconsciousness of childhood, are young immortals, beings destined to eternity, creatures placed on earth on probation for heaven—and that it will depend upon her whether the everlasting ages shall be spent by them in torment or in bliss. This is an all but overwhelming idea. One should almost think that solicitude about this matter would be so overpowering as to extinguish parental delight. But a mother cannot look at the babe that is feeding at her breast, and smiling sweetly in her face as if it meant the thanks it had not yet learned to speak—or watch his slumbers in his cradle, breathing as softly as if he lived without breathing at all—and at the same time feel her soul shiver and shudder in the dark shadow cast over her spirit by such a thought as "Oh, should you live to be a profligate in this world, and a fiend in the next!"

Instead of a reflection so harrowing to every maternal feeling, she exults in the hope that the dear babe will be a holy, useful, happy Christian on earth, and then a glorified immortal in heaven. Such reflections ought to be, at some times, in the mind of every parent. All should realize the sublime idea that their houses are the seminaries for eternity, their children the scholars, themselves the teachers, and evangelical religion the lesson. Yes, with every infant born into the family comes the injunction from God, "Take this child and bring it up for Me." It is one of God's own children by creation, sent to be trained up in the way he should go, that is, in the nurture and admonition of the Lord. Those parents who neglect the religious education of their children, whatever else they may impart, are more guilty than Herod. He slew the children of others; they slay their own. He slew only the body, they the soul. He slew them by hired assassins; they slay them themselves. We shudder at the cruelties of those who sacrificed their babes to

Moloch; but how much more dreadful an immolation do they practice who offer up their sons and daughters to Satan by neglecting their religious education, and leaving them to grow up in ignorance of God and their eternal destiny.

But can anyone, will anyone, teach, or teach effectually, that religion which she does not feel and practice herself? Therefore, I say, a mother's heart must be deeply imbued with piety if she would teach it to her children. Without this, can she have the will to teach, the heart to pray, or the right to hope? Mothers, can you conceive of a higher, nobler elevation to which, in your maternal relation, you can rise than when, to the opening mind of your wondering child, you give the first idea of God? Or than when you direct him to that divine Babe who was born at Bethlehem; who was subject to His parents; who grew up to be the Savior; who said, "Suffer the little children to come unto Me," took them in His arms and blessed them, and then died for their salvation upon the cross? Or than when you talk to them of heaven, the dwelling place of God and of His angels? Oh, to see the first look of holy inquisitiveness, and the first tear of infant piety, start in the eye; to hear the first question of concern, or the first breathing of prayer from infant lips! How has many a woman's heart amidst such scenes swelled with delight till, in an ecstasy of feeling, she sank upon her knees and breathed a mother's prayer over the child of her heart, while he looked wonderingly up and felt a mysterious power come over him which he could neither fully express nor understand!

Your religion, if it is genuine, will teach you at once the greatness of the work, and your own insufficiency to perform it aright in your own strength. Your business is to train mortals for earth, and immortal beings for God, heaven, and eternity. Even an apostle, in view of such an object, exclaimed, "And who is sufficient for these things?" Your work, as to its design, is the same as his; and you, like him, have to contend with the depravity of human nature, and all the difficulties arising from your own weakness and sinfulness. A mistake in either your sentiments, your feelings, or your example may be fatal to your children's eternal welfare. Cultivate, then, a trembling consciousness of your own insufficiency, and cast yourselves by believing, constant, and fervent prayer upon God. Be, in an eminent sense, praying mothers. Distrust yourselves, and, by believing prayer, secure the aid of Omnipotence.

Do not forget what I have already said, that affection is the golden key fitted by God to the wards of the lock in every human heart, to the application of which the bolts that nothing else could move will fly back and open with ease. Severity is out of place in anyone, but most of all in women. But beware of allowing affection to degenerate into a fond and foolish indulgence. A judicious love is as remote from this on the one hand as it is from moroseness and cruelty on the other. For if severity has slain its thousands, injudicious and pampering indulgence has slain its ten thousands. Fathers are apt to err in the former extreme, mothers in the latter. And it not infrequently happens that these extremes are played off against each other. The father, afraid that the mother will spoil the child by indulgence, adopts a harsh treatment to counteract the mischief of his wife's excessive fondness, while the wife compensates the child for the severity of the husband by her own excessive attention to his gratification. Thus, like the sharp frost by night and the hot sun by day, operating in spring to the destruction of the blossom on which their antagonistic influences are made to bear, the opposing treatment of the parents ruins the hapless child who is the subject of it.

Still, while I enjoin affection, it must not be allowed to impair authority. A parent must not be a tyrant, but neither must he be a slave to his children. It is a painful and, to the parents, a disgraceful spectacle to see a family like a state where rebellion reigns rampant, the father deposed, the scepter broken, and the insurgent children possessed of sovereign rule. And a mother as well as a father must be obeyed, and it is her own fault if she is not. A persevering system of government, where the reins are held tightly in the hand of love, will be sure to produce submission at last. But it must be a mixture of kindness, wisdom, and authority. Submission must be felt by a child to be a duty yielded to authority, and not merely a compliance won by affection. Authority must not stiffen into severity, nor love degenerate into coaxing. Commands should be obeyed not only because it is pleasant to obey them, but because it is right that they should be obeyed.

A judicious mother will exercise much discrimination, and will adapt her treatment to the disposition of her children. There are as many varieties of temperament in some families as there are children. No two are precisely alike in their minds and character any more than in their persons. One is forward and obtrusive, and should be checked and rebuked; another is timid and retiring, and needs to be encouraged and emboldened. One is more easily wrought upon by appeals to her hope, another by reasonings addressed to her fear. One is too close and reserved, and needs to have frankness and communicativeness encouraged; another is too open and ingenuous, and should be taught caution and self-restraint. Every child should be a separate study. Quackery should be banished from education as well as from medicine. One treatment will no more suit all minds than one medicine or kind of food all bodies. A woman who does not know the peculiar dispositions of all her children, and does not adapt her treatment to them, is a very indifferent mother.

The woman who would fulfill the duties of her relationship must surrender herself to her mission, and be content to make some sacrifices and endure some privations. Who can witness the patient submission of the mother bird to her solitude and self-denial during the term of incubation without admiration at the quiet and willing surrender which instinct teaches her to make of her usual liberty and enjoyments? A woman must be willing, for the sake of her children, to do, under the influence of reason and religion, what the bird does from the unintelligent impulses of nature. Her children are a charge for which she must forego some of the enjoyments of social life, and even some of the social pleasures of religion. She who would have a maternal power over her children must give her company to them. It is not for her to be ever craving after parties, or to feel it a hardship that she is denied them. The secret of her beneficent influence lies in a life of retirement. Hence the exhortation of the apostle in the text to the matrons of his time, "Teach the young women to be . . . keepers at home." I would not have a mother incarcerated in her own house, so as never to go abroad or enter into company. She who is devoted to her family needs occasional relaxation amidst the pleasures of society, and especially the exhilarating engagements of public worship. There are some mothers who are such absolute slaves to their children that they scarcely ever stir from home, even to the house of God. This is an error in one extreme, which might be avoided by method and dispatch. But those run into an opposite extreme who will not, even for the benefit of their children, give up a social party or a public meeting. The woman who is not prepared to make many sacrifices of this kind, for the sake of her children, her home, and her husband, should never think of entering into wedded life.

Be ingenious, inventive, and studious as to the best method of gaining the attention and informing the minds of your children while young. There are too many who imagine that education, and especially religious education, consists in just hearing a chapter read, a catechism taught, or a hymn repeated, and that when this is done all is done. The memory is the only faculty they cultivate; the intellect, affections, and conscience are wholly neglected. A Christian mother should set herself to invent the best mode of gaining attention and keeping it; and she should never weary it, or keep it so long that it wanders off itself. How ingenious was the device of Doddridge's mother in teaching him Scripture history by the Dutch tiles of the chimney place. The illustrated works which in this fertile age are perpetually issuing from the press afford advantages for conveying both secular and sacred knowledge, of which bygone times knew nothing.

Be familiar in your religious instruction. The freedom of incidental conversation, rather than the formality of set and stated lessons; the introduction of religious topics in the common intercourse of life, rather than the grave and forbidding annunciation of a change from secular to sacred subjects; and the habit of referring all things to God, and comparing the truths and maxims of the Bible with the events of every hour, rather than merely lighting a Sabbath lamp and forcing all things out of their channel when the season of devotion returns—these are the means of opening the avenues to the youthful heart, and rendering religion, with its great Author, the object not of aversion or terror, nor only of cold and distant homage, but of mingled reverence and love. "These words, which I command thee this day, shall be in thine heart; and thou shalt teach them diligently unto thy children, and shalt talk of them when thou sittest in thine house, and when thou walkest by the way, and when thou liest down, and when thou risest up."

Mothers, invested as you are with such an influence, often dwell upon your responsibility. With such a power conferred

upon you by God, you are responsible to your children themselves. Every time their infant or adult voices repeat that word,
"My mother," so sweet, so musical to your heart, they urge
their claims upon your best and most devoted attention. As it
sounds in your ears, it should awaken the deepest emotions of
your soul and the most faithful admonitions of your conscience. You are responsible to your husbands. They entrust
the education of their children to you. They seem to say, "We
will work for their support, and leave the early education of
their minds to you. We will hereafter share all the obligations
of instruction and the care of their minds and characters with
you, but at present, while they are so young, we devolve this
duty upon you." You are responsible to the church of God, for
family education is, or ought to be, in the families of the godly,
the chief means of conversion. It is a fatal error for Christian
parents to look to the ministers of religion for the conversion
of their children. And, alas! it is the error of the day. The
pulpit is looked to for those benefits which should flow from
the parents' chair. Our churches have weighty and righteous
claims upon parents, and especially upon mothers.

Nor does your responsibility stop here, for society at large
looks to you for that beneficial influence which you are capable
of exerting. I repeat here a well-known anecdote. Napoleon
once asked Madame Campan what the French nation most
needed in order that her youth might be properly educated.
Her reply was compressed in one word: "Mothers!" And it was
a wise reply. Not the French nation only, but the world needs
them: Christian, intelligent, well-trained, devoted women to
whom the destinies of the rising generation may be safely entrusted. The woman at whose domestic hearth, and by whose
judicious, maternal love, a family of industrious, godly, and
public-spirited sons, or of modest, kind-hearted, prudent, and
pious daughters, is trained for future life is an ornament of her

country, a benefactress to her species, and a blessing to posterity. I again and emphatically say, mothers, understand, feel, and remember your responsibility.

But hitherto, it may be said, the chapter does not answer to its title as intended for and addressed to young mothers. I will therefore now give it a special bearing upon their case. It has been my object, first of all, to set forth the subject of maternal duty and responsibility in its general aspect, apart from its relation to those to whom it is new, that they may see it in its widest and most comprehensive bearing before they are reminded of its special bearing on their case. This, I am aware, will give the appearance of a repetition in the second part of this chapter of some things that were advanced in the first. But such repetitions are sometimes beneficial. In addition, therefore, to what has been said on maternal duties in general, I shall now submit some other matters for your special consideration.

Too many, it is to be feared, enter upon this momentous business without consideration, and, as might be expected, equally without preparation or qualification. It is indeed a pitiable sight to look into the state of some families, and behold the hapless condition of the poor children who have the misfortune to be on the hands of a weak, foolish, and incompetent woman. Perhaps the cause may be traced one step further back, and it may be found that they are incompetent because their mothers were so before them. Thus the mischief perpetuates itself from generation to generation.

In all things it is of importance to begin well. The beginning usually determines the progress and the close. Errors, both in theory and practice, however long and pertinaciously persisted in, may, by intelligence, determination, and the blessing of God, be corrected. Reformation would otherwise be hopeless. But how much better and easier is it to avoid faults than to amend them! Many mothers have seen their mistakes when it was too late to correct them. Their children have grown up under the influence of a bad system of domestic government and maternal guidance, and have acquired a fixedness of bad habit which no subsequent wisdom, firmness, severity, or affection could correct; and the parents have had to pour out bitter but unavailing regrets that they had not begun life with those views of their duties with which they were closing it.

If a mother begins well, she is likely to continue well, and the same is true if she begins ill. Her conduct towards her first child is likely, of course, to determine her conduct with respect to all the following ones. How momentous is it, then, at this stage of her domestic history, to weigh well, and solemnly, and prayerfully, her responsible situation! Indeed it is quite clear that this subject ought not to be driven off by any wife till she becomes a mother. The very prospect ought to lead to a due preparation for the expected new duties; for these commence with the earliest anticipations of sustaining the maternal character. It becomes us to prepare ourselves for any situation into which we have a confident expectation of soon entering. Forethought is given to man for the purpose of meeting with propriety the situation and duties to which we are looking forward. The woman who never studies maternal responsibilities and duties till she is called actually to sustain them is not very likely to do herself much credit in that very important relationship.

Instinct will teach a parent bird, beast, fish, or insect all that is necessary for the well-being of its young; but it is not so with human parents. For study, reflection, forethought, and determination are indispensable for them. Unhappily, a young wife, in prospect of giving birth to a child, is in some cases so bowed down with an unnecessary solicitude about her own safety, and in others so absorbed with the preparations which are made for the physical well-being and the elegant habiliments of her promised baby, as to forget to prepare herself for those more important duties which devolve upon her in relation to the mind, heart, and conscience of the child.

A mother who wishes to fulfill her duties to her children should take special pains to educate herself for those momentous functions. She should read, to store her mind with knowledge; she should reflect, observe, and gain useful information from every quarter. Her principles should be fixed, her plans laid, and her purposes formed. She must cultivate all the habits and tempers which will fit her to teach and to govern. She must seek to acquire thoughtfulness, careful vigilance, quick observation, and discretion in various forms. Habits of activity, dispatch, order, and regularity are indispensable for her; so is the exercise of all the good and benevolent feelings. She must unite gentleness with firmness, and attain patience and the entire command of her temper. It is of immense importance also that she should have a correct knowledge of human nature, and of the way of dealing with the human heart. And, above all things, let her remember that piety is the vivifying spirit of all excellence, and example the most powerful means to enforce it. She should never let the recollection be absent from her mind that children have both eyes and ears for attention to a mother's conduct. Not content with preparing herself for her important functions beforehand, she should carry on the education of herself simultaneously with that of her children. There are few situations which more imperatively require preparation, and yet few that receive less.

Again, we often see in a mother such a solicitude about the health and comfort of her babe; such an engrossing attention to all matters respecting its physical well-being, united with such an exuberant delight in the child, as a child; such a mother's pride and joyousness in her boy, that her mind is diverted by these circumstances from all the serious thoughts and solemn reflections which ought to be awakened by the consideration that a rational, immortal, and fallen creature is committed to her charge, to be trained for both worlds. Thus her attention is absorbed month after month, while all this while her infant's faculties are developing. Its judgment, will, affection, and conscience, at least in their capabilities, are opening, but neglected, and its natural bias to evil grows unnoticed and unchecked. The very time when judicious care over the formation of character could be most advantageously exerted is suffered to pass by unimproved; passion is allowed to strengthen unrestrained, and self-will to attain a resoluteness which stiffens into obstinacy. And the careless mother, who at some time or other intended to begin a system of moral training (always saying there was time enough yet), when she does commence, wonders that the subject of her discipline is so difficult to manage. And then she finds that she has so neglected to prepare herself for her duties that she knows not how to set about them, or what in fact she has to do. An ill-managed child continues growing not only in stature and in strength, but in his wayward disposition and obstinate self-will; the poor mother has no control; and as for the father, he is too much taken up with the cares of business to aid his imperfect helpmate; thus the scene is exhibited, described by Solomon, of "a child left to himself." Another and another are added to this first-born, and are misgoverned, or not governed at all; and there are soon seen, in rude, disobedient, and ill-natured children, perhaps at length profligate sons and vain, silly daughters, the sad fruits of the want of maternal wisdom!

Young mothers, begin well, then. Manage that first child with judgment; put forth all your skill, all your affection, all your diligence and devotedness, in training him; and, the habit thus acquired, all will be comparatively easy with the others that follow. It is the novelty of that first child, the new affections which it calls forth, and the new interest it creates that are likely (if you are not careful) to throw you off your guard, and divert your attention from the great work of moral training. The first child makes the good or injudicious mother.

And as it is of immense consequence to begin your maternal excellence with the first child, so it is of equal importance to him, and to every one who is added, as I have already said, to begin early. Education, as has been observed, does not begin with the alphabet. It begins with a mother's look; with a father's nod of approbation or sign of reproof; with a sister's gentle pressure of the hand, or a brother's noble act of forbearance; with a handful of flowers in green dells, or on hills or in daisy meadows; with creeping ants, and almost imperceptible emmets; with humming bees, and glass beehives; with pleasant walks in shady lanes; and with thoughts directed in affectionate and kindly tones and words to nature, to beauty, to the practice of benevolence, and to the remembrance of Him who is the Fountain of all good.

Yes, and before all this can be done, before lessons of instruction can be taught to the child from flowers, insects, and birds, the moral training can commence: a mother's look, her nod of approbation or sign of reproof.

One of the greatest mistakes into which mothers fall is that of supposing that the first two or three years of a child's life are unimportant as regards his training. The truth is that in the formation of character they are the most important of all. It has been truly said that from the impressions made, the principles implanted, and the habits formed, during these years, the child's character for time and eternity may take its complexion. It is perfectly clear that a child, before he can speak, is susceptible of moral training. The conscience, or moral sense, may, by a judicious woman, be developed soon after, if not before, the child has spent his first birthday. So early may he be made to distinguish between what his mother considers right and wrong, between what will please and what will displease her. Why, the brute creatures will do this; and if they can be taught this, may not very young children? It is admitted that there is more of reason in many brutes than in very young children. Still, even very young animals may be trained to know what they may and may not do; and so may very young children. I often hear mothers say that their children are too young to be taught obedience. The mother who acts upon the maxim that children may have their own way for a certain number of years, or even months, will find to her cost that that lesson at least will not speedily be forgotten. Moral training may and should precede that which is intellectual. The cultivation of the affections and conscience should be the commencement and foundation of education, and will facilitate every succeeding effort whether of the child or of those who train or teach him.

There is in some women a timidity and a distrust of their own capacity, which paralyze or prevent the endeavors which they could make, if they would only believe in their own power. Every woman of good, plain understanding can do more than she imagines for the formation of her children's character. What she is deficient in, let her supply by reading; and no mother, however qualified, should neglect this. Everyone may learn something from others. Fearful, timid, and anxious mothers, be not afraid! Prayer will bring God's help and God's blessing.

Injudicious indulgence is the most common (as it is the most injurious) danger into which a young mother can fall. Be kind; you ought to be. An unloving, hard-hearted mother is a double libel upon her sex and her relationship. Love is her power, her instrument, and her talisman. She can do nothing, worse than nothing, without it. But then her love must be like that of the divine Parent who said, "As many as I love, I rebuke and chasten." Can you say "No" to a child when, with winning smiles, beseeching voice, or weeping eyes, he asks for what it is not good that he should receive? Can you take from him that which is likely to be injurious to him, but which it will give him pain to surrender? Can you correct him for his faults when your heart rises up in opposition to your judgment? Can you put him off from your arms, at a proper season for so doing, when he clings to your neck and cries to remain? Can you exact obedience in what is to him a difficult, but to you a necessary, command? Can you stand out against his tears, resolute in purpose, unyielding in demand, and first conquer your own heart, so stoutly resisting you, in order to conquer his? Or do you allow yourself to be subdued to put an end to the contest, and, by soothing his sufferings, foster the temper which ought to be eradicated at any pains and any cost? She who cannot answer all this in the affirmative is not fit to be a mother. There must be discipline in a family. A parent must be obeyed. Give this up, and you train your children for evil and not for good. Here again I say, begin early. Put on the soft and easy yoke quickly. The horse is broken in while still a colt. Wild beasts are tamed while yet they are young. Both the human species and animals soon grow beyond the power of discipline.

A young mother is apt to devolve too much of the care and early training of her children upon servants. Much of what may be called the drudgery of managing children must of necessity be committed to them; but a wise woman will have her children with her as much as possible. Next to mothers, nursemaids are the most influential class of the community, as regards young children. They and nursery governesses are, to a great extent, the educators of the community. They, when carrying the children in their arms, leading them out for air and exercise, attending upon them in the nursery, dressing or undressing them, or however they may be employed for them, are forming them in good or evil habits. If multitudes are spoiled by mothers, multitudes more are spoiled by servants; and some of the latter have undone all the good the former have done. Of what importance is it then that you should be careful as to the persons you admit to your families in this capacity, to whom you entrust your children's minds, hearts, and consciences; for depend upon it, they have the care of them as well as of their bodies!

Need I say to you that all you do in training up your children in the way they should go will bear directly or indirectly on their eternal welfare? If I seem to advert to this subject with a frequency that looks like tautology, let its tremendous importance, and its too frequent and too great neglect, be my apology. You will not overlook, as I have already remarked, the intellectual training of your children's minds, but their moral and religious education will, I hope, be with you the chief object of solicitude. Viewing your children as immortal beings destined to eternity, and capable of the enjoyments of heaven, you will labor even from infancy to imbue their minds with religious ideas. It is immortality which rescues from littleness and insignificance all that it appertains to, and hence arises in no inconsiderable degree the exalted honor of a mother.

She has given birth, by the sovereign ordination of the Almighty, not to a being of a mere momentary existence, whose life will perish like that of the beast of the field, but to an immortal! Her sucking infant, feeble and helpless as it may appear, possesses within its bosom a rational soul, an intellectual power, a spirit which all-devouring time cannot destroy, which can never die, but which will outlive the splendors of the glorious sun, and the burning brilliance of all the material part of heaven. Throughout the infinite ages of eternity, when all these shall have served their purpose and answered the beneficent end of their creation, and shall have been blotted out from their position in the immense regions of space, the soul of the humblest child will shine and improve before the eternal throne, being filled with holy delight and divine love, and ever active in the praises of its blessed Creator. Mothers, such is your dignity, such your exalted honor. Feel and value your rich distinction in being called to educate the sons and daughters of the Lord God Almighty, and to prepare the holy family who are to dwell in those many mansions of His Father's house which the Lord Jesus is gone to prepare. Give yourselves up to this glorious work. But be judicious in all you do, lest you produce prejudice against true religion, instead of prepossession in its favor. Let your warmest affection, your greatest cheerfulness, your most engaging smiles be put on when you teach religion to your children. Approach as nearly as possible to a seraphic form. Represent religion in all its beauty, loveliness, sanctity, and ineffable sweetness. Let them see it in your character as well as hear it from your lips.

Especially be careful not to enforce as a task what should be proposed as an object of hope and a source of delight. Let them see in you that piety, if in one respect it is a strait and narrow path, is in another a way of pleasantness and a path of peace. Do not inflict upon them as a punishment for offenses learning Scripture or hymns, and thus convert religion, which is the foretaste of heaven, into a penance which shall be to them like being tormented before their time. Especially do not make the Sabbath a day of gloom instead of gladness by such an accumulation of services as shall cause the day of rest to be physically more irksome than the common labors of the week.

And can it be necessary to admonish you again to pray for

and with your children? How have a mother's prayers been blessed to her children! John Randolph, a distinguished American statesman, who had been much exposed to the seductions of infidelity in the society into which he had been thrown by his position, thus accounted, to a gentleman with whom he was conversing, for his preservation: "I believe I should have been swept away by the flood of French infidelity if it had not been for one thing, the remembrance of the time when my sainted mother used to make me kneel by her side, taking my little hands folded in hers, and caused me to repeat the Lord's Prayer."

On the east of Long Island, in one of the most secluded spots in America, more than thirty years ago, a mother, whose rare intellectual and moral endowments were known to but few, made this simple record: "This morning I rose very early to pray for my children, and especially that my sons may be ministers and missionaries of Jesus Christ." A number of years later, a friend who was present described that mother's dying hour: "Owing to extreme weakness, her mind wandered, and her conversation was broken; but as she entered the valley of the shadow of death, her soul lighted up and gilded its darkness. She made a feeling and most appropriate prayer, and told her husband that her views and anticipations had been such that she could scarcely sustain them; that if they had been any more increased, she would have been overwhelmed; that her Savior had blessed her with constant peace, and that through all her sickness she had never prayed for life. She dedicated her five sons to God as ministers and missionaries of Jesus Christ, and said that her greatest desire was that her children might be trained up for God. She spoke with joy of the advancement of the kingdom of Christ, and of the glorious day now being ushered in. She attempted to speak to her children, but was so exhausted, and their cries and sobs were such, that she could say but little. Her husband then made a prayer, in which he gave her back to God, and dedicated all they held in common to Him. She then fell into a sweet sleep, from which she awoke in heaven."

The prayers of this mother have been answered. All her eight children have been "trained up for God." Her five sons are all ministers and missionaries of Jesus Christ, and the late Rev. George Beecher is the first of her offspring whom she has welcomed to heaven. One of her daughters has obtained worldwide fame by her pathetic story against slavery [*Uncle Tom's Cabin*]. In that lady and her work, as well as in her able and learned brothers, we see the fruit of a mother's prayers.

Take with you the following maxims, as summing up all that has been said:

Though a child's character is not entirely created by the circumstances in which he is placed, especially as regards his mother, it is powerfully influenced by them.

Education is designed to form character, and not merely to communicate instruction. A king of Sparta, when asked what it was in which youth ought principally to be instructed, replied, "In that which they have most need to practice when men."

Obedience is the first thing a mother has to teach; first both in order and time, and the foundation of all the rest. Obedience must first be taught as a habit, and soon after inculcated as a duty.

A mother should assiduously cultivate the spirit of curiosity in a child, and, instead of always calling him to learn, should prompt his desires to be informed.

Young children must be sometimes contradicted in their wishes, but never merely to teach them submission by taking from them something they are pleased with.

Habits of employment and a love of useful employment

should be taught to children; they are not so mischievous for the mere love of mischief as they are supposed to be. If they destroy articles, it is sometimes for the purpose of investigation, and more often still for want of proper employment, which ought to be furnished to them. In very early childhood a love of industry and honest independence may be instilled into a child by teaching him that it is honorable to be usefully employed. One little child may feel the pleasure and practice the duty of benevolence by doing something for the comfort of a tender babe still more helpless than itself.

It is of the first importance for a mother to establish in the mind of her child an entire confidence in herself—in her wisdom, kindness, and truth—as well as a sense of her irresistible authority.

Truth, sincerity, candor, and ingenuousness are cardinal virtues in children. Simplicity is the beauty of a child's character; and he should be taught from the beginning to act upon principle, and not for the sake of being well thought of or rewarded.

Domestic affections should be most assiduously cultivated. When the second baby is born, the first child should, if old enough to understand the matter, be congratulated, and taught to regard it as an acquisition by which his happiness is to be increased, and in which he is to take an interest in conjunction with his parents. The child who is taught affectionate obedience to his parents, and justice and kindness towards his little equals around the domestic hearth, is being trained to fill with propriety the stations and relations of future life.

The babe grows into the child, the child into the youth, the youth into the man, and the man into the immortal. And let it ever be remembered, and acted upon, that that immortal will be an heir of glory or a child of perdition.

Discipline in a family is what the public administration of

justice is to a state. Where it is wanting, there may be very good laws, but they will remain a dead letter, and the reign of crime and confusion will be the certain consequence.

Religion should not be regarded as one science among many, the inculcation of which is a part of good education, but it must be the vital principle diffusing itself through all instruction, all rules, all authority, all discipline, and all example. At what age is it proper, it may be asked, to begin teaching children religion? Their father and mother are, if true and consistent Christians, religion embodied; and as soon as they begin to know their parents they begin to know something about religion. A very young child is quite aware that his parents speak to One whom they do not see, and inquiring thoughts are awakened in his mind before he can express them in words.

And now, to sum up all, consider a mother's charge, an immortal creature; a mother's duty, to train him up for God, heaven and eternity; a mother's dignity, to educate the family of the Almighty Creator of the universe; a mother's difficulty, to raise a fallen, sinful creature to holiness and virtue; a mother's encouragement, the promise of divine grace to assist her in her momentous duties; a mother's relief, to bear the burden of her cares to God in prayer; and a mother's hope, to meet her child in glory everlasting, and spend eternal ages of delight with him before the throne of God and the Lamb.

But are mothers only to engage in this work of educating their children for God? No. Fathers, I speak to you, for the Bible speaks to you. "Ye fathers, provoke not your children to wrath; but bring them up in the nurture and admonition of the Lord." I have addressed this chapter to your wives, because on them first devolves the duty of training the infant mind, and preparing the children for your hands. Not that they will ever, or should ever, give up their assiduities or withdraw their influence. A mother's power is perhaps as great when judiciously exerted over the adult as over the infant child. But you, when the children are growing up, must join your solicitude and labors with hers. They are your children as well as hers. God will require their souls at your hands as well as hers. Are you exercising your authority, giving your instructions, pouring out your prayers, and affording your example, all for the salvation of your children? Is it your wish, your ambition, your endeavor, and your supplication that they may be religious men or only rich ones? Are you pouring your influence into the same channel as your holy wife? Are you helping or hindering her in her pious solicitude for the spiritual and eternal welfare of your joint offspring? Happy, happy couple, where there is a sympathy of feeling and similarity of sentiment in the most momentous concern that can engage the attention of man, of angels, or of God—religion; where the husband and the wife are of one mind and one heart, not only in reference to themselves, but in regard also to their children, and where both are engaged in training them up for everlasting glory! I can compare such a couple, in their benevolent efforts for their children's welfare, only to the two angels who were sent down from heaven to rescue Lot, and who, with holy and benevolent violence, took him by the hand to pluck him from the burning city, and conducted him to the place of safety prepared by the mercy of Almighty God.

After this chapter was composed and partly printed, I received the following letter:

Dear Mr. James,

In your next sermon to young women, will you kindly give some advice to commonplace mothers who, not gifted with extraordinary affection or extraordinary patience, are apt to be sadly worried with the incessant

and multifarious claims of a large family, especially
where a limited income imposes unremitting toil to ar-
range for ordinary domestic comfort, and the numerous
inmates of a small house almost preclude the refreshment of solitary closet intercourse with that Heavenly
Father who rewardeth openly. As a class, we would
gladly be instructed how to avoid, or at least to sur-
mount, the impatience and irritation so frequently en-
gendered by the perplexities of the nursery and the
school room; the hasty speech, the angry action, which
must be not only a hindrance to maternal influence, but
perhaps even a hindrance to the efficacy of a mother's
prayers.

Excuse the liberty I take in thus writing to you, and
with many thanks for your past valuable hints,

Believe me, dear Sir,
Yours very respectfully,
A Commonplace Mother

This letter claims and awakens my tenderest sympathy for
the class of mothers to whom it refers: women without the
advantages of wealth, the accommodations of a nursery, and
the help of servants to lighten the load of maternal cares, and
to assist in the performance of maternal duties; women who
must always be in the midst of the perpetually recurring trials
of temper to which, in such circumstances, a numerous family
of young children exposes them; women who may fancy
themselves, as to intellectual and other qualifications, only
"commonplace mothers." Let such women not despond, as if
they were but slenderly fitted for their duties. The writer of
this letter gives full evidence that she is not disqualified for a
mother's functions, so far as mental ability is concerned; but
perhaps she, and others in her situation, may have something
yet to learn and acquire as to temper and manner. It is evident

that she is in danger in these respects. The waywardness and freaks of unamiable disposition in her children produce petulance and irritability, and lead, perhaps, too often on her part to unseemly anger. A scold, slap, or shake sometimes takes the place of mild but firm expostulation and calm correction. To her, and to all in her situation, I say, what you need, and what you must put forth all your constant and determined effort and wrestling supplication with God, to obtain is the complete subjugation of your temper. You must bring this under control. You must acquire forbearance, patience, and calm serenity. It will cost you much trouble and much prayer to attain it, but God's grace will be sufficient for you.

I do not, of course, counsel you to contract that spirit of apathetic, easy indifference which lets children take their own course, and for the sake of a little ease throws up the reins of discipline. Still a mother must often have eyes and not see, ears and not hear. A fussing, fidgety notice of every little thing that goes wrong in the temper of all the children will keep her in perpetual misery. To all then who are in the situation of the "commonplace mother," I say again and again, with all possible emphasis, subdue your irritability, and acquire a calm, patient, forbearing, loving, and serene mind. God will help you if you seek it. You must not think such a frame of mind unattainable, nor allow your provocations and temptations to be an apology for your little sallies of bad temper.

The misfortune, perhaps, in the case of such mothers is that they did not begin well. The first child was not well-managed. Bad habits crept on, and now, with the family increased, it is difficult to break them. I have known even large, very large families where, though there were few domestic accommodations, by good temper, patience, and kindness mixed with firmness on the part of the mother, aided by a wise, kind, firm father, the children were all well-managed, and the parents happy.

As regards what is said about the opportunity for prayer, I can hardly admit a crowded house to be an excuse for the neglect of this. Every mother has at her command her own chamber to which, as to a little sanctuary, when the infant voices are hushed in sleep, she can repair and pour out her heart to God for her children, and perhaps breathe over some of them, slumbering on the bed at which she kneels, a mother's prayers. Besides, how much of prayer, silent and ejaculatory, yet sincere, fervent, and believing, may be presented to God without the formalities of devotion or the retirement of the closet!

I again say, let no mother despair because she does not possess high intellectual qualifications. The more of these she has, of course, the better, but a temper under control; a patient, loving, forbearing disposition; mild firmness; a gentle but constant maintenance of parental authority; and a judicious administration of rewards and correction will enable any woman to fill her place with efficiency, though she may think herself to be a "commonplace mother."

Chapter 12

*The Beautiful Picture of a Good Wife
in the Book of Proverbs*

"Who can find a virtuous woman? For her price is
far above rubies." Proverbs 31:10

If anyone desires a book which combines grandeur of subject with beauty of expression; the sublimest theology with the soundest morality; the widest variety of topic with an obvious unity of design; the most ancient history with the most fascinating poetry; the profoundest philosophy with the plainest maxims of human conduct; pathetic narratives with picturesque descriptions of character; in short, a book which shall as truly gratify the taste by the elegance of its composition as it shall sanctify the heart by the purity of its doctrines, and thus, while it opens the glories of heaven and prepares the soul for possessing and enjoying them, shall furnish a source of never-failing pleasure upon earth—I say, if such a book is sought, it can be found in the Bible, and only in the Bible, and that precious volume more than answers the description.

And where in all the range of inspired or uninspired literature can be found a delineation of female excellence, I will not say equal to, but worthy to be compared with, that which forms the subject of the present chapter? We have in it a picture about which it is difficult to say which is the most striking, the correctness of the drawing or the richness of the coloring. Both display a master's hand, and, though delineated three thousand years ago, it is still true to nature; and when we

302

have removed some of the effects of time, retouched some lines that have been clouded and obscured by the lapse of years, and given a few explanations, it is impossible to look at it without admiration and delight. It adds to the interest to know that it is the production of a female artist. It is the description of a good wife, drawn by the hand of a mother to guide her son in the selection of a companion for life. They are "the words of King Lemuel, the prophecy that his mother taught him." Who this king was is a matter of uncertainty. He was not, as some have supposed, Solomon. The original Hebrew has many Chaldaisms, which are found in no other part of the book of Proverbs, and afford a cogent argument that it was written by another hand, perhaps after the captivity. The whole passage is composed with art, a kind of poem containing twenty-two verses beginning, respectively, like some of the Psalms, with the letters of the Hebrew alphabet in their order of succession. Whoever Lemuel might have been, he had the privilege of a most eminent mother.

The admonitory verses with which the chapter commences, composed by this distinguished woman for her son when in the flower of youth and high expectation, are an inimitable production, in respect to their actual materials as well as the delicacy with which they are selected. Instead of attempting to lay down rules concerning matters of state and political government, the illustrious writer confines herself, with the nicest and most becoming art, to a recommendation of the gentler virtues of temperance, benevolence, and mercy, and to a minute and unparalleled delineation of the female character which might bid fairest to promote the happiness of her son in connubial life. What a pattern of maternal excellence was this king's mother! We may well imagine that in this inimitable portrait she drew her own likeness. What sons we would see, if all were blessed with such mothers as she was!

In taking up this delineation, I shall first consider the inquiry which introduces it. "Who can find a virtuous woman? For her price is far above rubies." This interrogation implies the rarity and the worth of the object sought. The question might have been more forcible in those times than in ours, for such a blessing was no doubt more scarce than it is now. True, the picture is so admirable that even now a perfect resemblance is not to be found everywhere. Yet, if extraordinary excellence is not often met with, happily that which is far above mediocrity is by no means rare. And why should there not be in every female bosom an intense desire to rise to a perfect conformity to this beautiful pattern? How much more to be valued by her happy possessor is this than all the jewels with which so many women are fond of being decked, or than the largest and the purest diamond in the mines of the east!

I proceed now to consider this exquisite delineation of "the virtuous woman." But really I feel as if to touch it were to spoil it, and as though comments were almost like painting the tulip, perfuming the rose, or attempting to add brilliance to the sun. Instead of following the order of the verses and adopting the regular expository method, I shall dislocate the verses and place them under separate headings and titles.

The authoress reserves piety for the climax or culminating point of her description, and winds up the whole thus: "Favor is deceitful, and beauty is vain, but a woman that feareth the Lord, she shall be praised." I shall make this our starting point. In the verse just quoted, the essence of true religion is comprised in that phrase, "the fear of the Lord," which means the cultivation and exercise of all right and holy dispositions towards God. Yes, this is religion, to have the heart right towards God. And we hold that this is not merely the gilded ornament that towers upwards to heaven, and crowns and beautifies the building at the apex, though it is this; but it is more than this, for it is the base of the whole structure, and supports the noble pyramid of varied excellences. It is this which makes them strong and stable, and ensures at once their proportions and their perpetuity.

True piety, instead of setting aside a single female excellence, clothes all such with a divine sanction, harmonizes the demands of God with the claims of man, converts the ordinary duties of domestic life into a means of preparation for that glorious world where the social ties no longer exist, and softens the cares, anxieties, and sorrows with which woman's lot in this world is but too often sadly oppressed. Whatever else a woman may be, without this she is lamentably deficient. "Favor," or, as the word signifies, gracefulness, "is deceitful, and beauty is vain." The face of a beautiful woman ought to be an index of the mind; and when all is fair on the outside, as it is said of the king's daughter in the Psalm, all should be glorious within. Never do an ill-furnished mind and an ill-favored heart appear more revolting than when seen united, but in contrast, with personal attractions. And yet how often do elegance of manners and loveliness of person conceal dispositions which are in perfect opposition to them, and bitterly disappoint the man who has been captivated by them, and who, in his choice of a wife, has been led by no other considerations than mere personal charms!

Let beauty have its due praise, and suppose what you will of it; even if all that the poets say of it is true, still the text tells you it is vain. Its nature is transient, fleeting, and perishing; it is the flower of the spring which must fade in autumn, and when the blossom falls, if no fruit succeeds, of what value, I pray, is the tree? The grave is already opening for the most elegant person who moves, and the worms are waiting to feed on the fairest face that is beheld. But religion is an excellence and a beauty which time cannot corrode, nor old age wrinkle, nor disease spoil, nor death destroy, but which, after living and thriving amidst the decay of all other things in this world, will flourish in the next in the vigor of immortal youth.

We next note her conjugal excellence. "The heart of her husband doth safely trust in her, so that he shall have no need of spoil. She will do him good, and not evil, all the days of her life." Confidence between man and wife is the basis of domestic happiness. There cannot possibly be happiness where this is wanting. Suspicion and jealousy must drive felicity out of doors. In regard to the virtuous woman, her husband trusts her chastity. Her fidelity is as inviolable as the covenant of the Most High, and her purity unsullied as the light of heaven. What a torment is jealousy in the bosom of husband or wife! Wormwood and gall are sweet to it. He trusts her fidelity in the management of his affairs, and knows that all his domestic interests are safe in her hands. With such a manager at home, he can go without anxiety to his daily business, travel to distant places, or remain, when necessary, away from home for ever so long a time. He shall have "no need of spoil," shall have no necessity through an improvident and unthrifty wife for despoiling others of their property. "He need not," says Matthew Henry, "be griping and scraping abroad, as those must be whose wives are proud and wasteful at home." She manages his affairs so that he is always beforehand, and has such plenty of his own that he is in no temptation to prey upon his neighbors. He thinks himself so happy in her that he envies not those who have most of the wealth of this world; he needs it not, for he has enough in having such a wife. Happy is the couple who have such satisfaction as this in each other!

It is too well known to be denied that, if many husbands make their wives wretched by their unkindness, many wives make their husbands poor by unthriftiness. Many a man has been tempted to cheat his creditors through the improvidence, bad management, and extravagance of his wife. The virtuous woman will study to do her husband good, and to avoid doing him evil, all the days of her life. She will be inventive, ingenious, and laborious to promote his comfort, his health, and his interest; will smooth his brow, when wrinkled with care, by her sweet words; will hush the sigh that misfortune extorts from his bosom; will answer with gentleness the sharp words that in moments of irritation drop from his lips; and will do all this not by fits and starts in genial moods, but continually.

But this is not all; for on looking onward in the chapter we find another reference to her conduct and influence as a wife. "Her husband is known in the gates, when he sitteth among the elders of the land." By "the gates" are meant the place of magisterial assembly and business, which in ancient times was in apartments over the gates of the city. In these public convocations a good wife will make her husband known, and add to his public reputation in various ways. Her prudent conduct in her domestic arrangements will enable him to leave home with confidence to attend to public business. She does not engross his company so as to prevent his becoming a public benefactor and blessing.

By the happiness which she imparts to him at their own fireside she sends him abroad not with a downcast look, as if he had left a heavy trouble at home, or carried it everywhere with him, but with a cheerful countenance, as though he had just come from the scene and seat of his chief earthly bliss. By her proper care of his personal appearance, in the elegance and neatness of his apparel (which in ancient times was the work of her hands), and especially by the force of her holy example sustaining and encouraging his excellence, she raises the honor and increases the respect of her husband. He is better known and more esteemed as the husband of such a wife. Can a woman rise to higher honor than to be so excellent and

estimable as to augment the public respectability of her
husband?

Still, let husbands take care that they do not shine only in
borrowed splendor, and stand indebted for all their esteem to
their wives. Let them so act, and be such men, that the honor
they receive on account of their wives shall be only an addition
to the greater honor that belongs to themselves. It is to the
comfort and glory of a man to be better known and more respected on account of his wife; but it is to his discredit to be
known and respected only by and for his wife. It is a poor,
mean affair for a man to go through society with no higher
qualification than his wife's excellence. Such a woman must
feel herself, though in one sense exalted, in another sense degraded, by being the wife of a man who has no public honor
but such as he derives from her. It must also bring misery
when the husband finds himself ever totally eclipsed by his
wife, except that indeed he is too stupid to feel it. Alas for the
wife of such a man! Let this induce care and caution in the
formation of the marriage union. Unequal matches are not
often happy ones.

Observe now her industry as a woman. "She seeketh wool
and flax, and worketh willingly with her hands. She layeth her
hands to the spindle, and her hands hold the distaff." This is
an allusion to the customs of the times, and is a description of
her personal habits of manual labor and energetic employment.
All textures of wool and flax, cotton and silk, were, before the
invention of machinery woven out of thread and yarn, spun by
hand with a distaff and spindle. Nor was this occupation confined exclusively to the laboring classes; for queens, princesses,
and peeresses disdained not to be thus employed amidst the
more courtly occupations of their rank.

It is well worthy of attention that out of the twenty-two
verses of this elegant poem, eleven are taken up in setting forth

the virtue and practice of the matron's industry in its various relations and duties. And her industry is represented as eminently utilitarian. Indolence is sometimes thought and said to be one of the failings to which women are exposed, especially in single life, and, more frequently, in high life. It is censurable even there; how much more in the state of matrimony! And those who give themselves up to it as maidens are in imminent peril of carrying the habit forward into the state of the wife, mother, and mistress. An indolent woman at the head of the domestic economy must throw all into confusion. It is neither asked nor expected that her energies should be expended on works which belong to servants; but an active female, even with servants at command, may always find something to do without stepping out of her proper place. The mistress of an establishment, especially if she is also a wife and mother, can never plead want of occupation as an excuse for personal laziness. What a sad example does such a woman set for her servants and her children! No vice is more contagious than this, nor is any example more likely to be imitated by those around her.

We next notice her thriftiness as a wife and female head of a family. "She considereth a field and buyeth it; with the fruit of her hand she planteth a vineyard. She maketh fine linen and selleth it, and delivereth girdles unto the merchant. She perceiveth that her merchandise is good; her candle goeth not out by night." From these verses it is apparent that in early times women were extensively employed even in buying and selling such matters as suited their sex, and, without withdrawing their attention from other duties, aided their husbands to increase the wealth and comforts of their families. This manufacturing in the house, this traffic with the merchants, this buying a piece of ground and planting a vineyard, sound hardly feminine in our ears; but they give us an insight into those times, and show how little the tyranny of man over woman, which afterwards, as time rolled on, prevailed in eastern countries, had yet been practiced.

Woman is here seen as man's companion, counselor and helper, even to her making provision for the support of the family. Modern customs render this to a considerable extent unnecessary. Woman's place ordinarily is the parlor and the nursery rather than the shop. Buying and selling are the business of the husband, and taking care of the family that of the wife; and the less, as a general rule, the latter has to do with the former, the better. It is an indelible reproach to any man to live in idleness upon the labors of his wife, and leave her to take care of their children also. A month's labor at the treadmill, or a month's penance upon bread and water, would be a suitable regimen for such drones. Yet necessity dispenses with ordinary laws; and where there are no children to be provided for, or where their comfort and education can be attended to also, it is by no means an unseemly spectacle to witness a clever and devoted woman occasionally at the side of her husband in the scenes of his trade. This applies, of course, only to small concerns, for in large ones there is no need of it. No wife will feel herself degraded by such occupations. The grateful and affectionate smile of her husband, and the consciousness that she is lightening his cares and aiding him to support his family, will be an ample reward for her labor.

It is, however, a great unhappiness for the laboring classes of this and other manufacturing towns that married women who are not only wives, but mothers are so extensively employed in our factories. In some cases it may be necessary, and even beneficial; but as a general practice it is fraught with much discomfort to the family. And in order to render it unnecessary, let the husband be more industrious, more sober, and more temperate in all things, and forego the earnings of his wife at the factory that she may be looking after her children, and providing him with a clean, comfortable, and well-ordered home. This would take away from him one temptation to frequent the alehouse.

We notice next her judgment and skill in her domestic arrangements. "She riseth also while it is yet night, and giveth meat to her household, and a portion to her maidens. She looketh well to the ways of her household, and eateth not the bread of idleness. Her candle goeth not out by night. She is like the merchant's ship; she bringeth her food from afar. She is not afraid of the snow for her household; for all her household are clothed with scarlet," or, as it should be rendered, "in double garments."

How many points are there here worthy of notice and imitation. She knows the value of time and redeems it, and makes the day as long as she can by early rising. Nothing wastes time more than unnecessary slumber. Sleep is a temporary death, and no more of it should be taken than prepares for a healthy resurrection in the morning. Even the rising of our Lord from the grave took place very early in the morning, as if, among the minor lessons He would teach us by the very circumstances of that wondrous and glorious event, one is that our own morning figure of the resurrection in rising from our bed should take place early. A slothful woman, who wastes the precious hours of her prime in bed, is a sad example to her family. How can she teach the valuable habit of early rising to her children and servants, or how can she "look well to the ways of her household, and give meat to her maidens," by setting in order her household affairs, if she leaves not her downy pillow till the day is far spent?

And then it is said of the good wife, "Her candle goeth not out by night." When the days are short and the nights long, she takes no advantage of this for the indulgence of sloth.

Though up early to lengthen the day at that end, she is not in haste to retire to rest and thus shorten it at the other. Each hour has its work, and the work of the hour is done in the hour. The ways of her household are the constant matter of oversight and inspection, and such is the fruit of her good management that, when winter comes, her servants and children need not fear frost or snow, for they are protected from the cold with both inner and outer garments. How interesting a scene it is on a bleak, cheerless day, when the east wind is piercing and the sleet is driving before it, to see a large family, through the activity of an industrious and kind mother and mistress, all warmly clad.

In a complete sense, "looking well to the ways of her household" must include not only good housewifery, but a proper attention to her servants' moral habits, their religious instruction, their attendance on the means of grace, giving them time for secret prayer and reading God's Word, the daily ordinance of family worship, the careful observance of the sabbath, anxious watchfulness over their manners, habits, and connections—in short, considering servants not as beasts of burden, not as mere mercenaries, but as a solemn and responsible trust for God and eternity. Who can have the claim to the title of a virtuous woman who does not feel this weight of family responsibility? And what a responsibility! Let every mistress read it, tremble, and pray.

I most urgently enjoin all the acquisitions of good and clever housewifery: of frugality without stinginess, plenty without profusion, attention without slavery, order without fastidiousness, dispatch without hurry, and elegance without extravagance. "This bear in mind," said an accomplished writer, in giving advice to his son as to the choice of a wife, "that if she is not frugal, if she is not what is called a good manager, if she does not pique herself on her knowledge of family affairs, and laying out her money to the best advantage—then let her be ever so sweetly tempered, gracefully made, or elegantly accomplished, she is no wife for a tradesman, and all these amiable talents will but open just so many ways to ruin. In short, remember your mother, who was so exquisitely versed in this art that her dress, her table, and every other particular appeared rather splendid than otherwise, and yet good housewifery was the foundation of all; and her bills, to my certain knowledge, were a fourth less than those of most of her neighbors, who had hardly cleanliness to boast in return for their awkward liberality." This is all true, and all good as far as it goes. But then it is not enough, for to this must be added all that moral and religious oversight and care which Mr. [Charles] Bridges (whose comments from his commentary on Proverbs were summarized in the previous paragraph) has so justly included in it.

I may now introduce her conduct as a mother. "Her children rise up and call her blessed." Happy are the children of such a mother, who receive the lessons of wisdom taught them by her lips as well as by the example of piety, prudence, and sobriety which she sets for them in her conduct. With their character formed under the plastic influence of her own, and the consciousness of how much they owe to her influence, they rise up around her with feelings of gratitude and veneration; when surrounded with families of their own, they teach her grandchildren to reverence her; and when she has descended to the tomb, they pour those blessings over her grave which they had during her life been accustomed to offer around her chair, or in their evening prayer for her welfare. Let it be the holy and honorable ambition of every mother to be crowned with the blessings of her children, which she who is foolish or sinful never can be.

Let every mother seriously ponder what she would really

wish her daughters to be, what by general consent they would
be praised for being, and that let her be herself. The mother
should be as perfect a model as possible for her daughters to
imitate.

In the last chapter I gave directions to young mothers in
reference to the early training of their children. Let me now
give a few hints to those whose children are growing up
around them, or have become young men and women. I say,
then, be much at home yourselves, and that is the way, if your
temper, spirit, and conduct are loving and agreeable, to keep
them at home. Make them fond of your society by causing
them to feel that you are fond of theirs. Throw an air of
cheerfulness over the circle. A mother's smile is the sunshine of
the domestic group, in which all delight to bask. Be happy
yourselves, and you will then make your children happy around
you. And yet let it not be a cheerfulness that degenerates into
levity. Nothing can be more unseemly than a frivolous mother,
indulging in undignified mirth, or frothy, gossiping, or slanderous discourse, in the midst of grown-up sons and daughters.
To be called a "rattle" is no commendation of a mother.

Of all subjects on which a discreet mother will never joke
with her children, love and courtship will be the last. A wise
and good woman will avoid all trifling with matters of such
delicacy and importance. To her sons she will exhibit in herself
the model after which she would wish them to choose a wife;
to her daughters, the pattern she would wish them to copy
should they ever become wives and mothers themselves. There
should be a high and dignified bearing, softened by the tenderest affection, and a kindness and affability uncorrupted by a
low familiarity. Her authority should ensure the prompt obedience of her children, whatever their age, as her wisdom should
attract their confidence, and her love their gratitude and affection. She must be thus their companion, counselor, and com-

forter, and, by the frankness of her own disposition, encourage theirs. They must be so treated as to be made to feel that they have no momentous secrets they could wish to conceal from her. And especially should she exhibit to them all the holiness, meekness, consistency, beauty and attractiveness of true religion; the sanctifying, humbling, spiritualizing power of genuine godliness in prosperity; and all its divine support and heavenly consolation in adversity, that they may be won by her example to piety, and thus rise up not only on earth and in time, but in heaven, and through all eternity, to call her "blessed."

She is not destitute of taste and elegance. "She maketh herself coverings of tapestry; her clothing is silk and purple." Though not addicted to pride in dress and vanity in ornaments, she maintains her rank and station in society by their external and conventional signs. Her wardrobe and her furniture are in keeping with her circumstances, her virtues, and her industry. And it is right that they should be so. Religion, my female friends, is not at war with elegance and good taste. It is itself the "beauty of holiness," and the richest and purest moral taste. Neither despise nor idolize these matters. Be neither a sloven nor a dressed doll, neither the slave nor the despiser of fashion; neither excite disgust by your want of attention to little matters of order, becomingness and ornament, nor court admiration by splendor and expansiveness. Be consistent with your station in all respects. Affect not the pride of meanness any more than that of magnificence. As for the elegant occupations for leisure hours of modern times, I refer to what, in former chapters, I have said on the subject of accomplishments.

Note her prudence in speech. "She openeth her mouth in wisdom." She thinks before she speaks, and therefore neither introduces a bad subject nor disgraces a good one by an improper manner of discoursing upon it. She has too just a sense

of the value of the gift of speech, and too accurate an idea of
the power of words for good or for evil, to employ them in idle
gossip, petty scandal, or slanderous backbiting. She is neither
too taciturn (knowing that speech is given to be employed),
nor too talkative (equally knowing that "in the multitude of
words there wanteth not sin"). The Apostle James says, "If any
man offend not in word, the same is a perfect man." This,
perhaps, is still more true of a woman, inasmuch as she is
thought to have a greater propensity to loquacity. The gift of
speech is never more adorned than when employed in the soft
and gentle tones of woman's voice uttering the words of wisdom and kindness, but never more dissonant and repulsive
than when her tongue is voluble in folly or falsehood, malice
or passion.

Have we not all known husbands, a large portion of whose
time has been employed in explaining the mistakes, correcting
the follies, healing the feuds, and repairing the mischiefs of
wives who opened their mouths without wisdom? On the
other hand, has not many an Abigail, by her discreet and
timely interposition and wise address, averted the storm that
was gathering over the family from the churlish language of
Nabal, her husband? Blessed is the woman who knows how to
charm to repose the troubled thoughts of an angry or a vexed
husband; who can discern when to be silent and when to
speak, and how, by the sweet tones of her voice, to lull his agitated mind, and drive the evil spirit out of his breast. Ah, it is at
home that this wisdom of speech is most wanted! What
stormy scenes sometimes arise from the absence of it, driving
peace from the family and filling it with harsh discord and
fearful strife!

Is benevolence no part of the spirit and conduct of the
virtuous woman? Let the text reply: "In her tongue is the law
of kindness. She stretcheth out her hand to the poor; yea, she

reacheth forth her hands to the needy." Her kindness begins with thoughts, goes on to words, and ends in works. In her heart, it is as a principle of charity; upon her tongue, as a law to dictate gentle, soothing, and pleasing words. She speaks, and her expressions are as the droppings of the honeycomb, or the falling of the dew. But her mercy is in her hand as well as in her heart and upon her lips. She does not merely say to the hungry and shivering, "Be ye warmed and be ye filled," but she gives them that with which to satisfy their hunger and clothe their limbs. And her kindliness of disposition is the golden thread which runs through all her life, and binds up all her actions, into not only a womanly but a saintly benevolence. Her spindle and distaff so industriously employed are used not for herself alone, but for the poor and needy. She is not so taken up with those within the circle of her family as to forget those who are without. Her benevolence is like a spring, which not only refreshes and fertilizes the spot where it gushes up and makes all verdant around its margin, but flows onward to carry its benefits to those at a distance.

She adorns herself with "silk and purple," and makes "coverings of tapestry" for her own habitation, and clothes her household; but then also, like Dorcas, she makes garments for the poor. How beautifully does this feature of kindness come into the portrait; how does this diamond of mercy sparkle amidst the other jewels of this charming character! What a blank would the absence of it have made! How should we have turned away, not with admiration but with sadness, from this industry, frugality, conjugal affection, good housewifery, maternal excellence, prudence, and elegance, if all these virtues had been exhibited in the iron setting of selfishness instead of the gold of mercy! If this woman, the pattern of all household virtues, had been presented to us as so swallowed up in her cares for her own well-provided household as to do nothing

for the starving and naked families around her, a dark shadow
would have fallen on her otherwise bright character, and its
luminousness would have passed at once, if not into total, at
least into partial eclipse. But it is not so. Mercy, like a midday
sun, rises upon the scene and sheds its luster upon all.
Christian women, you must be the brightest patterns of kindness and mercy which our selfish world contains, and add to
temperance, patience, and godliness Christian kindness and
charity.

Such a character cannot be unnoticed or unacknowledged,
nor can such excellence pass through the world without admiration and commendation. And I now, therefore, note the
honor and esteem with which she is treated. "Strength and
honor are her clothing, and she shall rejoice in time to come.
Her husband also, and he praiseth her. Many daughters have
done virtuously, but thou excellest them all. Favor is deceitful
and beauty is vain; but a woman that feareth the Lord, she
shall be praised. Give her of the fruits of her hands, and let her
own works praise her in the gates."

She seeks not human applause, and therefore acts no the-
atrical part, nor, for the sake of praise, does she affect display.
Content with the love and esteem of her husband, the veneration and affection of her children, and the respect of her
friends, she is not anxious to obtrude herself upon public attention, to shine in brilliant circles, or to have even her excellence made the subject of general commendation. Still, un-
sought praise will be given her. Spontaneous tributes and
freewill offerings of honor and respect will be paid her. Her
husband will be the first to perceive, and the foremost to acknowledge, her excellence. If a grateful man, he will make her
sensible of his just appreciation of her excellences not by mere
fondling and caresses, but by respect for her judgment and
character, by commending her to her children, and by bidding

them follow her example.

Cases sometimes occur of men so inferior to their wives, and so conscious of that inferiority, as to be jealous of their ascendency in the family, and envious of the talents and virtues they cannot imitate. A husband blessed with such a woman as is described in this chapter should not be backward on suitable occasions to let others know the estimate he forms of her character. True it is that a wise man will not be ever talking of his wife's excellences; but he will, at proper seasons, feel a pride and a pleasure in exalting her in public estimation, and the public will not fail to give her the fruit of her doings. "Let everyone," says Bishop [Symon] Patrick, "extol her virtue. Let her not want the just commendation of her pious labors. But while some are magnified for the nobleness of the stock from whence they sprang, others for their fortune, others for their beauty, and others for other things, let the good deeds which she herself has done be publicly praised in the greatest assemblies where, if all men shall be silent, her own works will declare her excellence." And to use the poetic language of another prelate (Bishop Horne), "The crown which her own hands have thus formed shall be placed upon her head as it were by general consent, even in this life; and her good deeds, celebrated in public assemblies, shall diffuse an odor as fragrant as the smell of Eden, or as the cloud of frankincense ascending from the holy altar. When her task is ended, the answer of a good conscience, and the blessings of all around, sweeter than the sweetest music, shall chant her to her repose, till, as she is awakened on the great morning of the world, descending angels shall introduce this daughter of Jerusalem into the joy of her Lord."

Such then is the character of the virtuous woman as delineated by the mother of King Lemuel. By expanding the miniature, as it was drawn by the pen of inspiration, into a

large and full-length picture, I have perhaps done injustice to
the subject. If so, let those who are of this opinion perpetually
and closely study the original as it is found in the book of
Proverbs. "There," says Matthew Henry in his quaint style, "is
shut up this looking glass for ladies, which they are desired to
open and dress themselves by; and if they do so, their adorning
will be found to praise, and honor, and glory, at the appearing
of Jesus Christ."

If, however, a wife devoid of all that constitutes her real excellence will run counter to this beautiful picture; if instead of
being the glory of her husband, she seeks to rival him, and will
either attempt to be in the domestic firmament the greater
light to rule the day, or to throw into eclipse him before whom
she should be content to be partially obscured; if instead of
being content to be praised by him, and deeming his approving
smile her worthiest object of ambition and her richest reward,
she should seek the gaze of admiration and the language of
flattery from strangers; if she is a wife who opposes wantonly
his tastes, or neglects his comfort; who condemns his opinion,
and contradicts him with asperity, and resents with unseemly
heat his real or unintentional slights; who exhibits indolence
and not industry in the management of his household, and
either by slovenliness allows all things to sink into uncleanness
and confusion, or by extravagance hastens on the approach of
poverty and ruin; who neglects even her children, and causes
them to rise up in grief and shame for their mother; who gives
her maidens constant occasion for reproach and complaint, on
account of her ill temper and worse conduct; who is restless
and uneasy at home, but gracious and engaging everywhere
else; who by her own conduct makes her husband happier everywhere else than at his own fireside; "or if she is a wife, using
her empire over her husband to turn him away from the Lord,
as the wife of Jehoram, whose fatal influence the Holy Spirit

paints in the single expression, 'Jehoram walked in the ways of the kings of Israel, like as did the house of Ahab; for he had the daughter of Ahab to wife'—a wife, in short, who constrains her husband to sigh in secret over the hour when he was blind enough to sue for her hand, and to look forward to the day when he shall lay before the tribunal of God the eternal wrongs she has done him—what plea can she offer for her conduct?" (Adolphe Monod).

There are some few things of a general character which may be worthy of notice in surveying this portraiture.

It is a very true and judicious remark of Mr. Bridges that the standard of godliness here exhibited is not that of the religious recluse, shut up from active obligations under pretense of greater sanctity and consecration to God. Here are none of those habits of monastic asceticism that are extolled by some as the highest point of Christian perfection. Nor does any other part of Scripture, either of the Old Testament or the New, set up a finger-post pointing to the convent. I repeat what I affirmed in a former chapter, that no single practice pleading the sanction of religion was ever the source of so much pollution and vice, or inflicted so deep a wound on morals, as monasticism. Woman's natural state is the conjugal one, into which she ought not to be, and is not usually, unwilling to enter at the call of Providence (with all due discretion), and for which she should assiduously prepare herself. Still, should there be some women of singular disinterestedness or exalted piety who, either for the benefit of near relations or from motives of zeal and mercy, and not from a superstitious notion of the superior sanctity of celibacy, shall be willing to forego the duties and felicities of the wife and the mother, who, I ask, shall forbid them? Such was the mind of the Apostle Paul, whose words on this subject have been so eagerly wrested in favor of erroneous opinions. "If I search," says Monod, "throughout the whole world for the type of the most useful, the most pure, the most Christian charity, I nowhere find all these conditions better fulfilled than in the good aunt who, by a marvelous sacrifice, accepts the fatigues and the cares of maternity without knowing its ineffable consolation; a mother, yea, and (it may be) more than a mother when the question is of serving and supporting, yet setting herself aside the moment the question is only of advantage and pleasure. Sad she may be, but her sadness is heavenly, and transforms itself completely into love and sacrifice. But if no family engagements bind you, extend your view further, towards finding a family who has need of you; comforting the afflicted; forming or supporting charitable institutions; seconding a pious minister in his labors; in short, in every good work for which God appears to have expressly reserved your liberty. Or embrace, for you may, a yet wider sphere. Embrace the world if you will, provided it be in the spirit of charity. In sum, accomplish your mission so faithfully that, when the hour of your death shall arrive, all may rejoice in the happy isolation which permitted you thus to devote yourself, and that amid the tender regrets which shall follow your mortal remains to the tomb, it may no longer be discerned, in the sacrifice which you have made, whether you were wife or sister, aunt or mother, relative or stranger."

It cannot fail, I think, to impress every reader of this beautiful description of the virtuous woman that the delineation chiefly regards the active virtues of the female character. It portrays the clever, energetic, and prosperous female, surrounded by circumstances that call forth her industrious assiduities, invest her with power, and array her with public honor, rather than the quiet, gentle, and retired sufferer, struggling with adversity or crushed by oppression, whose virtues consist of submission to the will of God and patient uncomplaining endurance of the wrongs of man, perhaps of her husband, and the brightness of whose character is admired by God and angels in heaven, rather than seen and extolled by men on earth.

To the latter women I would say, look up with believing prayer to God for the grace that is necessary to fill your dark sphere with the illumination of that holy virtue, which with lunar radiance shines brightest by night. Little of the glory of the character which I have been describing may fall upon you in the secluded shades amidst which you are called to dwell. In solitude, with no eye to pity, no voice to soothe, no hand to help, you may be called to drink the cup of sorrow. Well, drink it, as did the greatest and holiest Sufferer who ever passed through our vale of tears, saying, "The cup which My Father giveth Me to drink, shall I not drink it?" And the time will come when He who loves you better than you love yourself shall wipe away all tears from your eyes.

To those who by divine grace are copying the pattern set before them in this chapter, and are in circumstances to do so, I would say, cast the veil of gentleness, modesty, and humility over all these fine traits of active, energetic character. Let the passive virtues of your sex blend with and soften the active ones. Be sure to single out that lovely feature, "the law of kindness is on her tongue." With all this masculine energy in womanly conduct, unite feminine tenderness and softness. Whatever else in character you may be, still be a woman, with all a woman's grace and loveliness; and while as a wife, a mother, and a mistress you wield the authority and exert the influence which belongs to you, remember still that there is one in the family, I mean your husband, whose authority is still higher than your own, and that it is at once your duty, and will be for your happiness, meekly and gracefully, though not abjectly and crouchingly, to bow to him.

Young women, I beseech you to make yourselves familiar with this exquisite passage of Holy Writ. It must be a study for you. There is much, very much, to be learned from it. You will here see that piety is the broadest and most solid basis of all female excellence, and that, so far from interfering with temporal duties, it will, wherever it is genuine, quicken attention to them. Godliness is profitable for all things, and assists every lawful pursuit. There is not a single good quality in the character which it will not improve, and no one earthly interest, provided that it is legitimate, which it will not effectually promote. Do not allow yourselves to be imposed upon by the misrepresentations of its enemies, who will persuade you, if they can, that piety is unfriendly to general character, and inimical to personal happiness; that it enjoins unfriendly duties and forbids pleasures essential to youthful enjoyment. Upon candid examination it will be found that this objection to piety, like all others, is utterly unfounded. Is there a virtue or a practice which can adorn or bless humanity which it does not enjoin? And as for its most solemn (and what some would consider its most sorrowful) duty, repentance, I would remind you that this is not the only exercise of true religion; for there is the joy unspeakable of faith as well as the grief of contrition, and the latter leads on to the former, just as the shower in the sultry heat of summer portends and produces a cooler atmosphere. Religion forbids no pleasure but such as is injurious to the soul, and substitutes the substance of happiness for its shadows. It resembles a fine country in spring, where the hedges bloom and every thorn produces a flower.

Perhaps it will be thought by some a pity that a delineation of the virtuous man, equally minute, comprehensive, and impressive, was not drawn by the hand which gave us this picture of female excellence. In diminution of our regret, however, it is observable how much of what is here said may be copied into the character and conduct of the other sex. There is scarcely a rule of conduct here presented which may not, with a little change, be observed by the husband, the father, and the master. This virtuous woman's fidelity to her husband, personal industry, good management and diligence in her family, consideration for the comfort and necessities of others, kindness of speech and pity for the poor, courtesy to all, and especially her sincere and practical piety, all belong to her husband also, and are required of him as well as of herself. These virtues are appropriate to both sexes. They are the general principles of excellence, though adapted here to the female sex. And therefore we recommend that husbands study this portraiture, not only to see what their wives should be, but what is required of themselves also.

But who of either sex is sufficient for these things? None but those whose sufficiency is of God; and He will ever bestow upon docile and humble petitioners at the footstool of His grace that gracious aid which is equal to the exigency of every case. While enforcing your various duties, and calling upon you to form for yourself a character which, after exhibiting to the admiration of every beholder on earth its graceful proportions, shall endure with unfading beauty and undiminished grandeur through eternity, I would also remind you of your own indecision, feebleness of purpose, exposure to temptation, and consequent necessity of divine assistance. To obtain this help you must have faith in Christ, the source of all spiritual efficacy, and earnest prayer to God; and none shall seek this grace in vain.

I close this series of discourses on which, in consequence of the rarity of the effort and the delicacy of the subject, I entered, not indeed without some hope, but with much fear and trembling. So far as the pleasure of my own mind in preparing and preaching them, and the monthly attendance upon their delivery from the pulpit, were concerned, my expectations were more than realized. In laying down rules, pointing out defects, and, occasionally, in comparing the excellences and the faults of the sexes, I have had a somewhat difficult task to perform. And I can scarcely presume to hope that in the performance of it I have given satisfaction to all parties. I must be contented (and it is no small matter to be so) with the conviction that I have endeavored to hold the balance with a steady and impartial hand; and in this I have satisfied my own conscience. I have praised where praise was called for, and that was very often; but my commendation has not degenerated into flattery. I have blamed when blame was just, but it has been without acrimony. My object has been to promote the happiness of both sexes by improving the character of the one on which so much of the happiness of both depends, and to advance the welfare of society by purifying its earthly source. How far I have succeeded it is impossible that I should ever know, and in the absence of certainty I must be comforted with hope.

I have looked upon woman as related to both worlds, as being bound to this one by the ties of a wife, a mother, and a mistress, and to that which is to come by the grander and more enduring bond of immortality, and therefore as having to attain not only to social excellence, but to that which is individual in special relation to God, heaven, and eternity. I have contemplated you, my young friends, as the future wives, mothers, and mistresses of the next generation, and have endeavored to prepare you for discharging the duties of these momentous relationships.

It has been my aim in these sermons to open and prepare for you a smooth passage through this earthly state, gathering out of your way as many stones and planting as many flowers as I could. And imperfect as my counsels, and as defective as my views may have been, I am confident that if my advice is taken and my rules observed, though there may be much sorrow in reserve for you, there will not be wanting a large share of consolation and happiness. It will be your fault, not mine, if life is a dreary blank, a desert without an oasis, a wilderness without a spring. But I have looked beyond this world to that state where you will find yourselves with all those tender ties fallen from around you, and yourselves standing alone in your individuality and immortality. I am duly aware, and I wish you to be so, that you sustain a personal relation to God which requires an appropriate and prescribed line of conduct towards Him, and for the neglect of which no other duties, excellences, or merits whatsoever can be a substitute. It is not merely what you have been as a woman in society, or as a wife, mother, or mistress in your family, but what you have been towards God that will decide your lot in the day of judgment. You may have been the most exalted, noble, and learned of women, the most faithful of wives, the most devoted of mothers, and the kindest of mistresses; but if, with all this, you have not had repentance towards God, faith in our Lord Jesus, and true holiness, your domestic virtues, as they had in themselves no relation and in their performance no reference to God, will, in the end, meet with no recompense from Him, and instead of "Well done, thou good and faithful servant," you will hear nothing more than "They had their reward."

Young women, contemplate your situation as I do, and as I now present it to you. There, further than the eye can reach, stretches out the vast plain of earthly existence, with all its varied landscape, its numerous roads, its busy population, its duties, its pleasures, and its dangers. You are traveling across it, and need guidance, assistance, protection, and comfort along the way. Step by step you are going on, never stopping, but ever advancing, to what? To that boundless ocean of eternity which lies beyond, on which you must soon embark, and on which so many of your fellow travelers are every hour adventuring. Yes, yes, you are emigrants passing through time to embark for eternity; and ought you not, like other emigrants, to prepare for the voyage, and for the country to which you are going? Shall your attention be so taken up with the plain across which you are traveling as to forget your embarkation upon the ocean that lies beyond it? Does one of all the thousands who are now crowding to our colonies forget for a waking moment, after his determination is fixed, that he is soon to leave his country for one beyond the sea? Oh, no. And will you forget that you must soon (and how soon you know not, perhaps next year, or next month) emigrate to eternity? By what motive shall I induce you to prepare for eternity? By what? Only by itself. For if eternity is not enough to induce you to prepare for eternity, by what other motive can I hope to succeed?

I now, in conclusion, refer you to that day and that scene when the result of all ministerial efforts for the spiritual welfare of mankind, and of this minister's among the rest, shall be ascertained and made public. Before that dread tribunal you and I must appear. Not one single person of all who heard or who shall read these discourses will then be absent; and among the things to be brought into judgment will be this feeble, yet sincere and earnest endeavor for your spiritual benefit. In reference to some of you it will, I fear, be found that I have been "the savor of death unto death." But it is my prayer and my expectation that to very many I may be "the savor of life unto life." "For what is our hope, or joy, or crown of rejoicing? Are not even ye in the presence of our Lord Jesus Christ at His coming? For ye are our glory and joy."